C000095115

A Report of Trials Before The Right Hon. The Lord Chief Justice, and The Hon. Baron Sir Wm. C. Smith, Bart. at The Special Commission, at Maryborough, Commencing on The 23rd May, and Ending on The 6th June

James Mongan

A Report of Trials Before The Right Hon. The Lord Chief Justice, and The Hon. Baron Sir Wm. C. Smith, Bart. at The Special Commission, at Maryborough, Commencing on The 23rd May, and Ending on The 6th June

A Report of Trials before The right Hon. The Lord Chief Justice and The Hon. Baron sir Wm. C. Smith, Bart. At the Special Commission, at Maryborough - 1832
James Mongan
HAR05577
Monograph
Harvard Law School Library
Dublin: Richard Milliken and Son, 104, Grafton-Street. 1832

The Making of Modern Law collection of legal archives constitutes a genuine revolution in historical legal research because it opens up a wealth of rare and previously inaccessible sources in legal, constitutional, administrative, political, cultural, intellectual, and social history. This unique collection consists of three extensive archives that provide insight into more than 300 years of American and British history. These collections include:

Legal Treatises, 1800-1926: over 20,000 legal treatises provide a comprehensive collection in legal history, business and economics, politics and government.

Trials, 1600-1926: nearly 10,000 titles reveal the drama of famous, infamous, and obscure courtroom cases in America and the British Empire across three centuries.

Primary Sources, 1620-1926: includes reports, statutes and regulations in American history, including early state codes, municipal ordinances, constitutional conventions and compilations, and law dictionaries.

These archives provide a unique research tool for tracking the development of our modern legal system and how it has affected our culture, government, business – nearly every aspect of our everyday life. For the first time, these high-quality digital scans of original works are available via print-on-demand, making them readily accessible to libraries, students, independent scholars, and readers of all ages.

The BiblioLife Network

This project was made possible in part by the BiblioLife Network (BLN), a project aimed at addressing some of the huge challenges facing book preservationists around the world. The BLN includes libraries, library networks, archives, subject matter experts, online communities and library service providers. We believe every book ever published should be available as a high-quality print reproduction; printed on-demand anywhere in the world. This insures the ongoing accessibility of the content and helps generate sustainable revenue for the libraries and organizations that work to preserve these important materials.

The following book is in the "public domain" and represents an authentic reproduction of the text as printed by the original publisher. While we have attempted to accurately maintain the integrity of the original work, there are sometimes problems with the original work or the micro-film from which the books were digitized. This can result in minor errors in reproduction. Possible imperfections include missing and blurred pages, poor pictures, markings and other reproduction issues beyond our control. Because this work is culturally important, we have made it available as part of our commitment to protecting, preserving, and promoting the world's literature.

GUIDE TO FOLD-OUTS MAPS and OVERSIZED IMAGES

The book you are reading was digitized from microfilm captured over the past thirty to forty years. Years after the creation of the original microfilm, the book was converted to digital files and made available in an online database.

In an online database, page images do not need to conform to the size restrictions found in a printed book. When converting these images back into a printed bound book, the page sizes are standardized in ways that maintain the detail of the original. For large images, such as fold-out maps, the original page image is split into two or more pages

Guidelines used to determine how to split the page image follows:

• Some images are split vertically; large images require vertical and horizontal splits.
• For horizontal splits, the content is split left to right.
• For vertical splits, the content is split from top to bottom.
• For both vertical and horizontal splits, the image is processed from top left to bottom right.

A

REPORT

OF

TRIALS

BEFORE

THE RIGHT HON THE LORD CHIEF JUSTICE,

AND

THE HON BARON SIR WM C SMITH, BART

AT THE

SPECIAL COMMISSION,

AT MARYBOROUGH,

COMMENCING ON THE 23RD MAY AND ENDING ON THE 6TH JUNE

BY JAMES MONGAN, ESQ BARRISTER AT LAW.

DUBLIN
RICHARD MILLIKEN AND SON,
104, GRAFTON-STREET

1832

Chief Justice

THE RIGHT HON CHARLES FREVATT, C HH

Attorney-General,

THE RIGHT HON FRANCIS BLACKBURN

Counsel for the Crown

Mr ATTORNEY-GENERAL
Mr TICKELL, K C | Mr CLARKE
Mr MARTLEY, K C | Mr ABADIN

Crown-Solicitor, Mr GEATT

Clerk of the Crown, Mr GILL

CONTENTS

SPECIAL COMMISSION, &c

At eleven o'clock this day, Chief Justice and Baron Smith entered the Crown Court, and opened the Commission   The following Grand Jury were sworn

The Hon T Vesey, Foreman

Sir W D Burrowes, Bart	T B Kelly,
Sir E H J Walsh, Bart	Lewis Moore,
Richard Warburton,	Chidley Coote,
J S Rochfort,	F Thompson,
R Hamilton Stubber,	Hovendon Stapleton
J Pigott,	George Adair,
Henry Smyth,	W W Despard,
George Evans,	C L Sandes,
Jonathan Chetwood,	Myles J O'Reilly,
W C Cooper,	T Trench, jun and
A Weldon,	Wm Hamilton, Esqrs

The Chief Justice addressed the Grand Jury as follows —

GENTLEMEN OF THE GRAND JURY—It is scarcely two months since the gaol of this County was delivered at an Assizes which lasted from the 15th to the 27th of March, almost three times the period usually allotted.   During the greater part of that time, two Judges were engaged in separate Courts in criminal trials, the Crown Solicitor, under the orders of the Attorney-General, prosecuted in many cases connected with public disturbance, thirty-five cases were actually tried, there were twenty-four convictions, forty-seven were found guilty, five capital convictions have been followed by a commutation for the punishment of transportation, and twenty-six were sentenced to transportation,

B

twenty-four of whom have been transported yet your prison again is thronged, not with that class of offenders, whose crimes grow out of the frailties of man in his individual character, but, almost without an exception, with insurgents systematically confederated against the laws and institutions of their country.

In that short interval it appears, from the reports to the police department, that more than three hundred outrages have been committed of every class from murder downwards; in about sixty cases informations have been taken, and the calendar before us exhibits a list of one hundred and twenty-five prisoners already made amenable. Therefore it is that upon this extraordinary visitation of public justice, the Commission, which you have heard read, has been directed to the presiding Judges, in obedience to which it has been our duty to call you together.

Under those deplorable circumstances many duties devolve upon you as Grand Jurors, Magistrates, and Country Gentlemen, upon which it would be proper that I should address and exhort you but you have lately heard an appeal from this Bench upon all those topics, which you cannot have forgotten—an appeal carrying with it a weight, instruction, and persuasiveness, upon which, placed as I now am, I am not left at liberty to say more than that I will not by a worse than useless repetition, run the risk of effacing the profound impression made upon your hearts and understandings, and shall only call your attention, and that of all persons of all ranks assembled here, to a statement of the nature of those offences which the King's Judges are now commanded to enquire into, and of those laws which it has become necessary to put in force, and of the particular state of your county at this moment.

It is nearly sixty years since an extraordinary state of

crime called for a code peculiar to our country, and the Legislature was obliged to meet offences, (then of no recent date) inconsistent with civilized society by enactments which in other circumstances would be in repugnance to the principles of British jurisprudence —I speak of what are well known as the Whiteboy system, and the Whiteboy statutes—that system, as far as we know, originates in secret associations, and manifests itself sometimes by tumultuous assemblies, and sometimes by mischief, clandestinely and mysteriously perpetrated, and by means of both establishes that reign of terror under which a cruel despotism is exercised over mankind. Life and property are rendered insecure, the public peace is often violated and always endangered, and from a variety of conspiring causes, the people become deeply and fatally demoralised. The pretence has been the redress of grievances, some alleged to exist in one district, and some in another, but all substantially of the same character.—If a landlord looks for a good tenant, if a farmer proposes for a vacant farm—if a master hires a servant from another county or province—if a higher rent or lower wages have been paid than those confederates approve; if the tithes of the Protestant Clergy in one county, or the dues of the Roman Catholic Clergy in another, have exceeded that minimum which those confederates have established, all those have been represented from time to time as so many grievances, and the deluded people have persuaded themselves, or have been persuaded by others, to think that it was their duty to redress them.

No wise or good man will think or speak with indifference, or otherwise than seriously, and with regret, of the complaints and grievances of his fellow creatures. It is the lot of man in all classes to complain, and have reason to complain, and we are told that the sorrow to which we are born is as much a Law of Nature as that "the sparks fly upward."—Inequality of conditions has been in all ages and countries the dispensation of Providence, and necessarily leads to the humility of many, and the poverty of many, and all that human laws can do, is to mould the institutions of Society, so as to protect all men, however humble in their lives, properties and rights.— As to poverty, the duty of relieving and supporting the helpless poor, who have not " ceas'd in the land," is every where and particularly in Ireland, urgent, and there never was a period in which the energies of Government, the attention of Parliament, the talents of enlightened men, and the bounty of the benevolent were in such unanimous and active co-operation for the amelioration of their condition. But, with *them* we have here nothing to do I cannot recollect an instance in the experience of many years, (and perhaps it is a formidable view of our situation,) in which a man has been charged with an insurrectionary offence, whose crime could be traced to want or poverty. It is among the humbler classes, who either subsist by labour or exclusively by farming, or partly by one, and partly by the other, that the ostensible disturbers of the peace are to be found, they seek to regulate property upon a new theory, and subject its acquisition, and circulation, and enjoyment, to their own dominion, they certainly encounter a principle which some persons think it would be difficult, and if possible, dangerous to controul Whether that theory be right or wrong, whether the price of property and labour should be allowed to find its own level, or whether on the other hand it is not both safe and wise to deal with, and modify that apparent tendency of human affairs, are topics, not for this place, and upon which in any place, I should be incapable of judging but it does belong to this place and to you, and to me, to

lament that those delicate questions which the wisest statesman or lawgiver would approach with fear, and touch with
a trembling hand, should be subject to the rude decision of
a misguided and infuriated peasantry We must pity such
infatuation, but Gentlemen, it is not the causes of this
delusion we have to think of here, but the effects —Crime
and Misery—those inevitable consequences of popular
licentiousness both abound amongst you, and are traced, as
you will see, through all the means which have been always
adopted by the insurgents for accomplishing their objects.

Illegal oaths are administered by them, often by compulsion to unhappy wretches who attribute to them an obligation which they deny to more legitimate engagements.
Vengeance is denounced against all who refuse to join
their associations or resist their mandates, or give information of their crimes, by those means they become numerous, and the incessant and indefatigable plunder of arms
from all descriptions of loyal and peaceable subjects, soon
renders them formidable The destruction of property
follows, houses and barns, and granaries, are levelled, crops
are laid waste, pasture lands are ploughed, plantations are
torn up, meadows are thrown open to cattle,—cattle are
maimed, tortured, killed, those persons who incur their
displeasure are visited by parties of banditti who inflict
cruel torture upon their persons, mutilate their limbs, or
beat them almost to death. Men are deliberately assassi-
nated in the open day, who have in any way become
obnoxious to the insurgents, or opposed their system, or
refused to participate in their outrages, and sometimes the
unoffending members of a family are indiscriminately
murdered by burning the habitation of one devoted victim.
Entire classes are proscribed by them, especially those who
in any way, from the highest to the lowest department,

contribute to the administration of justice The humble being who earns his bread by serving the process of a Court of Law is held up to public hatred, and persecuted like a noxious animal. The witness who gives evidence in a Court of Justice is stigmatised as an informer, and devoted to general execration, and the Juryman is ordered on pain of death not to discharge his duty.

Whoever confines his estimate of the consequences of such a confederacy to the mere outrages and crimes it produces, has, I fear, but superficially examined the subject Such consequences may be occasional and transient, but the moral influence upon society of such a diseased state of human character must be deep and permanent The bad passions let loose, the charities of life extinct, those relations dissevered, which between the higher and lower classes are the offspring of reciprocal protection and dependence. Confidence displaced by suspicion, and fear and hatred in all classes vitiating and corroding the heart of man These are productive seeds which threaten a fearful growth, and if the mischief be not put down, every reflecting man will look forward to the necessary influence of such a state of things upon the future destinies of Ireland as operating far beyond the local disturbances of a provincial district.

It is quite plain that ordinary laws, calculated for civilized communities, are not applicable to a country so circumstanced , and one of the most lamentable consequences, which the offences of the people have produced, is, that thay have brought down upon their own heads the sanctions of a code, enacted expressly for the purpose, so uncongenial to our institutions, that shortly after the Whiteboy Act had passed, it received this construction, that though a permanent statute, its provisions are not in force in any district undisturbed by illegal associations;—except at such times, and in such places, it remains upon the Statute book disowned and inoperative, and as has been often said, rests like a sword in the scabbard till drawn by the crimes of the people. This law meets the principle of unlawful assemblies, in the first instance by enacting, that the mere act of association, without any other concomitant transgression, is a high offence, and subject to severe punishment.—I shall read to you the 15th and 16th George III. chap. 21. sec. 2. This is a very severe provision, and by it the mere assembling is a crime, although a hand should not be raised by any of the party But there is scarcely an act which can be done by persons so associated which the remainder of the statute does not visit with punishments more severe. Until very lately death was the common punishment of all such acts, but the legislature has substituted in its place transportation for life, or years, or at the discretion of the Court imprisonment and corporeal punishment —Several actions for which men in an undisturbed district would not be at all answerable, or if answerable, only liable to the slightest penalties, become subject to those awful sentences. Mere trespasses and acts which are not even trespasses, the mere attempt to commit a crime, though never perpetrated, the sending of a threatening letter, or delivering a threatening message, the slightest injury to property, an attack upon a dwelling house, without any injury to it, which is called by a phrase, I believe peculiar to this code, the assault of a dwelling house, are all made transportable offences, not only against those who commit them, but against those who "abet, succour, excite, ask, or require, or even endeavour to compel, or induce others to commit them" (2d, 3rd, 6th and 7th sec 1st and 2d William IV cap 44) Such are the formidable sanctions by which this code visits insurrection, but it goes farther, and as you well know, imposes new duties upon Magistrates, and gives them new powers calculated to enforce the execution of this law, by exertions beyond those required in ordinary times

It is but just to call such laws severe, but it is also just to call them merciful, they are founded upon two sound principles. the *prevention* of crime, and upon the known tendencies of unlawful associations to produce it In the case of individuals the progress from one offence to another is mostly gradual, but in the case of associated criminals, rapid. It is the nature of unlawful associations to inflame the passions of one man by the passions of another, and to bring into general action the collected vices of many. The man whose own temptation or frailty would be insufficient to urge him onward in the career of guilt, whose own reason or compunction might arrest his progress, is borne along with the torrent, bad example decides him, false shame hardens him, and he is precipitated almost necessarily into crime. It is, therefore, a humane as well a wise law which denounces a severe punishment against every offence of whatever nature which is likely to lead to a commission of the highest crimes, and its wisdom has been exemplified by the history of all those associations They begin by incendiaries spreading among an ignorant multitude the spirit of discontent.—The inequality of human conditions is represented as a grievance, every inconvenience of which they can complain, however incident to human society in all countries, is denounced as an abuse ,—they are taught to combine for the purpose of rectifying all those supposed wrongs, the confederacy requires arms, and procures them by robbery.—Rapine and violence thus become familiar.— The fear which never deserts conscious guilt makes them cruel and vindictive. Every moral principle is rapidly extinguished, every sense of obligation is lost, that consummation of vice to which an individual slowly habituates himself, a conspirator arrives at speedily, sometimes in a single day, and it has often happened that an unfortunate and deluded wretch, has in the morning, joined one of these confederacies as the champion of rights, and redresser of wrongs, and the evening sun has set upon him covered with crimes and stained with blood

I have already told you that this code is peculiar to Ireland, and I add that the experience of many years is at once a melancholy attestation of its necessity, and a convincing proof of its efficacy, and there is no instance (except where open rebellion has raged) in which those laws have not been found adequate to the suppression of the evil I can conceive that some will find it difficult to reconcile that opinion with the known and deplorable truths, that at the end of more than 60 years we are still struggling with insurrection in the third generation of those against whom those laws were pointed But it is not the province or within the power of such laws, as judges, and juries can administer, nor do those laws affect to annihilate such an evil as this. What may be its remote causes or remote effects—whether its roots strike deep, and threaten higher and more widely extended mischief, and if so, what course or system is best calculated to *eradicate* it, are questions awful and grave—they belong however to the statesman and the legislator, and not to us in this court of justice whose duty is to repress crime by enforcing the existing laws. Although the calls upon us for the discharge of that duty are, alas. too frequent, and although this mysterious engine of secret combination, shifted from place to place, continues to be wielded and worked by some invisible hand from time to time, now against one part of the Island, and now against another, yet those who have had the experience of many years of official and judicial life, can assure you that it has never been able to stand against the venerable authority of the laws vigorously and calmly brought to bear upon it   It is little more than a year, since the County of Clare has been agitated to a degree beyond what was ever known in Ireland, (short of civil war,) and the insurgents had almost, if not altogether, taken the field, but the course of justice at two assizes and one special commission, was (contrary to the apprehensions of many) found sufficient to put down the mischief, and I believe I am correctly informed in stating that at this moment, tranquillity is perfectly re-established in that county—that the misguided people have become sensible of their errors, and that confidence and good will are restored amongst those classes so lately arrayed in hostility against each other. Some of those who hear me, remember the insurrection of the Thrashers in 1806, when the entire province of Connaught with the exception of one County, and two Counties on the North West Circuit (Longford and Cavan) were overrun by insurgents, so formidable that the King's Judges upon a Special Commission could not move through the country except under a military escort, so formidable, that the sentence of the law could not be executed in one particular county town, till a general officer had marched from a distant quarter at the head of a strong force, to support the civil power, yet in the short space of one month that special commission in the midst of an inclement winter visited five counties, and in consequence of the firm administration of the laws, supported by the cordial co-operation of the magistrates and gentry —such was the triumph of justice that the insurrection dissolved before its influence, and from that period, for some years the Crown Solicitor of those counties had no case of public disturbance to prosecute In some years after that, similar disturbances broke out at intervals in Cork, Limerick, Tipperary, Kerry, Waterford, and Kilkenny, some formidable, and some made more particularly alarming by the existence of a war with France, then governed by the Emperor Napoleon All those counties were visited, as you are now, by special commissions, and all were pacified, some, I hope, permanently, some for a long time, and if there be others again infected by this moral pestilence, I trust that the same effects will follow from the same causes, and that the laws of the country will be always sufficient to subdue the disease and stop the contagion.

But let it be remembered that if that expectation should be disappointed, if the deluded people should continue incorrigibly to increase in wickedness as they have lately done, they may have to repent of the additional guilt of bringing down upon their country the operation of those stronger measures to which in cases of extreme necessity the Legislature has often resorted you all know what I allude to, and many whom I see, can remember as I do, the suspension of the Habeas Corpus Act, which at this moment secures the personal liberty of every man who hears me Many can remember the trial by jury, that institution long envied, and at last emulated by other countries, superseded in Ireland by the summary insurrection act, and the more summary court martial Every man who recollects those days, wishes that they may never return, but younger men of all classes only know them by description, and let them be assured that no description can convey an adequate notion of the horrors belonging to such a state of things Some of those who are disgusted and alarmed by the progress of insurrection, and impatient of the persevering follies and vices of the people, may look to such measures as a remedy more appropriate than our present proceeding, while the audacious and infatuated wretches now confederated against the peace of the country, may be taught by their more criminal instigators to despise a danger and defy a power which they have never experienced, but let both take counsel from those who have lived before them, and they will be told what a fearful thing it is to live in a country bereft of those free institutions, which, while they restrain, protect all classes of society in the enjoyment of their respective rights Such an evil is to be deprecated, but the time may come when it will be the least of two misfortunes, and the only means left to quell rebellion and avert anarchy. It is not unnatural that those who witness and suffer by daily and increasing outrages should think that time already arrived, and surely, on the other hand it will be expected by every constitutional man, that the Legislature will always pause to the last moment, and almost beyond the last moment, before it will adopt that course, which, however, the history of all countries shews *that the extreme danger of the commonwealth may call for and justify.* Whenever that day shall come *vae victis, vae victoribus.* Woe to the vanquished, woe to the conquerors

I have called the attention of those who hear me to the severity and effectiveness of the Whiteboy code, in the hopes of suggesting useful reflections to all classes of the community, but I must add, that a deplorable peculiarity of the offences and the laws which the Judges are now dealing with, and of the state in which we find this country, is the extreme difficulty of administering justice in that spirit of mitigating mercy, which, whenever it can be acted upon, constitutes our most pleasing as well as our most imperious duty Every one who has observed the ordinary administration of justice at the assizes against

ordinary offences, must have witnessed the anxiety with
which the circumstances connected with each culprit and
with his offence, are investigated by the presiding Judge
both during the trial and after the conviction, and if youth
and previous good character, or compulsion, or seduction,
or its having been a first offence, or the pressure of poverty
can be established in his favour, all discretionary punishments are graduated after giving their fair value to all such
favourable circumstances, and if the punishment be not
discretionary the judgment is merely recorded for the moment, and a recommendation to the executive government
is uniformly followed by a commutation of the sentence
from death to transportation or imprisonment, or from
transportation to imprisonment, and the duration of either
is abridged as far as is consistent with that necessary
example which is the great object of criminal law.—But
when justice has to deal, not with one individual trans-
gressor of a particular law to the injury of another individual, but with associations confederated against all law,
and all the institutions upon which society depends, there
is much difference, and the Judge who consults his consci-
ence will find, that, with a view to the good to be effected
by example, he is bound by the sterner duty of administering that code, whose principle is that *slight transgressions
in aid of insurrection are dangerous crimes.* The last Assizes
furnished more than one instance of this, but one in particular remembered by many who hear me. A very young
man was convicted of his first offence—an act certainly of
great violence, but not accompanied by actual cruelty.
He appeared to be a respectable youth, and his conduct on
his trial, was decorous and prepossessing,—he was an indus-

trious tradesman, not interested in landed property so as to connect him with that motive or pretence for unlawful association, and he was represented, I believe truly, to be the only support of a widowed mother. He is now doomed to transportation for seven years—and at the assizes the Judge refused to act upon the intercession of a humane and respectable gentleman, or to support any recommendation for mercy to Government. Afterwards the Lord Lieutenant referred to the Judge a petition from this unhappy person, supported by many attestations to his former character and good conduct and desired to know, whether in his opinion, " the convict was a proper object of mercy," and the Judge reported that he was not, and stated his reasons for thinking so   This man's crime was neither prompted by want, nor by anger, nor by revenge, or any of the ungovernable passions of youth, but was perpetrated in pursuance of the objects of that lawless association which still infests this country   In the day time he and two other men, armed with two hatchets and a scythe, took advantage of the supposed absence at a fair of the proprietor, and male inhabitants of a house where fire-arms were kept, burst into it, ransacked every part of it in search of those arms, broke the windows, demanded the arms with savage threats from the terrified females, raised those murderous weapons against them, and the prisoner struck a blow at one woman with a hatchet, which did not reach her, and probably was not intended to do so —They failed to get the arms—no life was lost—no wound was inflicted —no property was taken. But, one of the offences created by the Whiteboy Act was committed, and that was neither more nor less than an *attempt to put the arms of honest men into the hands of ruffians, for the purpose of overawing the laws, and bearing down the lawful institutions of the country*

Such was the crime exhibiting the sad influence of this infatuating conspiracy, even upon men of good dispositions and good character This young man's petition was unaccompanied by the profession of repentance—even by a pretence that the crime had been committed under compulsion or seduction,—by any abandonment of the principles of that confederacy to which he belonged, by any compunction for the offence, by any offer to surrender arms And when was it preferred ? Not after the defeat and humiliation of penitent insurgents, when Government is always happy to proclaim amnesty, and to dispense mercy but, while his unsubdued associates (as they had been doing indeed, at the very moment of his trial, and during the entire assizes) were spreading that terror and destruction through the country, which has continued almost up to the day on which I now address you, as the necessity of this Commission and the catalogue of crimes in this calendar too plainly testifies Mercy to him would have been cruelty to the public, and if I had advised it, (for I was the Judge) I should be responsible for all the too probable consequences of encouraging existing insurrection by impunity Every feeling man commisserates the fate of this victim, and wishes that he could have been spared , and some may censure the severity of his sentence , but let such throw the blame upon those who ought to bear it—upon his confederates, and upon those who set them on It is *they* who bring down Justice upon the deluded people, and shut *the gates of Mercy against* them,—they make the exiles, and the orphans, and the widows, whose wailing is heard through the land

From directing your thoughts to no pleasing view of our present situation, and to what I hope may be an instructive retrospect, and to a warning consideration of what, perhaps, is to come, I will conclude by recalling your attention to all that is in our power to do, and *that is our duty* Let us do that firmly and temperately—I say *firmly* and *temperately*, for in agitated times, it is hard to preserve the equable balance of the mind. Fear is a corrupting principle, and alarm operates in different and opposite directions—in such times, the influence of panic has led men, I am sorry to say, of all classes, to truckle to the insurgents, to decline those duties which the administration of justice calls for, or, what is worse, to discharge them in a spirit of base compromise, in the silly hope of securing, what could never be more than a temporary and precarious safety, or from the more abject motive of earning an ignominious popularity · on the other hand, panic is often the source of a blind, rash, indiscriminating zeal, an exasperating energy, more resembling the temper of war, than the stayed step and sober-minded character of Justice.—We should always remember that we are engaged in a conflict of law against outrage, and not of one violence against another, and that in proportion as the enormity of the offence calls for exertion, it also calls upon us to distrust, or at least to watch ourselves, and to proceed cautiously and circumspectly, not only because the punishments to be inflicted are heavy, but because it is impossible to approach the discharge of our present duties without a deep and personal interest in putting down the existing mischief—an interest which we are bound to neutralize by the coolest impartiality. In the discharge of my duties at the last Assizes, I had no reason to suppose that either of those imputations could, with truth, be alleged against the gentry of this county, but I have warned you against those extremes of error, which long experience in many places, tells me are the natural produce of distracted times, and the consequences of that demoralization which, once introduced into society, is never stationary Let us, therefore, co-operate in our several departments, in carrying into execution the laws of our country, and in the Grand Jury Room, in the Petit Jury Box, and on the Bench, enter into a covenant with ourselves, so calmly and scrupulously, to investigate every charge as to ensure the conviction of every guilty man, and the acquittal of every man whose innocence is manifested, or whose guilt is made doubtful.

TRIAL OF JOHN DELANY,

For Shooting at John Bailey.

About half-past ten o'clock, this day, their Lordships entered the Court The first prisoner put to the bar was John Delany who was indicted for shooting at John Bailey, at Inch, on the 27th of March last

JURY

J Warburton,	R Belton,	John Dunne,
J Tibeaudo,	B Thacker,	R Senior,
J R Price,	Henry Brereton,	Joshua Kemmis, and
Robert Fitzgerald,	James Price,	Mansell Dames, Esqrs

[In the selection of the Jury, the full number, twenty, were peremptorily challenged on the part of the prisoner, and only one was set aside by the Crown]

The ATTORNEY-GENERAL addressed the Court and Jury as follows —

My Lords, and Gentlemen of the Jury,—the prisoner, John Delany, stands charged with the commission of a capital felony; to sustain that charge, it will be necessary for me, on the part of the Crown, to lay before you, evidence which, in its substance and result, would have justified us in indicting the prisoner for murder if this were a case in which homicide had actually taken place.—This crime belongs to a class, the unfortunate prevalence of which, has induced his Majesty's Government to issue a Special Commission, under the authority of which we all act. I believe it is the only instance to be found in which a measure of such a character has ever been required by the condition of your county I have long known the Queen's County—I have perhaps known it as well as any part of Ireland, and to my mind, it is not only surprising, but almost unaccountable, how, in such a county, and among such a people, the spirit of lawless violence—the existence of illegal confederacies should have grown to such a pitch, as it has attained I have been acquainted with the habits of order, of peace, of subordination of the lower orders of its population. What a frightful change we now contemplate ! It is too true to be denied that there exists at this moment, in this county, a state of things, which has imperatively demanded the exercise of the utmost power, which the executive Government of the country possesses, to suppress the causes which have engendered this terrific, this pestilential spirit The administration of the law at the ordinary and accustomed periods, has failed to exterminate them; for notwithstanding the protraction of the last Assizes to an unusual period,—notwithstanding the signal success of the public prosecutions,—notwithstanding the numerous—the melancholy examples, which were made to the offended justice of the country,—notwithstanding the firm and faithful discharge of their duties by the Jurors of your county,—notwithstanding all this, in the short space of six weeks, a period of the year when there was full occupation for every industrious man, in that short period, the Government of the country has been compelled, by the iniquity and the extent of the crimes of the people, to issue this Commission to Judges of high rank, long experience, and exalted character, to administer the criminal justice of the country, and to call upon this county, through the constitutional medium of its Juries, to save itself

My Lords, I have said, that this state of things is in this county wholly unaccountable Were I to attempt to assign any rational cause for it, the attempt must prove abortive How is it possible for any reasonable, reflecting being for one moment to believe, that the commission of crime can be the means of obtaining any one good? But we are not put to reason, we have proofs and facts to convince us. Never, never can any consequence follow from a violation of the law, but mischief and irretrieveable ruin All that can be said on this subject may be expressed in a single sentence in an address of Baron Smith, delivered at the last Spring Assizes, and which I am happy to say has been published, and is in extensive circulation —His Lordship says, " no grievance, which the people can suffer would be " so great, as that which they would inflict upon themselves " by the subversion of the law "

But as I have said before, we are not put to reason upon the subject, for we have facts and actual experience to instruct us. With respect to the peaceable and well-disposed portion of the community, what is the consequence of the state of things, which I am thus exposing? It is this, that the security of life and property no longer exists, that they groan under an intolerable despotism—an uncontrouled and uncontroulable power, uncontrouled and uncontroulable for the present; but, I trust the time has arrived, when the law will put an end to this state of things, and restore the country to the enjoyment of tranquillity, security and peace

But what benefit or what blessing has these illegal associations conferred upon those who have been engaged in them? Has it remedied or alleviated any one evil? On the contrary has it not led many to expiate their crimes against the offended justice of the country by death and exile, leaving their wretched families in a condition of penury and wretchedness—But above all, has it not oppressed with a consciousness of guilt every member of their wicked associations? How can any man for an instant enjoy peace or repose of mind, who is conscious not only that he has committed flagrant crimes, but that his life and his liberty are under the controul and command of persons who are privy to his guilt, and who, sooner or later, will assuredly feel no compunction in appearing on the table, and aid the justice of the country against their wicked associates. Sooner or later that must happen. I remember in another county having, under circumstances, similar to those in which we are now placed, ventured to anticipate such an event.

Three months had not elapsed, when, as public prosecutor, I could have produced approvers, without number, ready and willing to give evidence against their guilty associates upon the condition of securing their own lives.

In your address, my Lord Chief Justice, to the Grand Jury, yesterday, your Lordship reviewed the history of that code called the Whiteboy Acts, which the condition of this country has made it necessary occasionally to call into operation. Few of us are so young as not to have witnessed many of the illegal combinations, which, from time to time, have infested this country. We have seen the misguided people enter into a conflict with the law between which and them there must exist an uncompromising hostility, for no Government can tolerate the despotism which they seek to establish. In other countries we have seen them gain a degree of strength which unquestionably in this country they have not yet attained, but one after another we have seen them share the same common fate: we have seen them dashed to pieces by the irresistable power of the law. Believe me, Gentlemen, that the time is come when it is the duty of every man to co-operate with those, whose duty it is to protect them in the enjoyment of their lives and liberties — The time is come when no honest man ought to remain passive — I know that these associations gain strength in their origin from a false estimate of the dangers to which they lead—they become formidable by degrees, and attain maturity and power, from the apathy and indifference of those who ought to unite to put them down. Independently of being negligent and passive, there are some base enough to connive at them—some are mad enough to court the protection of these illegal combinations, but, believe me, that those persons who are thus inactive and who thus crouch and truckle to them, will, if that state of things continue, be their slaves, and finally their victims — I tell them, that the time has come when even the narrowest view of self-interest ought to teach them, and inculcate upon their minds, that they should rally round the laws of their country, for the purpose of exterminating this illegal power—this intollerable tyranny.

My Lords, I had intended in the opening of the first case to be tried under this Special Commission, to have gone somewhat at large into a detail of the actual condition of this county, and into an examination of those laws which its present condition has called into operation, but, having heard and considered the address of your Lordship to the Grand Jury, yesterday, and having had an oppportunity, in which I rejoice, that the public participates, of reading and considering the various addresses addressed from that Bench, within the last year by Baron Smith, I feel that I would be guilty of a waste of the public time, if I were to enlarge more fully upon those topics If the testimony of your Lordships' great experience—if your earnest, your anxious, your almost paternal admonitions, fail to make upon the minds of these unhappy people, the deep, lasting, and salutary impression, that they ought, any argument or persuasion within my power to command must be utterly unavailing.

Gentlemen of the Jury —I am sure from your experience and intelligence, even if you had not heard the address from the Bench, yesterday, that you must feel that there is nothing which has fallen from me now, that can, or ought to effect the evidence of the guilt, or innocence of the prisoner at the bar, so far as regards his case My duty is now a very simple one—it is fairly to state to you the facts which will be laid before you by the witnesses. I told you that this is one of a class of those crimes which are engendered by the spirit of combination. The prisoner is a young man, we are not able to discover any private, any personal motive which could have led him to the commission of the act with which he is charged, the motive for the act must have been the furtherance of the illegal designs of those wicked associations which infect your country.

Mr J. Bailey, a man far advanced in years, who bears a most unimpeachable character, happened unfortunately to be a renter of tithes, and in the exercise of his legal right, he was obliged to make a distress From that period he appears to have become the object of a most malevolent conspiracy—he could not find labourers to do his work—he was consequently obliged, with the assistance of a pensioner,

of the name of Fleming, and of his own son, to work with
the spade himself, and was employed on the 27th March
last, in a field with them, covering his potatoes. Two days
before the occurrence of the transaction in question, an attack had been made upon his house, in the middle of the
day, for the purpose of obtaining his arms, and the assailants, were beaten off. In consequence of that attack, when
he went to work on the 27th, he and his son took with
them fire arms. The field where they were at work, is
about the distance of one hundred yards from his house—
about three o'clock in the afternoon of that day, two persons entered the yard close to his house These two men
were proceeding to go over the wall, but they turned back,
and one of them asked a boy, who was in the yard, the
shortest way to the field These two persons were each
armed with a blunderbuss, and one of them had a pistol.
On quitting the yard, one of them cried out, brandishing
his blunderbuss—" At last we have the arms ' During
this period their approach was perfectly discernible by Mr.
B and the other persons who were with him. The two
men advanced towards them, brought their blunderbusses
to a level, and when within about fourteen yards of Mr.
Bailey, they demanded his fire-arms. Mr B. and his son
were each armed with a pistol They endeavoured to discharge the pistols, but they missed fire. They immediately
fled in different directions—one of the men followed the son,
and the other followed the father just as the father had
leaped a ditch, the man who pursued him, fired his blunderbuss at him, and the contents lodged in his hip, and
thigh, and back. He fell immediately after: the other
man discharged his blunderbuss at the son, but that fortunately did not take effect, and the man then snapped the
pistol at him. The son fled to the road—he had approached

within a few yards of it, when he discovered a third man armed with a gun—to escape him he turned back, and the man upon the road fired at him. On changing his course, he was met by the man whose pistol had gone off, and he endeavoured again to discharge it, but missed fire.

This, Gentlemen, is the simple state of facts, which will be laid before you in evidence. I make no observation upon them—you will hear them from the witnesses—I have detailed them to you, as nearly as possible, according to the instructions that I have received

First Witness, *John Fleming*, examined by Mr TICKFILL. —I remember Tuesday, the 27th March last, I was on that day working for John Bailey, on the lands of Inch. Mr B. and his son. and a woman of the name of Judith Coyle, were with me as we were at work, we were alarmed by cries, which we heard from the house; we were about 100 yards, or better, from the house; the cries that we heard proceeded from Mrs. Bailey, we instantly looked round, and we saw two men running towards us, each of them had a blunderbuss in his hand, they were within about eighty yards of us, when we first saw them, they were coming straight from Mr. Bailey's house, they were then running, when they entered the field where we were working, and were coming near us, pistols were presented at them, they then halted, and they cried " Give up the arms." they partly halted, and then advanced to where we were, there was a gap at the entrance into the field, where we were, through which they went into the field,—that gap was about forty yards from where we were; when they came within about fourteen yards of us, they brought the blunderbusses to their shoulders, it was before they brought them to their shoulders that they demanded the arms, when they brought the blunderbusses to their shoulders, I saw them plainly cover Mr. Bailey and his son, Mr. Bailey and his son snapped their pistols at them, when they came within about fourteen yards of them, and they both missed fire; that was after they demanded the arms, it was when the two men had the blunderbusses at their shoulders that Mr. Bailey and his son snapped their pistols; when the pistols missed fire, young Mr Bailey retired from my side, and then one of the men fired after him, old Mr. Bailey ran also and leapt over a ditch, and the other man followed him and fired across the ditch at him; the man was about seven yards from me when he fired at him, I did not see old Mr Bailey until I leapt up on the ditch, after he called me · I went up to him and found him partly lying on one side; the blood was running from his wounds. I did not examine the cause of that blood flowing, Mr. Bailey stood up on one thigh, and I got him on my back and carried him home to his own house, I had the two men in my view constantly from the time that I first saw them until Mr Bailey was shot, the man who shot Mr. Bailey was within about seven yards of me when he fired, I did not see that man after that until I saw him a prisoner in Stradbally, that was about a month after this transaction, there were seven men more with him when I saw him in Stradbally, when I saw him among the seven men no person pointed him out to me, as the person who fired · [here the witness identified the prisoner, as the person who shot Mr. Bailey;] I am quite satisfied that the prisoner is the man that I saw fire the shot at Mr. Bailey, I am quite certain of it

Cross-examined by Mr. GRAYDON—This was about ten minutes after three o'clock in the afternoon, just before that young Mr. Bailey looked at his watch, it was a fine day, when I saw the men first they were running and continued to run until they came into the field, where we were, they opened right and left when they were coming up to us to take their object, I had seen them about a minute before they got into the second field, they had their hats on they had not great coats on, they attempted no violence towards me, Mr Bailey was to my right side when he was fired at, but he was partly to my front, young Mr Bailey was the first person that was fired at, the father and son took different directions, one went to the left and the other to the right, old Mr Bailey was out of my sight when the shot was fired at him, but the man that fired at him was not out of my sight, I never knew the man before, it is by his face and figure and speech that I identified him, but by his face in particular, I heard him speak in Stradbally, I did not hear him speak there before I identified him, the leaf of his hat was partly slouched down when I was going to Stradbally I had not the least idea that I was going to see the man that fired at Mr Bailey, I went to Stradbally because I was sent for, the Rev Hunt Johnson was the first person that I had any conversation with in Stradbally, I did not know what the prisoner's name was until that day; I saw him afterwards in Maryborough Gaol, when I saw him there, there were five or six more men with him, I had not the least doubt about him when I saw him in Stradbally; when I saw him in Stradbally my mind was made up, but I am very cool before I swear, it was the day that I saw him in Maryborough Gaol that I swore the informations, I was rather afraid until I was protected out of the country, for murdered I would be of course I was afraid at the time I was at Stradbally, I was sure of the prisoner in both places, after I came home from Stradbally I saw a reward offered, it was not up when I was going away, I thought whoever would take the prisoner would get the reward; the reward was £200; I did not expect to get the reward because I did not take him, I read the advertisement over and over, Mr Singleton told me that I would be protected, on the evening that he took my informations, at Maryborough Gaol, he sent me to Dublin

To a JUROR—There was a kind of a gap, where the shot was fired at Mr. Bailey, about four feet high, the man was about a yard and a-half from the ditch when he fired the shot

JUROR—You said something about knowing him by his speech, did he speak in the field before he fired? Yes; they demanded the arms.

Second Witness, *James Luttrell Bailey*, examined by Mr. MARTLEY—I am the son of John Bailey, he lives in Inch, near Stradbally, my father holds about 20 acres of land there; he holds other property there, as lessee of tithes to the college, he was obliged to make a distress for those tithes, after he put the cattle into pound, they were branded with the word " *Tithe*," this happened about 12 months ago; before that, my father was in the habit of employing labourers to till his land, after that, he found it very difficult to procure labourers to till his land; he could not procure any labourers in March last, he had only one labourer to assist him, that was John Fleming, before that, my father was not in the habit of working as a labourer himself, on the 25th of March last, I recollect that persons came to my father's house, to look for arms, I saw five men altogether; I believe they saw arms with me, I fired at one of them, I remember my father received a wound on Tuesday, the 27th of March last he and I were working about 100 yards from the house the day he received that wound, there was only one field between us and the house, John Fleming, and a woman named Judith Coyle, were working with us on that day, my father received the wound between three and four o'clock in the day, I saw two men turning in the direction we were in from the stable of my father's house. I saw them coming into the next field where we were, there was a gap coming into the field where we were, the two men partly separated when they came into the field, and they afterwards closed, my father and I were about ten yards asunder, when I first saw the men coming, I saw two short pieces in their hands, which I believed to be blunderbusses, I had a pistol in my pocket, when they were closing upon us, I snapped the pistol, but it missed fire, I then ran away, I then heard two shots fired, I did not see where my father ran to, I did not run in the same direction with him, I ran towards the road, I saw another person standing on the road, he presented a piece at me, with that I turned back and I heard a shot, when running back towards my father's house, I saw one of the two men that I first saw, he snapped a pistol at me, and missed fire, I saw the face of these persons distinctly, the prisoner at the bar is one of the persons that I saw that day; I am positive of that; he is one of the two men that I first saw; he had a blunderbuss, they had the blunderbusses partly to their shoulders I saw them point them, the prisoner was not the man that snapped the pistol at me, I afterwards saw the prisoner in Maryborough gaol, I swore informations against him that day, when I saw him in the gaol, there were three or four other men with him.

Cross-examined by Mr GRAYDON.—The two shots were fired nearly at the same time, when Fleming came back from Stradbally, I asked him if he had any news, he told me that there was a man in gaol that I would be glad to see, he did not mention his name; he bid me ask him no more questions, and he handed me a note from the Rev H. Johnson; Mr Johnson desired me in the note not to ask Fleming any questions; I recollect having seen an advertisement offering a reward, I do not recollect when I first saw it; I did not see Fleming in Maryborough, the first day that I went to Maryborough, I did not see Mr Johnson there, I went there another day, and then I saw the man and lodged the informations against him, I did not go to the gaol the first day that I went to Maryborough; the prisoner was not shewn to me more than once, I heard of the reward before I went to Maryborough, my father used to be talking of going to America, as the country was in such a bad state.

CHIEF JUSTICE —When these men pointed the arms at you and your father, did they say anything to you? They muttered something, but I cannot say what it was. Was it before or after you snapped the pistol at them? It was before. When you were in Maryborough jail, there were persons shewn to you? Yes, they were brought into the jail yard, and I was brought into a room to look at them through the window. When you saw them, did you at once satisfy yourself that the prisoner was one of the two men, that you saw in the field with the blunderbusses? I did, and I told it to Mr Singleton

Third Witness, *George Ramsay*, (an interesting little boy about 12 years of age,) examined by Mr. CLARKE.— I know Mr. John Bailey· I recollect the day that he received the wound, I was in his service at that time, he was trenching potatoes that day; his son James and John Fleming were with him, I was in the yard that day, when I was there, I heard two shots, before I heard the shots,

I saw two men come into the yard, each of them had a blunderbuss and one had a pistol, when they came into the yard, they ran to a pig yard, and laid their hands on a wall, if they got over it, it would lead to the field where my master was; they did not get over the wall, they came back and passed within a yard of me, one of them asked me the way out to the field, I did not tell him, they then went to the haggard, they passed me and turned to the left, I went into the larder and brought a young child with me, and I saw them going to the field that my master was in, one of them whirled the blunderbuss over his head and said, "We will have the arms!" I saw their faces distinctly in the yard, I would know them if I saw them again, the prisoner at the bar is one of them; I am quite sure that that is one of the two men that I saw in the yard he had a blunderbuss in his hand yesterday was the first time that I saw him since I saw him in the yard, I saw him yesterday in the jail yard, there were three persons with him when I saw him, I knew him immediately

Cross-examined by Mr. GRAYDON —I never saw him before the day that my master was shot, I heard my mistress crying out, neither Fleming nor young Mr Bailey asked me if I knew these persons? two policemen brought me to the jail yesterday, they did not tell me what I was going there for, there were four men in the jail, standing in a line, the prisoner was the second on my right hand; Mr. Singleton was with me, I looked at them only once, I knew the prisoner at once, I looked up along them straight, I got no hint, after I looked at the four men across, I went and laid my hand on the prisoner, I saw Mr. Adair, the evening that my master was shot, and I was desired not to talk to any body about it, I heard of a reward being offered; I don't know the time, I had no conversation with any body to-day about this business, but a gentleman told me to tell the truth, when I went to the jail, Mr Singleton said "Bring out three men besides John Delany!" that was the first time I heard his name mentioned.

CHIEF JUSTICE.—When the four men were brought out into the jail yard for you to look at, did they or any of them mention what their names were, or did any body in the yard mention the names? Not after they were brought out. After they were brought out, did any body in their presence mention the name John Delany? No

BARON SMITH.—When the four men came out, all you knew was that one of them was John Delany? That is all Did any body point your attention to his person? No.

Mr. GRAYDON.—After the men were brought out, did any one come forward, and ask the men "What is your name, and what is your name?" I heard no one asking that question?

Fourth Witness, *William Bailey*, (a boy of about twelve years of age,) examined by Mr. ARABIN—I am the son of John Bailey, I recollect the day my father was wounded, I was in the stable that day cleaning a horse, while I was there I heard mamma screeching, I came out of the stable and saw two men crossing the yard going to the haggard; they had a blunderbuss each, and one of them had a pistol, they said that they should get the arms. One of them furled the blunderbuss over his head, they got into the haggard, and went into the field next to that dada was working in; I heard two shots, that was about four minutes after I saw the men, I would know either of them; the prisoner at the bar is one of them, I am certain that that is one of the two men that passed through the haggard.

Cross-examined by Mr. GRAYDON—They were running, they did not ask me any question, I never saw the prisoner before that day, I was brought to see him in the gaol yesterday, Mr Singleton was with me, George Ramsay was with me; four men were brought out, I heard the name of the prisoner yesterday, and never before, it was after he was brought out yesterday that I heard his name, Mr. Singleton mentioned his name.

CHIEF JUSTICE —How did he mention his name? He said that John Delany was his name, George Ramsay was there, it was after George Ramsay and I had pointed him out that Mr Singleton mentioned his name, his name was not mentioned before I pointed him out, I did not hear it mentioned, before I pointed out the prisoner nobody asked the other men their names

Fifth Witness, *William Digby Lalor*, (Physician,) examined by the ATTORNEY-GENERAL —I know Mr. John Bailey, I recollect having been sent for to see him on the 27th of March last, it was near six o'clock in the evening, his son had dressed him before I saw him, I saw two wounds in his left hip, another in his thigh, another in his leg, and another in his back, [the witness here produced three very large slugs, which he said, he extracted from Mr Bailey] I saw Mr. Bailey last night, I think he is sinking, I think him in great danger of death, I think it impossible for him to attend here to-day, his wife was confined about nine days ago, I would not advise her to attend here to-day.

ATTORNEY-GENERAL —Now, my Lords, I offer them Judith Coyle, we have brought her here, and they may examine her if they please

(The prisoner's Counsel declined to examine her.)

Here the evidence for the prosecution closed.

EVIDENCE FOR THE DEFENCE.

Margaret Lalor, examined by Mr GRAYDON —I am the wife of William Lalor he holds about twenty-four acres of land, I know John Delany the prisoner at the bar, he was in my husband's employment on the 27th of March last, he had been one day in his employment before that, and he was in his employment the day after the 27th, and part of another day the 27th was on a Tuesday he was cutting rushes part of that day, and backing a ditch the remainder of the day I know he was at work in the middle of the day, I saw him between one and four o'clock, his brother was at work with him at the ditch, my husband was not at home and I was in care of the work, John Delany slept in my house that night, and he had slept there the night before, the next day my father-in-law sent for a man to work, and I sent him John Delany, I do not know where Mr. Bailey lives, I do not know where Inch is.

Cross-examined by Mr TICKELL —I first heard of the prisoner being taken up on Easter Sunday night I am sure my husband heard of it in the course of the morning; I knew the prisoner a year before he went to work with me, I do not know what part of the country he came from, it was on Easter Monday, I heard of his being taken, I heard that what he was taken for was for drinking, I never heard of his having been accused of firing at Mr Bailey, I did not hear it until he was kept in Stradbally, to the best of my knowledge that was on Easter Tuesday, when my husband came home I had no conversation with him at all, about John Delany being accused of firing at Mr. Bailey, I did not dive much into the business until I was summoned, before I was summoned, I told my girl that I thought this man was innocent; I was summoned last Monday, since I was summoned I told my husband that this man was innocent

CHIEF JUSTICE.—How did you come to know that the 27th was the day that Mr. Bailey was fired at? It was the day after the fair of Maryborough When did you first know what time Mr Bailey was fired at? When John Delany was put in The moment you heard this man was accused, did you know he was innocent? I did When did you hear upon what day Mr Bailey was fired at? Not until I was summoned What was the latest hour, that you saw the prisoner on the 27th? I saw him after two o'clock that day, and after three o'clock.

JUROR.—You don't know which part of the country he came from? I do not. Do you know his family? No.

Second Witness, *William Lalor*, examined by Mr. GRAYDON.—I am the husband of the last witness I remember the fair of Maryborough in March last; the prisoner came to me on the 25th of March, he remained in my employment two days and a half—the 26th, the 27th and part of the 29th, he was working with me on the 27th, I was not at home that day, I left him cutting rushes in the morning, I left his brother at work with him, I do not know what countryman he is, I sent him to my father to work on Wednesday the 28th, I paid for him, and therefore he was in my employment I do not know where Inch is.

Cross-examined by the ATTORNEY GENERAL—I never knew him until he came to my house to me about this time twelve month, he then worked a few days for me, I don't know that he has any settled place of abode I did not hear that he was charged with shooting at Mr Bailey, until he was brought from Stradbally to Maryborough. I do not know now upon what day Mr Bailey was shot, I cannot form a belief of the day he was shot, I never said a word to my wife about this business at any time, I am sure of that, I do not recollect that my wife ever said any thing to me about it, I left home on the 27th of March, a little after sun rise; it was on Sunday night the prisoner came to me, he slept at my house that night, I engaged him for the whole week, and he went away before the week was out; men came to him and took him away, because he would not get ten pence a day, I don't know where he came from.

Third Witness, *Daniel Delany*, examined by Mr. GRAYDON.—I am the brother of the prisoner, I was in the employment of Wm Lalor, on the fair day of Maryborough—the day after Lady-day, my brother was in his employment that day, my brother was cutting rushes on the 27th until breakfast time, and then he came to me, and was backing a ditch with me until night, he was the whole day working with me at that ditch, he was working with Wm Lalor's father on the 28th, on the day after, men came into the field, and said that he should not work any longer; he first went to William Lalor on the 25th of March, we met him in the morning, and agreed with him on the way; I do not know where Inch is.

Cross-examined by Mr MARTLEY —All my people live at Knockleague, that is about four miles from Wm Lalor's, I know William Lalor these 12 months; he knows the part of the country that I came from, I am sure of that, I went away at the end of the week I was working with William Lalor to plant my own potatoes, my brother was taken away from him by the men, my brother was working in William Lalor's field on Wednesday I was not at the fair of Maryborough William Lalor was not there, I am sure of that, my father and mother have been living at the widow Ryan's six or seven years, that is within a hundred perches of William Lalor's.

CHIEF JUSTICE ---Does William Lalor know them? He does Is your brother in the habit of living at the widow Ryan's? He is not

Maurice Deacon, examined by Mr. GRAYDON ---I hold twenty acres of land, I know the prisoner these five years, I know him well during that time, I always heard that he was quiet, sober and honest

CHARGE

CHIEF JUSTICE ---Gentlemen of the Jury,---the prisoner stands charged with maliciously and unlawfully shooting at John Bailey, and there is another count for maliciously and unlawfully shooting at James Luttrell Bailey The evidence is that he did shoot at John Bailey, and the evidence is that he did not shoot at James Bailey, but the evidence is that he was aiding the person who did shoot at him.

Gentlemen, this case divides itself into two views, the first is whether supposing the prisoner to be guilty, the offence is sustained in point of law, and the second is, supposing the offence to be sustained in point of law, is the prisoner Guilty? As to the first, I do not apprehend that there is any difficulty What the Attorney-General has very truly stated to you, the test by which, upon such an indictment, the law tries that question, is this —— If John Bailey had lost his life by that shot, would the homicide be murder? If it would, this indictment is supported. If on the contrary, it would be but manslaughter, this indictment would not be supported.

Gentlemen it appears upon the evidence, if you believe it, that the person who was fired at and his son both attempted to fire at the prisoner and the other person who was with him, a question might arise upon that part of the case whether their having attempted this violence against the prisoner, would give that turn to the transaction, that would make that homicide, manslaughter. In my apprehension there can be no ground for saying that it would.

It is perfectly clear that the attempt made by Mr. Bailey and his son to take away the life of the prisoner, was an attempt made by them either in resisting assassins, or in resisting men who had at that moment committed a felony by an attempt forcibly to take away their arms, this is, therefore, a case in which if a homicide had followed, by the death of Bailey, that homicide would, I take it, have been murder.

Gentlemen, the next question for your consideration, is this, is the prisoner the person guilty of this offence? And that depends upon the credit which you will give to four witnesses for the Crown, who have all sworn to his identity. In the first place, you are to consider the integrity of those witnesses, and whether if you are of opinion, that in point of morals, they are credible upon their oaths, and secondly, whether intending to swear truly, they have sworn accurately. If a reasonable and conscientious case be suggested to your minds, as to their having possibly made a mistake, you are bound to acquit the prisoner.

Now, Gentlemen, these four persons have positively sworn to the identity of the prisoner, but you will recollect this, that not one of them had known him before You will also recollect that the opportunity they had on that occasion was very short, a period of a very few minutes, and those very agitated minutes, certainly there are some men whose faculties are concentrated, and there are others whose faculties are prostrated by such circumstances.

But such as it is they have all sworn positively. Two persons have sworn positively as to what occurred in the field, and the other two have sworn positively as to what occurred in the farm-yard Now, although the *Corpus delicti* is not made out by the witnesses who saw the men in the farm-yard, yet, if they have sworn rightly they have shewn a very deliberate wicked intention, operating upon the persons who moved from the yard, and the witnesses as to what happened in the field, swear to the acting on that intention, and both swear to the same prisoner

Gentlemen, this prosecution, is encountered by a defence that is generally called an *alibi*. It is the best defence that can be made, if made to your satisfaction. In this case it turns altogether upon the testimony of witnesses contrasting their credit with the credit of the witnesses for the prosecution ---The credit of the witnesses is not necessarily contrasted with that of the witnesses for the prosecution, for the witnesses for the defence are swearing to facts which are either true or false, but the witnesses for the prosecution may have sworn truly, and yet be mistaken

Gentlemen, this defence is relieved from an imputation that very often rests upon defences of this kind

If a person whose attention is not called to a distinct transaction till a good while after that transaction has taken place, swears minutely and accurately to the day or the hour, it is difficult to conceive how any one's memory can be so tenacious and faithful, unless there be some particular reason for fastening the fact in his recollection.

But I think this case is relieved from that observation —— A person may be so illiterate as not to know the 27th day of March, and yet that person might have a distinct recollection of the day after Maryborough fair

Now the ear marks, (if I may so express it.) put upon the day in this case, are two one is that it happened upon the day after Maryboro' fair, and the other is that it happened the day after Lady day, which is one of the most notorious holidays in this country, and I believe it is not unusual to hire servants on that day If therefore, the *alibi* in this instance fails, it must fail upon the discredit of the witnesses, and not from any intrinsic objection to it

But, Gentlemen, you will apply the particular facts to the question of their credit I will only call your attention to one of them. At an early part of the testimony of William Lalor and his wife, it occurred to one of the Jury to ask what they knew of the prisoner? and they stated their utter ignorance of his family and their residence; but the brother of the prisoner swore that his father and mother lived within one hundred yards of them, and that they knew them well

Gentlemen these are the only preliminary observations which I think it necessary to make to you.

His Lordship then minutely recapitulated the evidence, and thus concluded —

Gentlemen that is the whole of the evidence. I have made some preliminary observations to you upon the nature of the evidence, and the concluding observations that I have to make are such as you hear from every Judge that ever addresses you from this place, and they are these you are not to find this man guilty if you have any reasonable doubt of his guilt, even though you may have doubts of his innocence, but if you have a moral certainty of his guilt, and see your way to it clearly without any doubt, both conscientious and reasonable, you are bound to convict him ---Such a doubt will always justify an acquittal, but no suspicion however strong will warrant a verdict of Guilty

When his Lordship concluded, the Jury retired, and in a few minutes returned into court with a verdict of--- GUILTY

The CHIEF-JUSTICE ---Mr Attorney-General, have you any thing to say ?

ATTORNEY-GENERAL.---Under ordinary circumstances, I should not think myself warranted in making the application which I am now to address to your Lordships ; but the situation of this county makes it my imperative duty, and it is a most painful one, to move your Lordships for immediate judgment upon the prisoner

The task of pronouncing sentence devolved on Baron Smith as junior Judge, who prefaced it by the following address

John Delany, the verdict, which has been just returned, imposes upon me a most awful and afflicting duty ; a duty, to the performance of which no habit has reconciled me, but which I now find as deeply painful, as it was thirty years ago, the terrific duty of announcing to my fellow-creature, that he has forfeited his life   Under such circumstances, I can only say, that it is a source of melancholy consolation, to reflect that you have had an impartial, fair, deliberate, and patient trial Your case has been heard and determined by a jury, composed of persons with whose principles and line of conduct, the transactions of the last assizes brought me in some degree acquainted; and whom I will describe as humane, unprejudiced, intelligent and conscientious. And how was this jury formed? It was constituted as favourably for *you*, as the most ample exercise of *your* rights, and the most sparing use of the privileges *of the Crown*, could make it. For, by peremptorily challenging twenty of the panel, you availed yourself of your privilege to its utmost limit. while, if I do not mistake, the Crown has not, in more than one solitary instance, asserted its right of causing a juror to stand by My Lord Chief Justice, in his charge, insisted on every topic, and made and dwelt on every observation on your behalf, which the evidence, or the law applicable to the case, supplied To that charge I listened with uninterrupted attention It was my duty to do so. Under any circumstances I should have done so. But I felt myself the more strictly bound to such attention, because his Lordship did me the honour of desiring, that if I dissented from any of his comments, or found him omitting what struck me to be material, I would suggest to him any impressions of this kind But in the opinions upon the law of the case, and observations upon the facts of the case which that charge contained, I entirely concur and am not aware of any omission which I could have supplied

You have been found guilty, under a statute which punishes criminal intention, even where the act, demonstrating this intent, has failed to accomplish its deadly, or sanguinary purpose.

In truth, you were near committing an *actual* murder. For how does the case stand? The wound was given about two months ago, yet, it was but yesterday that the last of the balls were extracted. The medical attendant informed us upon his oath, that it was quite impossible for the wounded man to appear in court. He even described him as in *a sinking state* So that in the moment in which I am addressing you, his situation is precarious; and perhaps his death is not unlikely. If he had died, let me suppose a few weeks ago, your trial on this day would have been for murder. And how would such a trial have terminated? The verdict which has been had, demonstrates that it would have ended in conviction and you would not only be now doomed to an ignominious death—but would not have many remaining hours to live.

Why am I warranted in pronouncing, that if death had ensued, you would have been found guilty of a murder? Because you have this day been found guilty of a murderous, or at least mischievously sanguinary and deliberate intent,—because, if upon the evidence which we heard, it had appeared that any death, ensuing on the wound you gave, would have been—not a murder but a manslaughter, (though of the most aggravated description) you would have at once obtained, and been entitled to an acquittal.

Between you and the wounded man, no private grudge appears to have previously existed Yet the jury, on the evidence, have found that you gave the dangerous—perhaps deadly—wound What seems to follow? That the sanguinary act, which we cannot trace to individual malice or ill will, must have originated in that turbulent spirit of confederated and lawless mischief, which is now maddening this county, and other portions of our distracted land

The jury, I repeat, have found your act to have been a deliberate one, and towards ascertaining whether the evidence sustained and justified such a finding, let us look to the evidence of the boys; *Ramsay* and the youngest *Bailey* We there find you and your associate, with loaded fire arms in your hands, entering the premises of your victim, and avowing the purpose of your visit, by triumphantly declaring that you would have his arms. No pistol had *then* been fired, or snapped at either. Before any such snapping had occurred, we have this evidence of an acknowledged purpose upon your part, a purpose deliberate, concerted, unprovoked. By your own confession, or rather boast, your object was to commit a felony, and homicide, committed in the prosecution of such a purpose, will be murder.

But, upon the proofs, we may reasonably conjecture that the plan was of some standing that the plundering attack, if not determined on, at least was thought on, long before That it originated in an offence against the combination code, committed by the elder Bailey, so long ago as in last Summer. The offence of meddling with obnoxious property, and presuming to farm tithes. Thus exactly, and deplorably, have those predictions been fulfilled, which I hazarded, from this bench, about a year ago

A more recent occurrence may have hastened the execution of your purpose. Some days before the wounding, an armed party had entered the premises of Bailey. One of the family resisted stoutly, and discharged a pistol at the aggressors It may then have been determined, that it was time to deprive the Baileys of those arms, which they seemed ready to make a spirited use of, for their protection.

The first Witness, Fleming, swore to a demand of arms, in the field which was the immediate scene of that outrage, of which you have been found guilty. Does this important part of the case rest upon the single, unsupported testimony of John Fleming? No if the clear and credible evidence of the boys is to be believed, the evidence of Fleming stands corroborated, not only by that of the younger Bailey, but by yourself. The statement of your having made a demand of arms in the field is corroborated by your having already, when you first entered upon the premises, avowed that your object was to possess yourselves of the arms, and exultingly anticipated your attainment of this guilty object. Consistently with this avowal, you made your illegal demand, when you had arrived at the potatoe-ground where your victim was, engaged in agricultural labours which were more or less beneath his rank, but which devolved unsuitably and chiefly upon himself and his son, because few or none would work for one who had presumed to deal with tithe.

How fatally—how ruinously dangerous it is, to excite the people to a refractory opposition to the law, and invasion of those rights, which that law has bestowed, and must protect!—In your case we behold a specimen, of the sad, and guilty, and penal consequences of such encouragement. In your, and similar cases, we but gather in that pernicious harvest, which the seeds that were scattered by such encouragement have produced. What is the early commencement, in your case? a prejudice against tithe property and claim. And to what has this quickly led? To an illegal combination to injure and destroy it, to aggression upon all who have an interest in upholding tithe, to a plunder of that species of property which may be made an instrument of farther mischief,—I mean arms, to the shedding of innocent blood, and lastly to the forfeiture of an excited and misguided peasant's life.

O that the infatuated peasantry would but see, that each member of those confederacies, which are destroying this fine country, by demoralizing its population, is stained with the blood of every victim, that is necessarily sacrificed to the outraged law! Yes, every conspirator against the law—is answerable to God for the lives which that Law is reluctantly obliged to take. Yes, all who are aware of the mischief which their proceedings were calculated to produce, yet excited such confederacy against the institutions of their country, will be fearfully answerable for the crimes which they have produced and sprinkled with the blood of those deluded convicts, whose deaths will have expiated their transgressions I will not say that all, who not reckless of consequences, but unfortunately blind to their approach, joined in fostering and encouraging such perilous combinations, are guilty and responsible to this vast extent but I do assert—that if they have the hearts of men, they must feel deep and keen remorse, for the effects which their improvident rashness has produced, and not content with abandoning their head-long and pernicious course, will endeavour to make tardy, and, after all, imperfect reparation, by diligent efforts to undo the mischief which they have done

What is it—that the frantic populace complain of? Either (as my Lord Chief Justice truly said) of imaginary grievances or of evils not arising from their laws or government, or from the conduct of their superiors, but from the unalterable (by them at least unalterable) *condition of human nature.* Do they murmur at the inequalities of rank? Then they are in array against what is necessary and useful. They murmur at the work and ordinance of God. But what God ordains cannot be ill and man's resistance to what God has willed—must be impious and evil.

Do I mean to say, that inequality of rank has no evils in its train? I do not mean to say so. The best of human good is contaminated with inseparable evil Such is, for the present the mysterious arrangement of Providence; such is the corrupt imperfection of our depraved and fallen nature. Until its purity be restored, we must rest satisfied with incomplete, and as it were adulterated good

Against wealth and rank, the present popular enmity seems pointed —and upon property, and its possessors,— upon those obnoxious higher ranks,—I admit that the ruinous consequence of popular disturbance might first fall. But trust me, in the end, upon the disturbers, the confederates, the lower orders, the community which those orders mainly form,—upon these would the destruction, which their madness is preparing, most overwhelmingly and irreparably fall. What have their perverted efforts hitherto achieved? I behold evil in abundance but look in vain for good

If I love the law,—if I would assert and vindicate it in case of need, even sternly and severely,—why is this the case? Because I love the people, whose best protector the Law is—O, why will my countrymen, abounding in virtues, in dispositions highly amiable, which even strangers are struck with, and acknowledge to be prepossessing,— why will they suffer those estimable qualities to be lost, and overwhelmed in the tempest of their violent and sudden passions, which it is in the power of every agitator to raise, and to let loose? They conceive that they are cordial and affectionate to one another. Why then will they form a league, to scatter crime, and death, and banishment, amongst those they love? The Whiteboy Code, for sixty years the disgraceful record of national turbulence and insurrection, why will the people make it necessary that we should retain? Only see what this turbulence occasions. The inevitable infliction of punishments perhaps heavier than the intrinsic nature and moral turpitude of the offence might seem to call for, but that what as individual offence is light, becomes weighty as an outbreak of insurrectionary combination. Why will the people, while they profess to love each other, combine to inflict these augmented penalties upon their friends?

I love mercy I feel how much I stand in need of it myself. But is mercy to be bestowed exclusively upon the guilty, and refused to the unoffending portion of our people? Strange would that mercy be, which by declining to point the wholesome severities of the Law, against those in turbulent array against it, deprived the innocent of security, of property, of their rights, their comforts, their morals, and their lives The law is roused, and when firmly administered, and assisted by the members of the community who are sound, I am persuaded, will ultimately prevail, and soberly triumph, and put down misrule But if it cannot do this as speedily as the urgency of the case requires,—if we must unwillingly have recourse to a more rigorous system one less compatible with our liberties, and less consonant to the spirit of that constitution which secures them — it is illegal confederacy and outrage, that will have brought this evil upon our people.

The learned judge then assumed the black cap, and solemnly, and with exhortations, pronounced the awful sentence of the Law.

COUNSEL FOR THE CROWN.

Mr Attorney General	Mr Clarke.
Mr. Tickell	Mr Arabin.
Mr Martley.	*Crown Solicitor,*—Mr Geale.

COUNSEL FOR THE PRISONER.	AGENT FOR THE PRISONER.
Mr. Graydon.	Mr Delany.

A part of Baron Smith's address to the convict, John Delany, proved predictive. On the 30th of May, a few days after the trial, the unfortunate Mr. Bailey died of his wounds.

TRIAL OF PATRICK NASH,

For Stabbing John Magee

SATURDAY —FOURTH DAY.

Their Lordships having come into Court at half-past ten o'clock this morning, and Patrick Nash having been put to the bar, a highly respectable Jury was sworn

The Attorney-General —My Lords and Gentlemen of the Jury, the crime with which the prisoner stands charged is one not only capital in its nature, but one of most peculiar enormity   The crime imputed to the prisoner, though there has not been a homicide, although the person wounded has not died, amounts in substance to the imputation of murder   Important as the case is, with regard to the unfortunate man upon his trial, there are circumstances, which, if any circumstances can, render it of still greater importance, and connect it with the dearest interests of the community   This is not a crime perpetrated through private malice, not prompted by any of the bad passions which stimulate to acts of violence and blood, but a crime perpetrated for the purpose of furthering, and advancing, and establishing projects, which, if they prevail, there must be an end of society itself   It is a crime perpetrated for the purpose of subverting those very principles

E

in which consist the authority of the law, the security for the life, the peace, the property, and the liberty of civilized man. We have already had at this Special Commission one trial originating in the same source, perpetrated for the same purposes the cause of the attack upon the man* in that case who was wounded, was his having been a lessee of tithes. The crime in this case has no connection with tithes, but it has the most intimate connection with the administration of justice My Lords, the immediate cause of the attempt upon Magee's life was this, that he had dared to take, or rather that he had dared to occupy with his uncle a house and farm, of which a Doctor Carter had been the tenant, and which he had been obliged, by threats of violence, to abandon why? because Doctor Carter at the last Assizes was produced as a witness for the Crown, to prove the dying declarations of a man who had been murdered. and Magee was to forfeit his life because he dared to inhabit the house and farm from which Doctor Carter had been expelled! Doctor Carter had shortly before the last Assizes let this farm to a man of the name of Jacob, who was the uncle of Magee, with whom he resided The farm is called Mayo, and is situated in one of the disturbed districts of your country The family of Jacob who removed with him to this house were, his sister, his niece, and his nephew, John Magee, upon whose life the attempt was made, which is the subject of this prosecution. They had no sooner removed to its occupation than schemes were laid for their expulsion About a week before the attack upon the life of John Magee, he was in the yard of a smith close to a forge, when he met the prisoner, Patrick Nash; the prisoner endeavoured to pick a quarrel with

* This man, John Bailey, died during the Commission.

him, he attempted to discover his name and afterwards to strike him with a stick · to escape from him John Magee went into the forge, there he was pursued by the prisoner, who attempted to strike him with the hammer, in the course of this affair the prisoner learned the name of Magee. On the Sunday next before the attack the prisoner with two other men, came to the house of Jacob they remained there for some time, and you will find that on coming in they introduced themselves as neighbours, and seemed anxious to cultivate an acquaintance with the family, but their conduct was so unusual as to excite the apprehensions of the inmates of the house. The particulars of what occurred that evening will be stated to you by the witnesses. The prisoner first represented his name to be Walsh, but afterwards said that his mother's name was Walsh, and he then represented his name to be Thomas Nash. Gentlemen, this is the substance of what occurred on the Sunday before the attack on Jacob's house About one o'clock on Good Friday night a party consisting of about thirty armed men attacked the house of Mr Jacob, it was a bright moonlight night when they approached it, and during all the time they continued there the house has all its rooms on the ground floor there are two rooms to the left, and two to the right the windows are between six and seven feet high the family were alarmed by a demand from the outside for admission upon a refusal to open the door the insurgents immediately dashed open a window and entered the house, they demanded arms; they put Magee upon his knees and swore him whether he had arms or not after having been sworn a second time, and again put upon his knees, he received a stab of a bayonet from the prisoner Nash, inflicting a wound which, but for the intervention of Providence must have proved fatal, the bayonet was fixed upon a gun, the point of it having struck against a rib was diverted from its direct course, and though it inflicted a wound of two inches in depth, it did not reach any vital part of his body, the young man notwithstanding this, got upon his legs, and was able to walk about for a few moments, he endeavoured to escape by the door, but in a short time the effusion of blood was so great that he fainted from exhaustion, and you will find that some of the party said that he was only pretending to be dead, and called for his immediate destruction. Ellen Magee, during the time that this was occurring, saw all that I have told you, there was a fire lighting in the house, she was ordered to light a candle, she was obliged to go with the party in search of the arms from room to room, the whole transaction occupied one hour, and if you believe her and her brother, they had the best means of identifying, not one, but many of the party. This, Gentlemen, is the detail of the facts that will be sworn to before you. Having thus briefly stated those facts without exaggeration, give me leave to ask, was I not right in representing this to be the case of almost unexampled enormity The other evidence which we will produce, will be to show you with what decision Magee and his sister identified these men. This, gentlemen, is the outline of the evidence which shall be now laid before you

John Magee examined by Mr TICKELL —I know the prisoner, Patrick Nash, I first saw him in the yard of a man of the name of Byrne, a smith that was a few days before he called on me, on the 20th of April last; I was then living at Mayo, in the house my uncle took from Doctor Carter my uncle's name is William Jacob I had been about four months living there before the 20th of April, when I first saw Nash in Byrne's yard, I told him that I lived at Doctor Carter's, he raised a stick up to strike me when he raised the stick, Byrne caught hold of him and brought him into the forge in a short time after, I went into the forge to learn his name, and the reason why he intended to strike me, I had not given him a word of provocation before that, nor did I ever see him before to my knowledge the minute I went inside the door he spoke some threatening words, and took a hammer in his hand, and was offering to come down to fight or strike me with it, the smith held him there again, and would not let him strike me. I went away then; I saw the prisoner again before the 20th April, it was on the Sunday before Good Friday, I saw him that day in my uncle's house where I lived I was speaking to him there; it was near duskish when he came in two men more came in with him, I saw these two men afterwards, they are prisoners on that Sunday my uncle asked prisoner what was his name I could not tell at that time where he lived he spoke some words about Whitefeet, he bid us not be afraid of them

CHIEF JUSTICE.—By whom were the Whitefeet spoken of? They were mentioned in the conversation.

To Mr. TICKELL —He said there was no fear of us to live in that neighbourhood, that there was no spite against us, in the course of that evening he said, that he would wish to be as soople a man as I was, that if he was as soople as me he would not fear any man, he said that he would wish to see some of what I could do I gave a leap on the parlour floor; my uncle asked him what was his name, he said it was Walsh, then my uncle said that he knew some good men of the name of Walsh, that he knew one remarkably good man of that name, the prisoner said afterwards that he did not wish to deny his name, that his name was Thomas Nash, and that his mother's name was Walsh, he shook hands with us all when he came in, and welcomed us to the neighbourhood, and he shook hands with us again when he was going away, they were about half an hour in the house on Sunday; when going away, they said they would call again, on Good Friday night last, about one o'clock, I heard a rap at the window it awakened me, I asked who was that, and they answered me, "we are your friends, open the door," I said what friends are you to call at this hour of the night, they said nothing but " open the door," I said I would not open it, that if they would come in the day I would open it, they then broke in the window, the sash, and the glass, and all was broken in, the under part of the sash was broken in, it was the window of the farthest off room was broken in, they entered the house through that window, about thirty men came in, they caught hold of me, and brought me into the parlour, there was a fire in it; they beat me with sticks there, I got several strokes of sticks, and boxes of fists, they made me go on my knees, and they put a book in my hand and compelled me to swear had I pistol, gun, or bayonet; I answered that I had no pistol, gun, or bayonet, this was when I was on my knees; after that they went away from me; I then got up and walked about the parlour, they came to me again, and put me on my knees and swore me over again about fire

arms, I bid them search, if they did not believe me; when
I gave that answer the prisoner Nash came forenent me
with a bayonet on a gun, and stabbed me with the bayonet
on the right side of the breast, he did this when I was about
getting up off my knees, when he was stabbing me he said,
" is not that a gun and a bayonet," I said "yez killed
me " after I got the stab I walked about the parlour, and
kept my hand on the wound, the wound was bleeding very
fast, I saw the blood coming, and I could not keep it in,
a short time after that, a man struck me in the side of the
neck with the breech of a gun which knocked me down when
I was stabbed, there were two candles lighting in the room,
there was a fire also in the room, and good light from the
windows, I was knocked down a second time, I got up
and went out to the porch door, I unbolted the porch door
and looked out when I looked out, I saw a good bulk
of people in the yard, I shut the door and bolted it again,
I moved a very short distance from the door, and laid my
back against the wall, and found that I was not well able
to stand against the wall, I then sat down on the ground
and leant back against the wall, a man came up out of the
kitchen, and stood over me with a gun in his hand,
I looked at him, and when he saw me looking at him, he
said, " Boys, he is only foxing, I will shoot him," my
sister came out of the parlour door, she had a short stick
in her hand, and she knocked up the gun; she jostled the
man at one side, and struck him in the head with the stick,
the man who had the gun in his hand wheeled about, and
made an offer to stab her, and I saw her falling, a tall
man of them who was present, bid him not to kill or touch
the girl; he said, " these people are strangers, and do

not know us," he said that they should kill himself if the girl would be killed, they went away then: 1 lay there in that posture against the wall, 1 found myself afterwards laid in the parlour, 1 saw the man who stabbed me with the bayonet, the prisoner at the bar is the man that stabbed me, 1 saw him again, in about a fortnight after that, in the gaol-yard of Carlow, there were thirteen or fourteen people with him when 1 saw him there, he was not pointed out to me

Cross-examined by Mr. GRAYDON—I slept in the room where the windows were broken in, I certainly was alarmed, the first of the men that came into the bed-room, caught hold of me, and hurried me into the parlour, there were people in three rooms, I could look into two rooms out of the parlour, from the time they knocked in the window, until I received the stab, was about 15 or 20 minutes, the candles were not lighting when they came in, I saw my sister light one candle, and I don't know who lit the other, the candle was lit by my sister at the parlour fire, I think the parlour shutter was not put up that night; I was not brought farther than the parlour until they swore me, I identified, I believe, thirteen of them, they were walking backward and forward, and by that means I saw them passing, there was a candle lighting in the parlour when I was stabbed, the candles were removed to every part of the house, my sister was taken away with the candle, every man that I identified, except one, I saw in the parlour, I was acquainted before that night with some of those I identified, I was acquainted with James Dowling, I saw a servant-boy, belonging to James Dowling, before that night, James Dowling was my next door neighbour, I knew John Dowling before that night, he lives close by me, I knew another man before that, he told me his name was Martin Brennan, I saw the young boy that came with Pat Nash the Sunday before, they were brought to where I was lying sick, to see if I knew them, I believe Pat Nash was not taken until the 30th of April, when I was brought to Carlow, there were about thirteen people brought out into the gaol-yard, and put into a row, I was placed in a parlour and I could look out at them through two windows, I was able to identify six of them, I swore against the six, I did not, at any time, say that there were more than six of those thirteen present that night, there were about thirteen persons shewn to me at a second time. I cannot say that they were the same persons, some of them were, and some of them were not the same persons that were shewn to me the first time, my sister was not with me when they were shewn to me the first time, I saw them a third time, there were two or three days between the first and the last time they were shewed to me my sister was not in the room with me, at any time that I was looking at them.

Did you ever go into the yard where those persons were? I did. Did you ever walk along the front of them when they were ranged as you describe? I did. Did you ever say this to one of them, "I believe I will keep you," I did not say that or any thing like it, but what I said was, "you were with me that night." I was quite positive as to the six the first time I saw them, and I said so at the time, I don't know why the gentlemen showed them to me again, the police asked me, on Saturday, the persons who were with me, and I did not tell them, I told the police that I knew some of them, and that I would have them taken, but that I would not tell them who they were, after I had been at Carlow gaol, I was brought to Maryborough gaol, there were only five or six brought out the first time, they were left standing, and there were as many more brought out again, there were others brought out after that; when they were altogether there were about twenty-eight in it; out of the twenty-eight I picked out, I believe, seven, I swore against those seven, among those seven there were none of the six I saw in Carlow, I cannot tell whether I did or not swear against a person of the name of Thomas Lawler, for I cannot recollect the names of the men I swore against, When did you first see Owen Brennan? Very shortly after Good-Friday I mean that I saw Dowling's servant-boy, for I could not give him a name, I knew him right well, I saw him in Maryborough, for I swore against him there, that was not the first time that I saw him after Good-Friday, for he was brought before me the Saturday or Sunday after, he was brought into the room where I was lying sick, to know whether I would know him or not, I did know him, but I did not charge him when he was brought into my room. Does it not appear extraordinary, that your neighbour, who gave you his name, should be the person to come forward to attack you, and the strangers remain behind? I do believe it a very strange thing Have you not heard that the common practice of those persons, who act in this way through the country, is to put forward the strangers who are not known? Yes, I have heard of such things. You went to the door after you received the stab? I did. You opened the door? I did Now, must not the person who gave you that stab, have known that you were not killed? He knew best himself Might he not have taken care that you were killed? He might have given me another stab or ten more, if he pleased. Then the man left you a living witness to convict himself?

I was of opinion that I could not live many minutes, and, perhaps, he was of the same opinion

CHIFF JUSTICF—Did you at any time, mention to any body who it was that stabbed you? I did Did you mention any name? I recollect I described him by the name of Thomas Nash. Did you see Nash, when the man said you were foxing? I did not

When this Witness was about to go off the table, he thus addressed the Court, "My Lords, as the Lord has left me my health, I would not wish that this man should be punished severely"

Second Witness, *Ellen Magee*, examined by Mr. MARILEY —I am sister to the last witness, I was living with my uncle at Mayo, in April last I know the man that told me his name was Tom Nash, the prisoner at the bar is the man; it was on the Sunday before Good-Friday that I first saw him I saw him at the gate of my own yard between twelve and one o clock he was a good while at the gate, he went into the field and helped me to put in the cows, he asked to come to see my brother, to get acquainted with him, he did not come into the house the early part of the day, when I first saw him, he came into my uncle's house when the candles were lit, he remained a good while in the house that night, when he first came into the house he said, that again this day twelve months, there would be no Protestants left alive in Ireland, rich or poor, and that any that would be left alive, should go to America, he said that Doctor Carter or his family never should come there his manner appeared friendly to me; when he came in he shook hands with us all, and welcomed us to the place, he shook hands with my uncle, my mother, my brother, and myself.

CHIEF JUSTICE.—Was it before or after he made use of

those expressions that he shook hands with you? It was after

To Mr. MARILEY —He shook hands with me before he came in at all, he took leave of us in a friendly way, and he promised to call again on the Thursday following, the next time that I saw him after that was on Good-Friday night. I saw him come into the room where my brother was, between one and two o'clock, I had been in bed before that, I sat up a good while, and put down a good deal of turf, and it was kindled well, I had been asleep before those people came into the house, I saw that night about thirty people altogether it was in the parlour I first saw them that is the room I slept in, I saw them come out of the room where my brother slept, and bring him down to the parlour, I lit a candle, and one of the men lit another about three or four men came into the room, and as he was putting my brother on his knees, he was arguing with them, he said he would not go on his knees, and that he was ready to fight any one of them, they forced him on his knees and struck him I saw the prisoner, Nash, come in with a gun in his hand I saw him take hold of the gun in this way (describes the way in which he held the gun) there was a bright bayonet fastened on the gun, and he stabbed my brother in the breast with it, the prisoner called himself Tom Nash the night he came into us, and welcomed us to the country, my brother went out of the parlour after he was stabbed, I found him after that at the porch-door he was looking at a man, he was lying and bleeding, we took him out of it, when they were all gone; he could not speak then, two of them struck me, and put me on my knees, when they put my brother on his knees, they asked him for arms, when they put me on my knees they asked for arms

CHIEF JUSTICE —Can you recollect the words they used? Some of them, when Nash stabbed at my brother he said, "is not that a gun and bayonet"

To Mr MARILEY —They remained about an hour in the house they were saying that they would shoot me, I fell when there was a stab of a bayonet made at me, my brother was then lying at the porch-door

Cross-examined by Mr WALKER —Before I went to Mayo, I lived beyond Carlow, my brother saw this man who called himself Nash, on Sunday morning, I shewed him to my brother, out of the window there were three men at the gate I said that there were three men at the gate wanted to come in I told him there was a man there who said his name was Nash, who wanted to come in, my brother looked out then Nash was out with me before that I don't know whether my brother heard me mention the name of Nash or not I cannot recollect that I ever saw Nash before that. he came up and shook hands with me, and he and two other men went with me to put the cows into the field, when my brother looked out, he did not seem to know Nash, I saw him several times again that day, between that and the time that he came into the house, when I would go to the well for water, or anywhere, Nash would come with me Nash was talking to me at the time he said this thing about the Protestants, my brother was in the parlour, near the fire, at that time, he spoke to me more than once about Protestants, he spoke to me at first about the Protestants when I was going with the cows into the field; he did not speak to me in the parlour about the Protestants more than once, and that was when he stood up to go away

CHIEF JUSTICE.—When he spoke to you in the parlour about the Protestants, how did he say it, whom did he address himself to? To myself. Was it merely to yourself? Yes Could the rest of the company hear it whilst he was saying it to you? They could not Why? Because he was speaking easy The hour that he was there he appeared friendly to you? He did and he said no one would offend us. Are you a Protestant? I am. Can you account for his saying such a savage thing to you who are a Protestant? He told me at the time, that he heard I went to Mass, Did you ever go to Mass? I did, I often went in to Mass, when people were at their prayers, to look about me

To Mr WALKLR —Where was your brother when he mentioned that to you about the Protestants? He was near the fire. Were you ever a Catholic? I went to Mass a few times. the reason was, that when I went to Church, there was stones thrown at me, it was my own prayers I said, when I would say any in the Chapel, he told me that he heard I was a Roman Catholic, and that he liked me the better for it, Mr Giff, a schoolmaster, came to the house, and spoke to me about going to Mass, several Protestants asked me what made me go to Mass, and I told them I would go to Church if they would keep the people from throwing stones at me, Nash told me he would not tell me that about the Protestants, only that he heard I was a Catholic, and he said that nobody would meddle with my brother, or my uncle, he said this in the morning. and at night also He was making love to you? He shewed a great deal of it after. When he was standing up to go away, he said that about the Protestants, and he said that he would die easy if he had Joe Fennell's arms. that was part of the whisper, Joe Fennell is a stout man, a Protestant, who lives in that country; before he began to whisper me, he asked my brother to give some leaps, and he said that he would like to be acquainted with him, my brother was asking his name. I can't recollect the first name he gave, but he afterwards said he would tell the truth, and that his name was Thomas Nash, while he was whispering me, my brother and my uncle were talking to the two other men; when he went out, my brother asked me what he was saying, I told my brother what he was saying to me, I told him all that he said to me, I was speaking loud enough for my mother to hear me, but my uncle is deaf, I told my uncle that there was no fear of us, as they thought I was a Catholic, my brother laughed at what I told him that Nash said to me my uncle said that he did not think there would be any fear in our staying in the country Nash was telling me how well he liked me, and how well the people in the country liked me because I was a Catholic, he said that he would call on the Thursday forenoon, he said that loud, I said to him that he was welcome, and that if he called before night I would let him in my brother said that any time he would come he would be welcome, my mother also said that he would be welcome. I asked my brother for money to have punch for him when he would come, my brother said there was no occasion to have the windows built up, as the people were so civil, Nash did not tell me the place he lived in but he said he lived near us, when the men were shewn to me at Stradbally, I picked out ten prisoners among a crowd Mr Singleton reckoned them, he wrote down their names as I picked them out; Nash was not among those men. I went to Carlow, there were a good many men shewn in the Gaol of Carlow, I picked out three men in Carlow my brother was not with me when I picked them out the first time the men were shewn me, I picked out the three men, my nearest neighbour is James Dowling; I went into his house the next morning, when he saw me going in, he ran into the room, and lay down on his face, on the bed, he struck his head against the side of the door as he was going away from it, the girl asked me did 1 know the man, and 1 said that 1 was a stranger, and asked for a *hapworth* of milk, that was Dowling's servant girl· 1 came off when 1 got the milk, 1 went in for the milk, but 1 did not intend to use it, 1 intended to look at Dowling, but 1 could·not when he ran away; 1 did not wish to let any one know that 1 did not like to go into his house, 1 did not say any thing to Dowling, as 1 thought that the girl might mistrust that I knew Dowling, 1 told her that 1 was a stranger, 1 never remember having identified a man as being at my brother's house, who was afterwards discharged, such a thing never happened for the men that I identified were kept, 1 recollect a man asking me, on the morning after the attack, what 1 was crying for, but 1 did not answer him, 1 swore against Nash before he was taken, 1 swore that the man's name that stabbed my brother was Thomas Nash; the first place 1 saw him afterwards, was in Carlow Goal, he was the first of the three men that 1 pointed out there

To a Juror ---Nash said that he liked me very much, and that he would like to be acquainted with me, one of the men that were with Nash called himself John Moore

Chief Justice.—Did that man say any thing about Protestants? He did. To whom did he say it? To myself, as he was sitting on the chair with me. Before the evening, did you tell your brother what Nash said to you about the Protestants, I did not like to tell him, for he might go out and be disputing with him Did your brother, your mother, and your uncle, or any one of them know that you were in the habit of going to Mass, They did Did they ever find fault with you for going to Mass? No, they bid me go whenever I would not be let go to Church. Had you a stick in your hand the night of the attack ? I had, and I struck a man with it that said he would shoot me, and made a stab of the bayonet at me

Third Witness, *Thos E. Burke* examined by Mr CLARKE.—I am a Surgeon, I recollect having been called in to see John Magee on the Sunday after the attack occurred, I found him in a very low state, I found a punctured wound in his breast, the view I took of it was, that the instrument which inflicted the wound struck some hard part, and was turned aside, or it must have penetrated the lungs, I did not consider his life was in danger, but at the same time it was a severe wound, I did not probe the wound, because I thought it might be very bad to do it

Cross-examined by Mr. BRADY —The bayonet passed in a descending direction, a person on his knees might have received such a wound, I had no conversation with him, except so far as I was professionally concerned

CHIFF JUSTICE.—How long did you attend him, I attended him a fortnight, when I left him he was nearly perfectly recovered.

Mr. BRADY —Was it such a wound as must have been inflicted with very considerable force ? I think there must have been a great deal of violence, he had the appearance of contusion upon other parts of the body, I am astonished how he escaped.

Fourth Witness, *William Jacob* produced and sworn

ATTORNEY-GENERAL —My Lords, I do not mean to put any questions to this man on the part of the Crown, they may cross-examine him on the other side if they please.

Witness cross-examined by Mr MURPHY —I recollect the night that my house was attacked, I was living there in and out of it a couple of months before that night, but not constantly there   Do you happen to know a man of the name of Patrick Nash? If the man's name be Pat Nash that called to the house, I know him, I did not not know him until that night, when I asked him his name, he said that his name was Walsh, but that his mother's name was Nash, but he afterwards said he should not deny his name, and that his name was Nash   I never saw any whispering going on between him and my niece, but there might be whispering unknown to me, I do not recollect she ever told me that he was whispering anything to her   I recollect the Sunday night that he was at my house   if he was whispering to my niece that night, I might not have seen it, I am sometimes deaf when I get cold in my head   Do you keep arms in your house?   Yes, a case of pistols, and I had a sword that night that was taken from me   had the sword in my bosom at the time it was taken from me, the pistols were hid, I cannot say that I knew any of the fellows that came to my house, because they used to knock me down when I would look at them, my neighbours might be there and I not know them, because I used to be knocked down; I saw all the fellows, I was reared a Protestant all my life time, and I am a Protestant still, my niece was reared a Protestant, but she went to mass some odd Sundays   Did you ever encourage her to go to mass?   When she was going to church the people in the streets of Carlow assaulted her, they hated her because her grandfather took a priest, she summoned them to the Court at Carlow, and the gentlemen there would not do her justice, then she thought it would be safer for her to go to mass, when she would not get law, and when the people were attacking her, she has been at church with myself since I came to Mayo, I heard that she was at chapel on Good-Friday, I never knew Nash until the evening he came to visit me, he did not say any thing uncivil that evening, it struck me that he was a civil sort of fellow, but they are very deceitful people there they welcomed us to the country, and said that nothing should happen to us, but we found afterwards that they were deceitful and treacherous people, and that they would murder us, two young men came with Nash to my house on that Sunday evening, he pretended that he wanted to see my nephew, he asked my nephew to do something, and my nephew *cotch* hold of his toe and leaped over his leg my nephew is a very active fellow, I have not made up my mind to go back to Mayo after this trial, there was no violence done you that night? How do you know

Fifth Witness, *Margaret Magee* sworn.

ATTORNEY-GENERAL —My Lords, I do not mean to examine this witness, we produce her for the Gentlemen on the other side to cross-examine her if they please

Witness cross-examined by Mr BRADY —I am the mother of the two first witnesses, and the sister of the last witness I was in the house the night it was attacked, I was there on the Sunday night before, on that night three young men came into the house off the road the candles were lighting they were sitting at the parlour fire, I saw my daughter speaking to one of the men Have you ever seen any of those young men since? I am not able to identify that I saw them, I was at Carlow Gaol, there were persons shewn to me there, I identified one man that I saw on Good Friday night, I was not at Stradbally I identified but one man, and that man I saw on Friday night, I do not know what the young man that was speaking to my daughter, was saying, I had no curiosity to know what they were speaking of, I don't recollect that I asked her what the men were saying to her; if she told me what that man was saying to her, I do not recollect it; I don't recollect that my son told me anything that the young man was saying to my daughter, the young man said that we were all welcome there, when he was going away he said he would call again, I slept in the parlour on Good Friday night; I had been asleep before the men came, I did not leave the parlour until I went to look for my son, the men were running backward and forward a great many of them, I saw my son on his knees, and he was bleeding; it was a dreadful scene, I saw him on his knees twice, the candles were lighting and there was a good fire, some wet turf was put on before we went to bed; my son did not speak for some time, I had no conversation with him that night as to the persons that were there, I heard him say that he knew a great many of them, but I cannot say whether it was that night or the next morning Did your son say anything at all to you that night? Yes—he said, "mother I think that there is as much of the life in me "as that I will recover." He was very hard set to speak at all.

EVIDENCE FOR THE DEFENCE.

First Witness, *William Walsh*, examined by Mr. GRAY-DON, I reside at the prisoner's house, I was sowing potatoes for him, I am working with him since spring, the prisoner, and his brother, and his mother, and sister, and I, eat supper together on Good Friday night last, in about an hour in the night we went to bed and remained there until morning, I cannot guess the hour that we went to bed because I am no scholar, it was an hour after night-fall that we went to bed, the prisoner Pat Nash slept with me all night in the bed, and there's not a turn ever I awoke but I found him in it still his brother went to Tullow that night with a load of coals about night fall, it was about six o'clock in the morning when the prisoner and I got up out of bed

[When Mr Tickell was about to cross-examine this witness he thus addressed the Court—" Please your Lord-"ships, I am not used to law, and I hope you will not " allow your Counsellor to *Cross-hackle* me "]

Cross-examined by Mr. Tickell—How long before Good Friday had you been working for him ? I found him every turn I awoke in bed, and that is all I have to say. Did you work three weeks with him before that ? I cannot say. Did you work for him three months before that ? All I have to say is that every turn I awoke I found him in the bed Did you work for him six months before that ? I cannot say, all that I have to say, I said Had you been working for him for twelve months before ? I cannot exactly say, all that I have to say I said. How often did you turn in the night ? I lay on my right side the whole night, and every turn I awoke I found him still—please your Lordship that is all I have to say. Do you know the name of Nash's mother ? Biddy Bergin, I did not know her before she was married, I have no house there, no wife, nor any people at all, I have been always sleeping at Nash's since I left my own house six or eight years ago, we had potatoes and herrings for supper that night

CHIEF JUSTICE —Was Biddy Bergin ever married to a man of the name of Walsh? Never

A JUROR —Was it in an inside room you slept? That is all I have to say, that every turn I awoke I found him in bed.

Second Witness. *Mary Blanchfield*, examined by Mr WALKER.—I know James Dowling I lived with him on Good Friday last, in Mayo, as his servant; *I saw him going to bed on that night*, at night-fall there are two rooms in his house, he slept in the INSIDE room, I did not lie down at all, there was a cow taken from us the night before, and I staid up lest they might take another. James Dowling could not leave the house the whole night without my knowledge, he did not leave it, he has a servant boy of the name of Owen Brennan he went to bed that night, *he slept in the inside room*, he did not leave the house that night, I called him before sun-rise, he could not leave the house that night without my knowledge

Cross-examined by Mr MARILEY —The cows were in a house forenent the dwelling house door, the cow-house is about ten yards from the dwelling-house I staid up on Saturday night to watch the cows, until my master was taken out of bed, I was not in bed when he was taken, *all the rest of the family were in bed but myself*, the servant boy was taken on Sunday morning no one watched the cows on Sunday night, James Dowling and the boy came from the fair of Ballyragget, where they were looking for the cow, it was on Friday they were looking for the cow, I kept a sharp eye on the cows on Friday night

Mary Conlan came there that night to look for a pail of milk, she remained there that night, she and my old master sat up with me that night we never opened the kitchen door the whole night, from the time that I put the bar on it the boy slept in the old man's room James Dowling's wife went to her father's house that evening her father's name is Paddy Moore, she returned home on Saturday morning she went to her father's, because her mother was unwell, I think another reason why she went to her father's house was, because Pat Daly was abusing her, Pat Daly has gone to America since James Dowling was taken, Pat. Daly was accused of stealing the cow, I can't tell the day that Pat Daly went off I saw him on Laster Sunday and I never saw him since, the cow was not found since I know where old Mr Jacob lives he lives about eighteen perches from James Dowling's house, there is a window in the room that my master slept in, I know a young woman, called Ellen Magee, I remember seeing her in my master's house the day after this business happened, she went there for some milk, my master was sitting on his chair at the fire when she came in, I saw him go into the yard after that, I heard no noise that night, I heard on Saturday morning that people attacked Mr. Jacob's house, my master was taken on Saturday night, I did not hear what he was taken up for that time, I heard after that he was taken on suspicion of beating John Magee, I heard that on Sunday. I knew that it was impossible for him to be at Mr. Jacob's that night, because I knew he was in his own house all night, I told Mr Carter that he was at home all night, I cannot tell what time I told him, I did not get a summons on that night; Mary Conlan got a summons; we came here together. I told her I had to clear my master, I know William Walshe, I saw him here to-day; he lives in Gartin with his brother, and father, I did not know that he was to be examined here to day, I know his father has land, and that he lives along with him.

CHIEF JUSTICE —Does James Dowling's house lie on the side of the road? It is in off the road about ten yards. Is Jacob's house on the same side of the road with James Dowling's? It is. Did you hear any steps of people on the road that night? I did not.

To Mr MARTLEY —I am sure my master went to the fair of Ballyragget to look for a cow, he left home on Friday Morning, between six and seven o'clock: he was out with coals the whole of Thursday night, he came home on Friday morning, between six and seven o'clock, and he set off immediately to Ballyragget.

Margaret Conlan, examined by Mr BRADY —I spent Good-Friday night at James Dowling's, I came for a pail of milk there that evening, Mrs. Dowling went to her father's that evening, I saw her when I was going to the chapel when I got to James Dowling's house that evening he was at the fan looking for the cow after going there, I went to the chapel, when I returned from the chapel at night-fall, I saw James Dowling asleep in the lower room, two of the children went to bed with him; my uncle, James Dowling's father, did not go to bed that night, we all remained up that night to mind the cows, there was a hole in the door, and we used to look out at the cow-house, we heard no noise that night, I laid my head on the settle-bed when the larks were singing, I heard the lark singing.

Mary Murphy, examined by Mr. MURPHY.—I live at Turrow; that is about half a mile from Mr. Jacob; I live with my father and mother there, I know a man of the name of William Dunne, I recollect Good Friday last: I recollect having been in his house that night, William Dunne's house is about half a mile from Mr. Jacob's I went to William Dunne's house between six and seven o'clock in the evening, there was a child of his in the agonies of death, I went to see the child, and remained in the house all that night, William Dunne did not leave the house that night, I remained up all night, he slept in a bed near the fire all night, I did not leave the house the whole night.

Cross-examined by Mr CLARKE —I am not a relation of Dunne's, the child was sick a good while before that, I remained there two nights before that, I went home on Saturday morning, I heard of this business the Saturday after it happened, when he was taken up I told several that he was an innocent man, I can't tell any one that I told it to, we had a candle lighting all night, I did not doze at all the whole night.

John Willoughby examined by Mr WALKER —I reside at Mayo, I know the prisoner nine or ten years, he lives about a mile from me as far as I was acquainted with him he never did anything bad, if he took any drink he would be a little wicked, I know William Walsh, he has no house

Cross-examined by Mr. TICKELL —I never heard that he was in Gaol I heard that there was a man that he had some law-suit with Did you ever hear that he was charged with any crime? I heard that he struck a man Did you ever hear that he was accused of robbery? I heard that he took money that a man gave him

William Willoughby examined by Mr. GRAYDON —I know William Walsh I know that his father and mother are dead, I know the prisoner four or five years, I don't know what sort of character he bears

CHARGE

CHIEF JUSTICE.—Gentlemen of the Jury, the prisoner, Patrick Nash, stands charged with wilfully, unlawfully, and maliciously stabbing John Magee, with intent to kill and murder him, with an intent to maim him with an intent to disfigure him with an intent to disable him and, with an intent to do him grievous bodily harm, and if you believe that he did stab him at all, and also, that he stabbed him with any one of those intentions, you ought to find him guilty but if you believe that he did not stab him at all, or that he did not stab him with any of these intentions, you ought to acquit him: if upon the whole of the case, you have any reasonable doubt, you ought to acquit him, but if you have not a reasonable doubt of his guilt, it is a case, I need not tell you in which justice calls for an example The test of an indictment of this kind is this — If the wounded man had died of the wound given by the prisoner and if, in contemplation of law, that homicide would be held to be murder, then the charge is supported; but if in the event of death having taken place, the prisoner would be only guilty of manslaughter, you are bound to acquit him In this case there is not a particle of evidence that would make it an excusable homicide, or reduce the homicide to manslaughter The case would be simply that of a man, at the head of thirty others, attrociously butchering an unoffending man in the dead hour of the night

Gentlemen, before reading my notes, I will make a preliminary observation or two, as to the questions raised upon the whole of the evidence. If John Magee and his sister be credible witness, that is, if they are both honest and accurate, they have supported the case for the prosecution completely, and you will then have to consider the defence that is made by the prisoner. Now that defence is two-fold, it consists, first, of an *alibi* proved for himself, and of two *alibis* proved for two other persons against whom John and Ellen Magee have sworn informations, but who are not now on trial. As to the *alibi* that he relies upon for himself, it altogether and exclusively rests upon the testimony of William Walsh and, Gentlemen, you will have to weigh the credit of John and Ellen Magee both as to honesty and accuracy, against the credit of this only witness for the prisoner. Gentlemen, the crime was committed by some person or other, on the night of Good Friday, a very notorious day, a night likely to be remembered by the circumstance of its having been a day of prayer, and also, by a fair having been held on that day in a neighbouring town. The prisoner at the bar was taken up upon this charge on the tenth day after the crime was committed, and of course his charge was made known to him when he was taken up. Now the difficulty under which persons are placed, when they are taken up upon a stale charge, does not belong to this case. If a man be taken up at the distance of a year, or half a year, from the time at which the transaction which forms the subject of the charge against him has occurred, it may be next to impossible that he should be able to recollect or prove where he was upon the day or night when the crime was committed, but you will judge whether a period of ten days falls within that observation or not, and, also whether William Walsh has given you such satisfaction on that head, as you have a right to expect from the prisoner, under such circumstances

Gentlemen, you are next to consider the cases of Dowling and Dunne, as to whom John and Ellen Magee have also sworn possitively, and if you should believe that they have perjured themselves as to Dowling and Dunne, that is, have intentionally sworn falsely against them, there can be no doubt that that would contaminate them at once, and you would be bound to reject the whole of their testimony, but it may be, that they have sworn falsely, as to those two men, and yet not have perjured themselves. It may happen that they have made a mistake as to them and then that physical falsehood, (to speak pedantically, perhaps,) that swearing against them under a mistake, has not the effect of annihilating their credit altogether, as to the prisoner against whom they have sworn, but it has only the effect of affecting their accuracy, and it is for you to consider how, in a capital case, you can safely act upon the evidence of persons convicted of that inaccuracy. But Gentlemen, that observation is to be taken according to all its circumstances. You will recollect, that between John Magee and his sister, they have sworn against a good many persons, and if they have sworn rashly, as against some of them, it might happen that those against whom they have sworn rashly, are persons that they had little or no opportunity of seeing before, and then you would have to consider whether their kowledge of Patrick Nash is not of a nature that would leave it possible that they should not be mistaken as to him, at the same time that they might be respectively mistaken as to the others, and you will consider what were the opportunities which they had of knowing Nash's person, and the persons of the others however, mistakes upon oaths are awful matters, and if you should believe that such have been made, you ought not to run the risk of convicting the prisoner, unless you have a moral certainty, free from all doubt, that there can have been no mistake as to him

Gentlemen, I shall read to you now my notes of the evidence, which are very voluminous, but every word of which requires your attention, and as I go along 1 shall endeavour to assist you in applying my preliminary observations to all parts of it, as they bear upon the prosecution and defence

Having made these preliminary observations, his Lordship read over his notes of the entire evidence to the Jury.

The Jury having retired for a few minutes, returned into Court with a verdict of *Guilty*

On the last day of the Commission, (Wednesday, 6th June,) in passing sentence, Baron Smith addressed the prisoner as follows —

Patrick Nash, you have been found guilty of a crime of no common magnitude, an offence at once henious in its own intrinsic nature, and, unfortunately, the more calling for severe example, from its connexion with those attrocious practices, and that criminal and lurking system, which this Special Commission has been issued to put down.

Upon some of its circumstances I am, therefore, reluctantly obliged to dwell for, of punishment, (especially that which is capital) example is the end, and example is promoted by comparing the punishment with the character of the offence, and showing that the former is but commensurate, and therefore just

I cannot utter the word '*example*', without recollecting how thinly attended this town and tribunal are.

Acquainted as I am with the propensities and habits of our people, considering too, how naturally a great number of prisoners for trial would attract a numerous assemblage of anxious relatives and friends, independently of those whom curiosity and interest might bring together, I can scarcely look upon this sparing attendance as undesigned I can scarcely avoid considering it as a manœuvre, the result of a command as a feature of that system which the law is endeavouring to crush He must be blind, who does not catch more than glimpses of a deliberate plan, to disparage, in the eyes of the people, the administration of the law His memory must be frail, who, if he be old enough to remember, can forget, that such a plan prevailed in periods big with threats, which were afterwards soon and bloodily carried into execution

The tribunals were then, in many instances, deserted, as if the law were something in which the people had no concern. A contemptuous aversion to it, was then, by secret agitators, instilled with mischievous purposes, into their minds

To estrange them from the law, was to place them beyond the reach of admonition and example, and impose upon their credulity by misrepresentations of the way in which justice was administered, calumnies, which, if on the spot, their ears and eyes would have refuted

Is it possible that similar plans and projects are revived? For the sake and interests of the deluded people, I wish it may not be so

What was the first feature of that criminal transaction which has placed you in the pitiable situation in which you stand?

That threatening conduct and manifestation of ill-will upon your part which occurred near the forge, where John Magee first met you, he not being then acquainted with your person or your name

This deliberate ill-will does not appear to have had its origin in dispute or private grudge, but to have belonged to your feelings, as a member of an illegal combination

What was the next proceeding? Your scheming and deceitful visit, for which a Sunday was made choice of, and of which, I fear, the object was two-fold

First, by an insidious welcome, and highly amicable tone, to lull the fears of the new inhabitants of Doctor Carter's house, and dissuade them from securing themselves by their intended barricade Secondly, to reconnoitre the premises, and make choice of the best point and mode of attack, and entrance

In the next place, on the fifth day after, followed that sanguinary outrage, the plan of which must have been laid some time before, while the day selected for carrying it into execution was Good Friday a choice which seems to add impiety to crime

The attack was made in the dead hour of the night, on a family which had given you no offence, and to which *you* had so lately given a treacherous and beguiling welcome

The object, at least the principal object of that act, was to obtain possession of their arms Thus your offence at once connects itself with the disturbed state of the Queen's County, and was committed in furtherance of one of the objects of those illegal combinations, out of which its disturbances have arisen

Of felons present, and mutually aiding and assisting one another, the act of one is, in contemplation of law the act of all. So that though it were one of your accomplices who had stabbed, you would have been guilty of the wounding

But you gave the wound yourself. It was inflicted by your own hand.

You accompanied it, too, with an unfeeling jeer.

The young man, in answer to a demand, said that there was no gun or bayonet in the house you replied, "is not *there* a gun and bayonet in the house?" at the same time stabbing him, in voucher that there was

The very words would tend to show, what however has been proved, that the wound was not accidental.

The wounded man cried out at once that you had killed him. The gush of blood immediately, and soon after, his utter helplessness, and weakness, so great as to be followed in a short time by a swoon, seemed to confirm the truth of his declaration that he was slain

Was any pity or compunction shown ? Was any assistance given him? Was anything done, which might lead one to suppose that the wound was accidentally, or even rashly given ? Was any thing attempted towards obviating the mortal consequences of the wound? On the contrary, upon the evidence, he appears to have been left to die

Had he died, those who by encouraging violaters of the law, raised a spirit which has not hitherto been controlled or laid,—those who framed and organized that confederacy of which you have been a member, those, I say, would have been morally accessary to the young man's death. As it is, they may be well considered to have been accessary to yours

Thus upon the evidence for the prosecution, your case appears to stand I wish it stood more favourably. To whatever, in the way of comment, would be insisted on, my Lord Chief Justice called the attention of the Jury, on your behalf.

You resorted to what is called an *alibi* defence, but the

Jury, in convicting you, disbelieved the witnesses who were produced, and under circumstances which seemed to imply a charge, of, subornation. A charge, however, which *may* attach, not on you, but on your friends.

I am afraid it is no uncommon practice with unhappy convicts, under circumstances whose sad solemnity calls imperiously for truth, to make protestations of an innocence, which they are not warranted to claim. At best, they found this claim upon some immaterial distinction,—some distinction without difference,—between the offence, as laid in the indictment, and as proved. Thus the man who was but present and *assisting* when a mortal wound was given, goes out of the world asserting his innocence of the murder.

An evasion of this kind would not be open to you. And it is sinful—it is uncharitable, to depart from life, bequeathing a legacy of anxiety to the Jury which found guilty. A man, through penitence, may have obtained the absolution and remission of his sins, and in *this* sense, through the efficacy of his Saviour's merits, be as innocent as the child unborn. But if when thus redeemed, and purified, and washed clean, at the very threshold of eternity, he utters that worst of falsehoods, a delusive equivocation,—does he not defy the God of truth, and stain his soul with a new sin, his repentance of which is fearfully intercepted by his death?

My unhappy fellow creature and fellow sinner,—(for unworthy sinners we all are,—but all have a righteous advocate before God,)—I conjure you penitently to reconcile yourself to your heavenly Father, through the all powerful and Divine atonement of His beloved Son.

The death and merits of that Son are sufficient for your salvation. without them we must all irretrievably be lost.— Praise His Holy Name, who has already saved you from committing murder.

And now, sustained by the ineffable consolations of religion, and in pious confidence of the infinite mercy which it declares, hear meekly and firmly, as becomes a Christian Man, not my sentence, (God forbid!) but the sentence of the Law.

The sentence was then pronounced. Towards the conclusion of his address, Baron Smith became deeply affected He evidently struggled with the violence of his emotions, frequently pausing, in order that they might not overpower him. When the prisoner, whose conduct had previously been unmoved, though not unbecoming, perceived this sympathy on the part of the Judge, he also became affected, and bending his head upon his hands, began to weep. The Lord Chief Justice appeared deeply penetrated by the sad solemnity of the scene, and at the affecting and fervent prayer which terminates the sentence, both Judges, with tears in their eyes, bowed their heads reverently to the bench. The concluding words were nearly choked by the strength of Baron Smith's emotion. The unhappy prisoner bowed submissively, as if grateful for the sympathy of the Judges, and retired in silence from the bar The whole scene was an affecting one.

TRIAL OF WILLIAM WOOLAHAN,

For Burglary in the House of Thomas Terrot.

28th May, 1832.

First Witness *Thomas Terrot*, examined by Mr. TICKELL. —I live in James's Town, in this County, I remember Sunday the 13th of this month, my house was attacked about twelve o'clock that night, my house joins another house, my wife, my children, and myself were in bed, the house that joins mine is Tom Brady's, I heard a stone thrown against Brady's door I heard a voice say " that is not the house he is in," they then came round to my door I then leapt out of bed in my shirt I stood at the door, and I had a thing like a knife, and I said I would make fight before I would let them in; I broke out into Brady's house through the wall, and made my escape, it was a very thin wall made of clay, I saw a man come up to Brady's door with a stone in his hand, and he struck the door with the stone in his hand, I saw the man through a slit that was in the door, it was one of the brightest nights I ever saw, I heard them in my own house at this time, I saw this man turn away after he hit Brady's door with the stone, he stood on the road opposite the door, I opened Brady's door and this man struck me on the side with a stone, his name is Will Delany; I then made my escape to Mr Miller who lives within a quarter of a mile of my house, I had only my shirt on, Mr. Miller was then in bed, I cried out through the window that my house was attacked I cried out to him to give me a gun he did give me a gun, and he himself came on with me presently: on my way back I called for Jacob Howe to come to my assistance, I returned to my own house from Howe's house: when I was going towards my own house I saw a flash of powder from a pan, I heard a great noise from the men that were at my house, Mr Miller was with me at this time I observed a great many persons on before us, Mr Miller and I went on, and they came on to meet us, as we went close to them there were two flashes in the pan, when they fired at us I snapped the gun, and I desired Mr Miller to fire, they were rushing on us at this time, I saw a pistol and a large white pole, Mr. Miller asked them what they wanted, and they rushed in and said "we want you," they seized Mr Miller and dragged him in towards the yard, he fired a shot at one of them, and he dropped to the ground, when he dropped I gave him a blow of the breech of the gun and he fell into the ditch, I saw nobody do any thing to Mr Miller any further than drag him into my yard, it was before he fired that they were dragging him into the yard, it was while they were dragging him that he fired, I received a blow of the white pole on my hand, I saw the man who struck me with the pole; the prisoner at the bar is the man who struck me. I had seen the prisoner often before this night, I knew his name and person both previous to this attack I had gone in search of a man with Mr Miller and Jacob Howe.

Cross-examined by Mr DARCY.—I am a day labourer; there is only one room in the house I inhabit, I have no arms in my house, the neighbours were not in the habit of coming into my house for a month before that, but before that they were in the habit of coming in to see me. I told Brady that I would know Delany, I did not tell him I would know Woolahan, and that he was the man that gave me the blow, I told Brady before I left the house that I knew William Delany, it was after it was all over, that I told this to Brady, I saw nobody else on the road that I know, out of the whole number, I lodged my examinations next day. I heard nothing about a reward, I heard that the prisoner was taken the next day on some part of Mr Miller's land. we fired three shots. Mr. Miller one, Jacob Howe one, and myself one, I know a man of the name of Thomas Delany that is in custody for this charge, I know him long, I heard that a man of the name of Bartholomew Malone is charged with this offence, I knew them as well as I knew Woolahan, I did not mention that they were there, because I did not see them. I have been living in the neighbourhood about twelve or thirteen years

Second Witness, *Elizabeth Terrot*, examined by Mr. MARILLY.—I am the wife of the last witness. I remember the night my house was broken open, I was asleep before it was broken open. my husband awoke me when he heard the noise, he made his escape by breaking through the partition that separates Brady's house from mine: some of the persons broke open my door and got into the house, they lit a candle when they came in; there was a shot fired in my house that night. I was sitting on the bed when the shot was fired, the flash of the fire came across my face, one of the persons who broke into the house offered violence to me, he was going to strike my child that was sick, and I called out to him not to strike my dying child, he pushed me and put me on the foot of the bed, he put his hands under my clothes and ill used me with his hands, I could see his face well; I would know that man if I saw him now, I am certain that the prisoner at the bar is that man, I would know him in a hundred, then more of them came into the house, they asked for a gun and for my husband, and they searched the house when they lit a candle, I have five children of my own and a nurse-child, I did not see the prisoner take any thing from the house, I think they were in the house better than a quarter of an hour

Cross-examined by Mr BRADY.—I never accused any one before of any offence, I did not know any of the men but one, when I heard the noise I put on my petticoat and took the child in my arms, I was in bed when the shot was fired; it was in my children's bed I was; I had got out of my own bed before that, I did not see the person that fired the shot; he was standing very near me when he fired, I was about a yard from the fire of the gun; it was fired over the bed where I was sitting, I cannot say that it was fired at me, I don't think there was a candle lit when it was fired, I did not see the man that fired the shot, I only saw the flash of the gun, I could only see his body, I could not see his face, it was before the shot was fired the man laid hands on me, they did not all go out at the same time, Woolahan and another man were the last that left the house; the only thing that was said to me by any of them, was to ask me for my husband and the gun, Woolahan was the man that asked me for my husband and the gun he asked me the question several times, I had known Woolahan two or three years before that, I knew him well, but I never had any conversation with him, I did not know his name before, I knew neither his Christian nor his sirname, my husband was acquainted with him 1 think he was more intimate with him than 1 was, he knew his father and his people, and where they live, 1 cannot say that he was acquainted with him so as to talk to him when he would meet him, my husband told me that he knew Woolahan; 1 often heard him speak of him before this came about at all, it was about the prisoner's father my husband often spoke to me, but he never spoke to me about the prisoner himself, my husband spoke to me about the prisoner's father, because he was about buying apples from us, 1 told my husband 1 knew Woolahan, he asked me which of the Woolahans, 1 could not tell him, because 1 did not know his Christian name; he asked me was it the soldier, and 1 said it was not, my son told me it was William Woolahan; my son was present when my husband was talking about this, that was the time he told me he was Wm Woolahan, my husband asked me if 1 knew any of them, and 1 said 1 knew Woolahan, 1 did not know then that his name was William, till my son told it, 1 knew his name was Woolahan these two years, he remained near me at the bed after the shot was fired, until another boy came up and said, "come away sergeant," and with that he hit me on the nose and went away, the other boy remained three or four minutes after.

CHIEF JUSTICE—At the time this man was offering violence to you, were you on the bed? 1 was Where was your son? By my side in the bed And he saw the violence offering to you? He did. Did your son then tell you what the man's name was? No

Mr BRADY —Do you mean to say from the first time he came to you and pushed you on the bed, that he remained with you until he quitted the house? He did In the same place on the bed? He was standing before me, and

I had an infant child on each arm, he was standing on the floor, but he did not leave the foot of the bed

Third Witness—*James Terrot,* (a very delicate looking little boy,) examined by Mr CLARKE—I am the son of Thomas Terrot I recollect the night my father's house was attacked, I was in bed when the house was attacked, my two little sisters were with me in bed, there are two beds in the house, I was awoke by the rapping at the door, I saw ten or twelve persons come into the house, they came to the bed to me, and they asked me where was my father, and they demanded the gun, my father at that time had gone into Brady's house; they fired a shot then, they beat me on the head, then they lit a candle and they looked for the gun, and when they could not get it they blew out the candle, I saw a man that night that I had seen before, I saw him at a dance, and I saw him at Mr. Trench's working. I would know him again if I saw him, (Witness was desired to look round to try if he could see that man,)—(lays the rod upon the prisoners head.) that is the man, I am quite sure that the prisoner at the bar is the man that was in my father's house that night, when he came near me, my mother said, "are you going to kill my dying "child," he then pushed her against the bed, he raised a crook over my head and another boy caught it behind his back, and said, "don't murder him," the prisoner was the man that held the crook over me, the man that saved me was the last person that left the house, I saw nothing done to my mother but that she got a push from Woolahan; about a quarter of an hour after I left the house my father came back, after putting on his shoes and stockings he took a pistol of Jacob Howes' in his hand and walked out; I did not see him again until next morning.

Cross-examined by Mr Murphy—I was in the hospital till Friday morning last. I knew what I was coming here for. I knew it was to prosecute Will Woolahan, I knew him a good while, the moment I saw him I knew him. I never saw him at my house only that night, I never heard my mother speak about him only since he came to gaol; before he was put into gaol I never heard her speak of him, that I am quite sure of, I knew nobody else that was in the house besides Woolahan. It was after the shot was fired Woolahan held the crook over my head, when they went away I said " Oh! mother, mother, the Monday " man's son murdered me "

Do you remember any thing else you said to your mother ? I said that Woolahan thought to murder me with a crook. What did your mother say when you said that ? She said---" Oh James, you and I paid for all " All these people were going through the house ? They were And Woolahan among the others? Yes Was he walking about the house among the others ? He was Did your father say any thing to you in the morning about the people that were there ? No Did you hear him say anything to your mother about it ? I did not Did you see your father after he first got out of the house that night ? I did while he was putting on his shoes and stockings. At the little time that he staid there did you say anything to him or to your mother about who was there ? Not a word that I can recollect I did not hear my mother say anything to my father, nor my father say anything to my mother about them, nor did either of them say anything to me; I did not ask my mother if she knew anything about them.

CHIEF JUSTICE —When you said to your mother that Woolahan thought to murder you with a crook did you mention Woolahan's christian name? I did not say Will. Woolahan.

JUROR.—How long before Woolahan left the house did he hold the crook over you? Not long, he went out very soon after. When he was holding the crook over you where was your mother? I cannot tell, the candle was not lighting then

To BARON SMITH —The door was at the end of the house where you could pick up pins off the floor it was so bright.

CHIFF JUSTICE.—While all this mischief was going on your father was not there? He was not When he came back and was putting on his shoes and stockings, did he, and you, and your mother, talk to each other at all about the business? No. When did you say to your mother that Woolahan was going to murder you? I said it to her at the fire when they went out Did you say Will Woolahan? No. I did not at any time tell anything to my father and mother about who were there but what I told my mother at the fire. Was there any time at all that your father, and mother, and you, spoke about this and that you told them any thing about the people that were there? No. Up to the time you came to Maryborough are you quite sure you never said any thing about who it was that did this mischief, except that Woolahan thought to murder you with a crook? I don't know that I did

Fourth Witness, *Elizabeth Terrot*, (a child about ten years old)— I know a man of the name of William Woolahan I saw him often—(Here the witness identified the prisoner)—I remember the night my father's house was attacked, I saw Will Woolahan there that night, I was sleeping at the foot of my father's bed when they came into the house   I heard a shot fired   there was no candle lit when it was fired, I saw Woolahan before I heard the shot, he was over my mother, and he was asking her where was the gun, and where was my father, he raised a white crook over my brother's head, and was going to hit him with it, but another boy came at his back, and whipt the crook out of his hand, and bid him not to murder him, my mother was lying down on her back, on the foot of my brother's bed—she had one child on one arm, and another on the other arm, I don't know the names of the persons that remained last in the house, the boy that remained last bid us shut up the door and not look after them.

Cross-examined by Mr MARA—Immediately after the men went away I had no coversation with my mother about who was there; I did not hear my father say any thing about the men that were there, only that the fellows struck him with a stone, I knew Woolahan a good many Sundays before that, I did not know the two last men that left the house.

CHIEF JUSTICE.—Did you know either of the two last men that left the house?   I knew Will Woolahan, but not the fellow that bid us shut up the door

Mr MARA—Did any body ever speak to you about what you were to tell?   Not one   Did any gentleman ever speak to you about this business?   Yes   Mr Adair and Mr Trench   These gentlemen did not speak to me together, Mr Adair spoke to me in my own house, and so did Mr Trench

Fifth Witness, *Thomas Miller*—Examined by Mr ARABIN—I recollect the night Terrot's house was attacked

I saw him that night at my house, he was in his shirt; he alarmed me, I was in bed when he came, I got up and went with him, I did not wait to dress myself, I went down the avenue with him, I had a pistol and a bayonet, and he had a gun We went on to Terrot's house, when we came to the gap coming into Terrot's yard, I saw the flash of a pan about forty yards from me; I saw about twenty-four or twenty-five men after I saw the flash of the pan they ran towards us I desired them to stop I asked them what they wanted, and they said, "We want you," one of them snapped a gun, and another of them snapped a pistol I had a double-barrel pistol, and I turned to the man on my right, and shot him, when I was turning about to shoot the man that had a hold of me by the shirt collar, the man that missed fire at me with a horse pistol struck me in the arm with it, that blow of the pistol knocked the pistol out of my hand that I had, I endeavoured to regain the pistol, and I got a blow of a stone in the jaw that knocked me down; Terrots gun missed fire, and he ran back to call Jacob Howe, when I was knocked down, two fellows held me down, while the rest pounded me with stones, I got home before I saw Terrot again.

Cross-examined by Mr Darcy —I did not find the body of the man I shot, I did not search for him, because I was not able.

Juror.—Did you know any of the party that was there that night? I did, six of them.

Here the evidence for the prosecution closed

EVIDENCE FOR THE DEFENCE

Timothy Woolahan examined by Mr Brady —I am the father of the prisoner I recollect the day he was arrested, it was on a Monday, he slept the night before in my house, he came home that night at half after ten. I know that was the hour because the early coach was passing a little after he came in, I am not sure whether it was up or down the coach was going, he was eating his supper when the coach passed

CHIEF JUSTICE.—How far is your house from Terrot's? About a mile and better

Cross-examined by Mr MARTLEY.—Had you seen your son that day before he came home in the evening? I did not see him that day from the time he eat his breakfast till he came home to his supper, he went to mass to Monasterevan, that is not our parish chapel. it was not a great deal after dusk-ish when he came in, I was just after lying down my wife was not in bed, she gave him his supper my family consists of my wife, and another son, and the prisoner my other son's name is Patrick he was at home that night. Patrick was home a long time before night he dined at home that day we all slept in the same room, the prisoner fell asleep before I fell asleep, I heard him different times in the course of that night, whenever I awoke I heard him snoring How did you know which it was he or Patrick was snoring? I knew it was he. There is no lock to the door of my house, nothing but a bolt I believe it was six o'clock when I got up he got up partly about the same time, my son was taken up this-day-fortnight. I did not see him since, till I saw him now. I had no communication with him since, Mr Trench, and other Magistrates lived near me; I did not tell them that my son slept at home that night.

Patrick Woolahan examined by Mr BRADY.—I am the brother of the prisoner, I recollect the day he was arrested, it was on a Monday morning, my brother slept with me in my father's house that night, he came in about half past ten o'clock; I was in bed about five minutes when he came he was in a little before the coach passed

Cross-examined by Mr TICKELL.—I was in the army, I was quite sober the next morning, my father and my step-mother were in bed when my brother came in.

BARON SMITH —Was your step-mother in bed? She was Did your step-mother give him his supper? It was not necessary for any of us to remain up to give him his supper.

To Mr TICKELL.—I did not go to bed as early as my father and step-mother, because I was diverting myself with the neighbouring children Who were the children? Oh! it is impossible for me to tell who the children were When I came in after amusing myself with the boys and girls, I found my father and my step-mother in bed I took my supper when I came in, and I took to my bed directly, as there was nobody up. When my brother came in, I told him his supper was by the fire, I was in bed about five minutes when he came in. he soon went to bed, and stopped there until morning, I asked him where he was, and he said he was leaving his measure for new shoes, he did not tell me where, I was at Monasterevan chapel that Sunday, I dont know whether my brother went to mass that day I am quite sure I did not dine at home that day, I did not return home until between five and six o'clock. When your brother came in, did you ask him where he had been? I did not You swear that? I do. Did you not say just now that you did ask him? No sir, you will recollect yourself, if you please, it was the next morning I asked him where he was Did your father ask him where he was? No. Did you hear any noise in the house that night? No. and if a straw merely stirred in the house I would hear it When did you hear of his being taken up? I heard it the next day. Then, I suppose, you went immediately and told those who had taken him up that he was at home the whole of that night? I treated it as a very light business, I thought no more of it than that bit of paper You have been in the army? I have How came you to leave the army? Misfortune What do you mean by misfortune? I am afraid to lie in my bed lest I may be taken out of it What do you call a misfortune? If a man fell and broke his neck, would not that be a misfortune.

[The demeanour of this witness, during his cross examination, was extremely indecorous]

Robert Cassidy, Esq examined by Mr BRADY —I live more than half a mile from the Ballybrittas road, I was at home on the night of Sunday, the 13th of this month, I heard the noise of the coach that night it passed some time before eleven o'clock, I don't know exactly where Woolahan resides, it was the coach from Dublin, I was standing on the steps in front of my hall-door when the coach passed, I particularly recollect having heard it, as it struck me as an indication of fine weather, and I observed it to my servant.

Fourth Witness, *Thomas Bracken*, examined—I am a farmer, holding some land, I know the prisoner well, he has been working with me part of three months, and I knew him for a year working with my neighbour, Mr Fawcett, he was at work with me the Saturday before he was taken since he came to work with me I found him sober, quiet, and honest, and diligent at his work, both before me and behind my back.

Cross-examined by the ATTORNEY GENERAL—This neighbourhood of your's is a good deal disturbed? So I heard Do you believe the neighbourhood of Ballybrittas to be disturbed? I must believe it when I hear of it. Have any of your people quitted your employment? No. Have you heard that Mr Trench's labourers left his employment? I did hear that they turned out and left his employment. How far does Mr Trench live from you? About two miles. Did you ever hear of any persons being suspected of these practices? No. Do you believe that there are respectable people engaged in them? I can form no opinion about that. Have any people, upon your oath, acquired a bad character in consequence of having been engaged in it? I don't know—I think they are all as good characters now as they ever were—I don't know any thing about that. Upon your oath, do you believe the prisoner to be a man of good character? By the virtue of my oath, since he came to me, I know him to be a quiet honest boy, and I heard of his being a man of good character.

Mr Brady—My Lords, we had Mr Fawcett in attendance last week to give the prisoner a character, but he unfortunately is not here this day.

Mr Mara—examined by Mr Brady—I am Agent for the prisoner. I issued a crown summons for Mr Fawcett, he was attending here for this trial, he asked me if I thought he could go away with safety—I told him that he was summoned, and that he was bound to attend.

CHARGE

Baron Smith—Gentlemen of the Jury, the prisoner at the bar, *William Woolahan*, is indicted for a burglary, with intent to steal. Upon the face of such an indictment, nothing appears, connecting the alledged offence with the disturbances which infest this country, but as I proceed in my recapitulation of the evidence, we shall perceive that a connection of this kind exists, if the witnesses for the crown have told the truth   Indeed this connection can be suggested in a moment, by observing that the property intended to be stolen was arms. The Baron then proceeded to sum up the evidence, beginning with the testimony of Thomas Terrott. His Lordship said, that in making such observations as appeared to him to arise out of the evidence, instead of aiming at any methodical arrangement, he would make them as they occurred, for fear they should escape him. Without recapitulating, from the learned Baron's statement, the proofs which have been already given, I confine myself to the outline of his lordship's charge, and the observations and comments which he interspersed   He observed upon the uncommon brightness of the night, and Terrott's previous acquaintance with the prisoner's name and person   On the other hand, he reminded the Jury, and appealed to their experience for the truth of the suggestion, how apt the class, to which this prosecutor belonged, was to confound the distinctions between certain knowledge, and strong belief, to mistake powerful conjecture and persuasion for absolute and undoubting certainty , to mix up what, at the proper moment for identification, they perceived and observed, with what they afterwards heard from others, or with circumstances which subsequently fell under their own observation   and thus assisted, to manufacture for themselves a sort of counterfeit and spurious certainty, which the law does not recognize   It was the bounden duty of a jury to correct these mistakes· to stand between the prisoner and their effect   and to reduce what a witness called certainty, to mere belief, if, upon the context of his evidence, it appeared that he had not distinct and solid grounds of certain knowledge   On nothing short of such genuine and certain grounds could legal evidence, for example of identification, against a prisoner, be raised   How would he apply these principles to the present case ?   Terrott said that he was struck on the hand with a white pole, and that the prisoner was the man who gave the blow   It was in a moment of considerable alarm and confusion that this blow was given   Now observe, next morning this witness missed a fresh, white pole, or spade-handle from his house   Some of his family told him that the prisoner had been in the house, and had removed this white pole.   It might form an important inquiry for the jury, whether the witness had irregularly assisted himself, towards identifying the prisoner, in this way   Whether, at the moment when the blow was given, he thought the striker resembled Woolahan, the prisoner   Whether, next morning, when he missed his pole, and heard that Woolahan had taken it, he said to himself, Woolahan must have been the man who struck me, I *believed* so last night, I am *certain* of it now   This would not be a legitimately certain identification, it would be a white staff, and some family hearsay, identifying a prisoner   It would be, so far as this testimony goes, concluding that Woolahan was guilty, because the blow was struck by a man *resembling* him, with a pole *resembling* one which had been removed from the witness's house, by some one who, *as he heard*, was Woolahan.   He would now anticipate, more or less, upon the proofs, for the purpose of, as it were, converting or transposing his observations, and inquiring whether, in undertaking to identify the prisoner, the other members of Terrott's family derived undue assistance from communications made to them by him   thus, whether he told them that he was struck with a white pole, by a man whom he believed to be William Woolahan.   That thereupon his family told him that a pole of this description had been removed by a man from the house That they, already perhaps *believing* this man to be Woolahan, and *he* already *believing* Woolahan to be the man, he and they, respectively, composed a certainty out of these two beliefs I am not, continued the Baron, asserting that this was so, I am only recommending to you to inquire whether it was so and to recollect, that the law will not allow us to piece and patch up a certainty, by tacking together different beliefs. Terrott admits that he was confused He adds indeed, that he was not frightened. We however find him act the part of a seemingly frightened man, when he escapes into his neighbour's house, breaking through a partition wall in order to effect his escape He certainly swore his informations on the morning after the outrage for that an outrage was committed, let the aggressors have been whom they may, is abundantly ascertained by the evidence of Mr Miller. But though Terrott swore his informations on the next day, it does not appear that he did so, before he and his family had been making mutual communications to each other. Another observation seems pertinent to this inquiry, how far the identification of the prisoner, by Terrott, rests on satisfactory foundations it is this—manifestly Terrott placed confidence both in *Howe* and *Brady* He made communications to both He told both of the blow which he had received He told neither who the person was that struck it why this omission? Was it that he was wholly ignorant, or quite uncertain who the striker was? Was it that his belief had not yet strengthened itself into a supposed certainty, by family communications? While the conflict was going on, Terrott was liable, by his own admission, to fall into a mistake, for he admits that he mistook his intimate and associate, *Howe*, for a person of the name of M'Donogh Yet *Howe* he saw almost continnally. The man who struck him, and who, he says, was Woolahan, he saw but for a moment

The learned Judge then proceeded to comment on the evidence of Elizabeth Terrot, the first witness's wife By her own account she was in a state of great alarm The scene was calculated to produce alarm Her husband had fled, the door was broken in the room was crowded, her children were threatened and beaten, indecent liberties were taken with her person, a shot was fired close by her, and the whole transaction occupied scarcely a quarter of an hour By the bye, in her informations before the magistrate, this witness swore that an attempt was made to violate her person. In her evidence on the table, though she swore to indecencies, instead of swearing to any attempt at violation, she negatived it nearly showing at the same time, that there was nothing to prevent such an attempt, or to prevent its being successful There was also something obscure in one passage of her testimony, She seemed to say this, that she knew but one of the party, and that her son told her.

Another part of this woman's testimony seemed not undeserving of observation, though what ought to be the result of such a scrutiny, might be another question, whether it ought, or ought not to be a distrust of the witness's credit She said, that in the morning her husband asked her if she knew any of the party who came into the house, she answered that she did, that she knew Woolahan, then she said William Woolahan. Again she represented herself to have said that she knew Woolahan "was in it," without mentioning any Christian name That thereupon her husband asked her, which of the Woolahans? She said it was not the soldier, and her son James told her it was William Woolahan, James told her this in her husband's presence —Now could such communications, in such an order, have taken place? Could she have told her husband that William Woolahan was there, could he then have asked her which of the Woolahans and could the son have thereupon told his mother, that it was William, she having the moment before told her husband, in this child's presence, that it was William who was there?—But this is not all, how could the wife thus inform her husband that it was William Woolahan who was there, when, in another part of her evidence, she declared that she never knew Woolahan's Christian name until her son told her what it was, and that this was not until after her husband's return?

The prisoner is not only entitled to the benefit of any doubt which the Jury may entertain, of the veracity of a prosecutor's witness but of any doubt which they may feel of such witness's accuracy Now, in one part of this witness's evidence, she said that for two years she had known that the prisoner's name was Woolahan, though she did not know his Christian name, until informed of it by her son, in the presence of her husband In another part of her evidence she most distinctly stated, that though for two years she had known Woolahan, " to see him," she never knew him by name, never knew either his Christian or his surname. She moreover said, that it was not while her son was by her side in bed, or during the night, that he apprised her of Woolahan's Christian name, but in the morning, in her husband's presence, and in consequence of his inquiries, and not before Now what does the next witness, the son, say? He denies having heard his father or mother ask any questions of each other, about Woolahan, he denies having himself told that the name of the Woolahan who came into the house, was William; he denies having on that morning himself known what his Christian name was. Elizabeth Terrott, a child of ten years old, also identified the prisoner. She did so, on no great previous length of acquaintance. The child merely said that she had known him "a good many Sundays." Of the communications made by her brother, she gives an account different both from that given by him and by her mother.

She represents her brother, on the day after the outrage, to have told her that Woolahan's name was William, and *to have made this communication in the presence of her mother; and not in the presence of her father.*

Thomas Miller added nothing to the evidence against the prisoner. From *Thomas Bracken* he received a very good character, and having appealed for one to a Mr Fawcett, he was shown to have used all due diligence in endeavouring to procure his attendance, and to have had every reason to expect it. He has, however, continued the Baron, Gentlemen of the Jury, been disappointed, and this disappointment calls on you to investigate the other evidence with the more care. The prisoner's father and brother too have proved an *alibi* defence, and if we suppose them, upon the other points, to have sworn the truth, the evidence of Mr. Cassidy adds something material, as to the time. Nor is that portion of Bracken's testimony immaterial to this defence, which represents the prisoner, as having been accustomed to sleep at his father's on Saturday and Sunday nights. I fear I do not risk encountering a different opinion upon your part, if I admit the evidence of Patrick Woolahan, the prisoner's brother, to be little entitled to credit from a Jury   His story is not too credible, his tone, manner, and deportment are every thing which they ought not to be   I will not say that a fabricated defence ought in no degree to disparage a prisoner's case   But it must not be suffered to produce too unfavourable an effect upon it   We ought to recollect that a prisoner does not prove his guilt, by encountering the charge against him by a false defence   The accusation, and the defence against it, may both be false   The accused may be innocent, but he may be so circumstanced as not to have the means of demonstrating this innocence by a true defence, and, feeling his life to be at stake, he may not have virtue enough to refrain from attempting to save it by a falsehood   Again, *he* may not be the suborner   His friends, against his will, or without his knowledge, may have sacrificed their consciences to their wish to save him   He ought not to suffer death, because others may have incurred the guilt and less heavy penalties which the law attaches to false swearing   He ought not to be convicted of an untrue charge, because he may have encountered it by an equally untrue defence   His father too gave *alibi* evidence on his behalf   This becomes the more suspicious, if you believe his associate witness and son, Patrick Woolahan to have sworn falsely   But still however, the perjury of Timothy, the father, would not be a necessary consequence of that of Patrick Woolahan, the son   The former evidence would lose its corrupt prop, but still might contain within it marks of intrinsic strength and truth   The detected falsehood of a defence should do little more than throw a Jury back upon the evidence for the prosecution, the sufficiency of which they are still bound to scrutinize   Here, the evidence against the prisoner consists merely of the testimony of the members of one family, a husband, who appears, from his own testimony and that of Miller, to have been somewhat rash and hasty,—a wife, under the natural controul and influence of that husband — and two young children, under the controul, persuasion, and influence of both. They would naturally be comparing notes; and accordingly, they appear to have done so: and yet, after all this, can we say that their testimony has left no room for animadversion? May we not conceive things to have proceeded thus?—My husband, says the wife to herself, thinks that the man who struck him with the white pole was William Woolahan, and my husband must be right. And now I remember that one of the party took a white spade handle out of the house, and I suspected it to be William Woolahan at the time, now *I am sure* it was he. My wife, says the husband, saw a man take a spade handle out of the house, it must have been that which I was struck with I thought the man who struck me was like William Woolahan, *I am now sure* that it was he My father and mother, says James, the child, think that William Woolahan was the man who was going to beat me, my father and mother must be right *I am sure he was the man.* My brother James, says the still younger sister, told me that William Woolahan was in the house my father and mother say the same; they could not all be mistaken *I am sure* he was in the house Thus, one belief may have been pieced up with another, and a certainty manufactured and patched up of these The lower orders are extremely slovenly in this respect, and very much given to confound knowledge with strong belief, and impose the latter for the former, upon juries, and upon themselves But such counterfeit certainty is not what the law requires. It must be unassisted, it must be undoubting, it must be acquired at once, and on the moment, not grow up by degrees, ending in certainty, after having begun in mere belief But under these cautions and refinements many a guilty man may escape No doubt this consequence will follow, but the law knew this when it established its rules, and to those rules it is our duty to adhere What are those rules? The following, amongst others —That doubt shall acquit a prisoner —that nothing short of *legitimate* certainty shall be received as evidence against him But the law would be defeated, and the country would be destroyed, if such scrupulous niceties were to prevail On the contrary, the law is defeated if they *do not* prevail, for those niceties are enacted by the law. The country too is destroyed, if niceties do not prevail, the neglect of which is the subversion of the law I do not say that urgent circumstances may not sometimes call for a temporary suspension of the law, or that the country must be destroyed by such—not permanent suspension But I deprecate the necessity, and warn the people not to produce it The security of the country will be best consulted, and the law most eminently triumph, when it refuses to abandon its mild maxims, though the country be disturbed,—when those who administer it refuse to swerve from its humane principles, though the tumult and violence of insurrection be at their doors

The Jury found the prisoner—GUILTY but recommended him to mercy in the following words —

The following is the Address of JOHN DUNN, Esq (one of the Jury) on recommending the prisoner to mercy —

My Lords—My fellow-jurors have selected me to convey to your Lordships their humble recommendation of the prisoner, William Woolahan, to mercy Although I am deeply impressed with the conviction of my very feeble powers to convey to your Lordships their wishes on the occasion, yet the duty is so congenial, and in such perfect accordance with my own feelings, that I have not for a moment hesitated to comply with their desire. The grounds on which we humbly and most respectfully beg to recommend the prisoner to mercy are, it appearing in evidence that a crown summons was regularly served on a witness for the prisoner, which has been disregarded, and the very proper conduct observed by him during the lengthened trial he had undergone. The extraordinary times in which we are assembled, the alacrity, I may almost say, the cheerfulness, with which the jurors of this county have given their attendance—the manner in which they have discharged their very important duties—when, my Lords, all these circumstances are considered, and that the prisoner's Jury are unanimous in their recommendation of him to mercy, they trust they are not too sanguine in entertaining hope that their recommendation may be favourably received.

ATTORNEY-GENERAL.—I feel that the recommendation of the Jury carries with it great weight, and is entitled to the most serious attention of his Majesty's Government, and I can give this assembled County the fullest assurance that the distinguished Nobleman who is at the head of that Government, anxious as he is to put down the spirit of insurrection, is desirous that this may be done by administering justice in mercy, and convincing the misguided people that the law can spare as well as punish. For my part, I shall with the respect and deference with which it becomes me to regard such a recommendation, give it all the weight which my furtherance of it can insure. Let me, however, advert to one or two facts connected with this case, that my views of it may be distinctly understood and appreciated I will first observe on the grounds of recommendation put forward by the Jury, one of them is, that there was a witness for the prisoner absent Now, I confess, that that is a ground of recommendation to which I can give little value; if that fact had been stated before the trial was called on, I most certainly would have given ample time to secure his attendance, such a matter therefore, I am free to confess, has no weight with me. Were I to act on the presumption, that the evidence of a witness not produced is of any value, it would be in effect a re-trial of the case without the power or means of investigating the truth. But there is another ground of recommendation to which I feel the utmost deference to be due, and that is the demeanour of the unfortunate man during his trial. I am persuaded that there was not a person in Court who witnessed it, that was not impressed with the belief that he was truly penitent and contrite; and I should hope that his example in this respect may make on the minds of those engaged in illegal associations, a salutary impression. There is another ground on which the recommendation of the Jury may be supported, which, though not used by them, it becomes my duty to state. The attack upon Terrott's house was, as your Lordships have judicial notice of, perpetrated by a great number of persons. I felt it due to the justice of the country to select one of this number, whose conduct evinced a greater degree of atrocity than that of his associates. From the sworn informations, I was induced to think it probable that Terrott's wife would have proved the actual violation of her person, however, I am bound to say, that although her evidence imputed grossly indecent familiarities to the prisoner, yet, that that dreadful crime does not appear to have been perpetrated. Upon these various grounds, I am now about to do an act upon my own responsibility, which, I trust, will be sanctioned by the head of his Majesty's Government in this country—that act is to entreat the Court, unless your Lordships see reason to the contrary, instead of pronouncing, to record sentence of death on William Woolahan.

BARON SMITH then said —

William Woolahan, I am relieved from the terrible necessity of pronouncing the capital sentence upon you. The humane recommendation of your Jury, and clemency of the Attorney General, as representative in this instance of the mercy of the Crown, enables the Court to merely *record* the judgment of death against you, and hold out to you a hope that your life will not be taken.

To have the power to do so, affords me the most sincere and heartfelt gratification

Chiefly upon your account, my poor, repentant, and therefore interesting young man

But also because it is delightful to behold a Jury, who having begun by a firm and honest performance of their duty, end by earnestly soliciting the mercy of the Crown.

And because it is no less gratifying, to find the representative of the Royal clemency, respond to this benignant feeling of the Jury, and promise his benevolent efforts to have it carried into execution

Especially one must feel gratified by such proceedings, when we have judicially heard an allegation that the panel was arrayed partially, to the injury of the prisoners, that panel from which has emanated this merciful recommendation.

Nor is this the only recommendation, which has proceeded from this panel

From it also issued a recommendation of *James Dowling*.

And here also, I believe I may consider the king's Attorney-General as not disposed to thwart the humane wishes of the Jury

These occurrences are the more acceptable to my feelings, because both the recommendations, and the acquiescence in them, have been in cases precisely and eminently of the class which has been throwing this county into disorder, and because such lenient conduct, both on the part of the Juries, and of the prosecution, would negative all idea of excitement, prejudice, or over keenness, against persons upon trial for offences of the insurgent kind

Indeed it has appeared to me, that the *uniform* conduct of the Juries at this commission, exculpated them fully and honorably from any such imputation Fallibility must attach upon every tribunal that is merely human, but the Maryborough Juries seem to have acted intelligently, conscientiously, and justly, and it is not for you, or Dowling, to say, that they have not conducted themselves humanely

Though your offence may not, upon the indictment, appear to have been of the whiteboy class, yet upon the evidence it was so It was the act of a collected number, and the burglary was committed with a view of obtaining arms.

You were indicted capitally. This arose from the Attorney General's having reason to apprehend, that you had aggravated your offence by offering violence to Terrot's wife But this turning out not to have been the case, he has most readily assented to the humane wishes of the Jury.

To the Crown, and to that Jury, you are indebted for your life The heavy punishment of exile, which you must endure, will have been inflicted on you by those, who generated those tumultuous conspiracies in which you joined.

Your offence has not been altogether free from aggravations. The blow which you gave to Terrot, your indecencies towards his weakly wife, and ill usage of his child, I must reckon amongst these

You appealed freely for a character, to a gentleman of

the name of Fawcett you did all in your power to procure his attendance, and had every reason to reckon on it He however did not attend On this absence, the Jury seem to me to have acted well They would have been **wrong** to use it as any ground for an acquittal This would have been to decide the question, not on the evidence which they had heard, but on the possible import of evidence which they had *not* heard.

But they used the fact as an ingredient, in their motives for recommending you to mercy.

The Jury did not suffer themselves to be withdrawn from the path of mercy which they had chosen, by the unbecoming demeanour of your brother They disbelieved the evidence which he gave *for* you. Possibly they believed the evidence which his tone of contumacy and turbulence gave against *himself* evidence not only against his character, but which might less lead to a belief that you were not at Terrott's, than to a strong conjecture that he *was*

A good character, notwithstanding the absence of Mr. Fawcett, you *did* receive And what, amongst other things, did this, demonstrate ' The speed, and completeness, with which innocence can be depraved, and the people demoralized, by the perversely diligent efforts of coarse and vulgar agitation.

But you received a character which has stood you in far greater stead, then that which issued from the witnesses you produced You received a character, through God's mercy, from yourself, which weighed more with your upright Jury, than all the rest That character was given, most impressively, by your deeply penitent demeanour. A softness which *manifestly* had its source, not in cowardice, but good feeling' a softness which melted at the presence of your father, at every matter which reminded you of your transgression, at every thing calculated to affect a generous and a contrite heart

Let us observe the power of God, manifested in a way which we are continually overlooking A power which never neds, and seldom uses miracle, to achieve its will, but accomplishes a great and gracious purpose, by the very simplest and most ordinary means Of the marks and tokens of that contrition which He inspired and accepted—of these simple indications, and their effect upon your Jury,—He formed an instrument of sufficient efficacy for the preservation of your life

I thank God, that I have not a yet more painful duty to perform, than that of announcing that judgment of death must be recorded against you

COUNSEL FOR THE CROWN

Mr. Attorney General	Mr Clarke
Mr Tickell	Mr Arabin
Mr. Martley	

COUNSEL FOR THE PRISONER

Mr Darcy.	Mr Murphy
Mr Brady	Mr Mara

Agent—Mr. Mara

TRIAL OF

THOMAS DELANY, BARTH MALONE,
JAMES DEEGAN, MICHALL MALONE, and
JERLMIAH WEIRE

For assaulting and breaking in the dwelling house of
Thomas Terrott

29th May, 1832

Elizabeth Terrott, Examined by the ATTORNEY-GENE-
RAL 1 remember the night of the 13th May, nine or ten
men entered my house that night, 1 saw two of them
with arms, my husband made his escape before they got
into the house, he broke through the partition that separates our house from Brady's and got away.

Cross-examined by Mr. DARCY —1 know all the prisoners, but 1 did not know them that night, 1 know them
these twelve or thirteen years, there was a candle lighting in the house for a few minutes, there was no fire lighting in the house, there is a window in the house beside
my bed, it has four panes, the door was broken in; they
were walking up and down the room.

Second Witness, *Thomas Miller*, examined by Mr Tickell ---I know Thomas Terrott; he lives about a quarter of
a mile from me, I remember the night of the 13th May,
Terrott came to me that night about twelve o'clock, I was in
bed when he came; he cried out that his wife and children
were murdered, I immediately got up in consequence of
that. I opened the door for him, and gave him a gun, we
came to Jacob Howes' house, I went forward to Terrott's
house, Terrott overtook me, we went to the yard of the
house; there is a space between his house and the road
there is a gap there, I was at the very gap when I saw
about twenty four or twenty five of those people on the
road, they were about forty yards from the house, they
were going on towards James's-town, they were going
that way at first, I saw the flash of a pan; we were both
in our shirts, they came running back, I desired them to
stand back, and the rushed on without attending to me,
one of them snapped a gun, and another snapped a pistol
and they had a hold of me in a minute, I had a double
barrelled pistol, I shot one man and I turned round to
shoot the fellow that cocked the pistol at me, and the pistol
fell out of my hand, I then got a blow of a stone, after
firing at the first man I turned round to fire at another,
after being knocked down with a stone I got up and I
was knocked down again with another stone, then two of
them held me down on the ground while others of them
pounded me with stones and kicked me, they looked at
me in the face I suppose to try whether I was dead or not;
by this time Terrott and Howe came and fired shots at
them, they got my pistol and the bayonet too, I then
got home to my house, it was as light a night as ever
came I think, I saw the five men in the dock among the

party that night, (identifies the five prisoners,) Michael Malone caught hold of me by the shirt, Thomas Delany kicked me, Jeremiah Weire put his face within a few inches of mine, I dont say that Weire struck me, I saw him look at me when I was down, the other two were partly at my back, but they were not together, I mean Bartholomew Malone and James Deegan, they did not stay any time at my back, I am perfectly sure that they were there, I know some of them since they were little boys Weire I know since he was a little boy I know Tom Delany since he was a little boy, I know Michael Malone two or three years, I know James Deegan six or seven years, and I know Bartholomew Malone four or five years; I think the Malones are cousins, when Delany gave me a kick, I said " Tom dont kill me ," I did not hear him say any thing.

Cross-examined by Mr. BRADY —I am a farmer, I have been always a farmer, I was a yeoman once, I have killed only one in the course of my life, I don't know who the person was that I killed, I had a good view of the man I shot, I don't know that there is any reward for valour of this kind, I have not heard of the Lord Lieutenant's offering a reward for a person who would signalize himself, I'll engage you would not go into the same place I did for five hundred guineas, I never heard of any one getting a reward, Colonel O'Donoughoe took my informations I knew him before, I saw him since, I had nothing to do with him but giving my informations, I gave him my informations the day after the thing occurred I was not very often drunk, I am not an habitual drunkard, I have never been so drunk as not to be able to walk, I don't think I was drunk these five months, I drank a tumbler of punch that day after my dinner, and that is all I drank by the virtue of my oath when this business occurred I thought it was twelve o'clock by the appearance of the night and the length of time until it was day I saw a good many persons there, I know only six out of the whole of them I did not see any thing in the hands of these men, one man had a gun fastened in a block, and another man had a pistol there were nine or ten about me in the struggle, some of them stood about the man that was shot, there is nothing in the world I would rather be than a farmer, I have the best landlord on earth, that is Lord Portarlington, I said that the man I shot was like a man of the name of M'Donough, I said that at first, but he was a little taller I think, I know M Donough these seven or eight years Terrot and I had a little difference about a ditch, it went before magistrates, and he said he would leave it to myself I don't well remember what took place before the magistrate

To a JUROR —When I mentioned the name of M'Donough I had an idea it might be him I was not able to go out the next day but I was able to go out in a couple of days, there was a great deal of blood about the place I bled a great deal myself

Third Witness. *Thomas Terrot,* examined by Mr MARTLEY.—My house was attacked last Sunday night fortnight I was in bed at the time I heard a blow of a stone come against Brady's window Brady's house was separated from mine by a mud wall, there are two distinct doors, when I heard the noise I bounced out of bed and stood at the door, I broke out into Brady's house through the wall, and got out of Brady's house I saw people about my own house before I got out they were forcing in my door I got out on the road and from that to Mr

Mr Miller's house, Mr Miller came with me towards my own house, when I came near my own house they were coming out of my yard, and going on towards James's Town, I observed a shot, they came back and faced us when they saw us, I saw arms with some of them, they presented arms at us, and snapped and missed fire, they then rushed at us, I snapped a gun and missed fire by this time they rushed up to the gate. I stood in that spot until the man that Mr. Miller shot dropped I remained standing for a moment, and then ran back for Jacob Howe, they had got away from Mr Miller when I came back, I was not able to distinguish any of the people that were about Mr. Miller, I found the door of my own house broken in, Jacob Howe returned with me

Cross-examined by Mr Murphy —Mr Miller and I had a difference once, but I was his friend notwithstanding, and I left the thing entirely to his own oath because I believed him By virtue of your oath did you not say at Ballybrittas that you would not believe him? I never did say that upon my oath. You know all these men very well? I do they are all my neighbours, if they were as near to me as the rest that night I would see them, I was on the road going away when Mr Miller was knocked down, I did not see him knocked down, I heard heavy blows, I think there were three or four men about Mr Miller when he fired the shot, I cannot swear but there were nine or ten about him, I cannot tell how many were in the yard, I can swear that three or four went off the road, when Brady's door was struck with a stone one of the men said, " Damn you that is not the door," I suppose they had a stranger because they struck the wrong door, I know Wm Delany very well, he knocked at Brady's door, by the virtue of my oath I think it was to let him know that there was a sentry at the door and not to let him look out, I was in the yard

Mr MARTLEY.—Have you seen Mr Delany since in the country ? I have not

Fourth Witness, *Daniel Hodgens*, examined by Mr CLARKE —I was stationed at Ballybrittas, I was in Dublin on the 13th of this month and returned on the 16th I made a search for a man of the name of Wm. Delany, I did not find him

ATTORNEY GENERAL.—My Lords, we have Brady here and the Gentlemen on the other side may examine him if they like. (*Prisoners Counsel declined examining Brady*)

The evidence for the prosecution closed here

EVIDENCE FOR THE DEFENCE

First Witness, *Elizabeth Moore*, examined by Mr. D'ARCY —My husband's name is Wm Moore. I live in Inch my husband is alive my son's name is James, my daughters names are Biddy, Catherine and Margaret, I know the prisoners Thomas Delany and Bartholomew Malone. I am not in any way related to Thomas Delany but I am to Bartholomew Malone, I recollect Sunday evening the 13th of this month, I was in my own house that evening and in my bed, my husband was in bed before me, my son James was also in bed, my daughter Margaret was in bed last, my other two daughters were not at home in the evening that evening Tom Delany opened my door and came in, a man of the name of Michael Maher was with him, I got up when they came in, that was about nine o'clock Tom Delany said "good night Mrs Moore, I am sorry to annoy you out of bed." he asked me if I saw Bartholomew Malone; I told him I did not, he asked me where were the girls, I told him I did not know, that I supposed they were gone to their sister my two daughters returned home in about a quarter of an hour aferwards with Bartholomew Malone and their first cousin Sally Dooley, they remained in my house and and prevailed on me to go to bed, about an hour after they came in Delany, Maher, and Malone remained opposite the fire, my bed room was behind the fire, I slept none, and I heard them chatting all night, but I don't know what they said. they left my house at day light, I heard them going away, Delany and Malone were acquainted with my daughters some time before, I suppose they were courting my daughters

Cross-examined by the ATTORNEY GENERAL—There is only the kitchen and my own room in the house; my husband slept with me in the same bed my daughter Peggy slept with me till she was called up, and I went to bed, the door was not locked it was only latched; there are two beds in the kitchen, I got up when there was nobody up in the house and my door was opened I dressed myself and sat at the fire for about an hour I left Peggy in bed she was asleep inside, and Sally Dooley went up and awakened her, she dressed herself and I went to bed, the girls were coming backwards and forwards for milk in the course of the night, my son was in bed in the kitchen, he was awake when they came in he did not get up, he was nearer to the kitchen door than I was; I dressed myself from top to toe I found my daughters in the house

when I got up in the morning, my son was not in bed
when I got up, I am sure he was not in the field when I
got up, when I got up in the morning all my daughters
were in the kitchen, and Sally Dooly was with them,
Sally Dooly had been sleeping in my house during the
course of that week, James's town is about five miles from
my house, she slept at my house on Saturday night and
Friday night I believe she left my house at about 10 or
11 o'clock on Sunday, I don't recollect that she dined at
my house on that day, Peggy and her father and I and
James dined at home that day, I can't recollect whether
my other two daughters and Sally Dooly came home to
dinner or not, but I saw them in the evening before they
went away, it was three hours and more before I went to
bed, that they went out, they went out a short time after
coming home, Tom Delany lives in James's Town and so
does Bartholemew Malone, I believe Tom Delany was
courting my daughter Catherine, I never saw Maher
before that I was only just settled in bed when they came
I am not a good sleeper at any time I could not close my
eyes a wink on Saturday night my husband slept part of the
night, I heard my son James say that he did not sleep, I
heard him say that he was annoyed by the girls and the
men, my husband was up before me By the virtue of my
oath my husband got up before me that morning, I was
awake when he got up, no one breakfasted with me on
Sunday morning but my own family and Sally Dooly
Sally, Biddy, and Catherine, went to mass that day,
Margaret did not, I don't know that my husband went to
Mass that Sunday, Margaret and I staid at home all day,
James went to Mass to Stradbally and so did the girls

James returned home from Mass and I had his dinner for him when he came home, he got his dinner by himself, the girls did not come home with him; I cannot tell whether they came home before or after him, my husband and Margaret dined along with me, I am sure there were only three of us dined together, I am positive Biddy and Catherine and sally Dooly did not dine at home that day, James and Margaret, and my husband and myself supped together, and we then went to bed

Second Witness, *William Moore*, examined by Mr Brady.—I know the prisoners, Thomas Delany, and Bartholomew Malone, I know Delany about half-a-year, and Malone a quarter of a year, I have three daughters unmarried, myself, and my two daughters, and my son, went to Stradbally to be examined by the police, I was in bed when these men came to my house, I believe it was about 9 o'clock, Delany, I believe, was the first man came in; he raised the latch and came in, another man of the name of Michael Maher came in that I never saw before, I did not see him that night, I saw none of them coming in, but I heard them, I knew Delany's voice, I knew that another man came in, because I heard them talking, I never saw him till I saw him a day or two after that night, when he told me it was he that was in it, the company remained there 'till the supper was got ready for them about 12 o'clock, my daughters came into the room to bring out milk for supper, after the supper I desired them to go to bed to my son, and not to go home that night, I fell asleep after, and I awakened when it was a bit in the day, and they were going out preparing to go home; I did not see them, I only heard them talking, just as I was going out of my room, they were going out of my land; I know that, because I looked out after them and saw them. I know that Bartholemew Malone was there by his voice I heard him sleep, and I called in Sally Dooley to know if it was he was asleep

Cross-examined by Mr. TICKELL —I asked Delany and Malone what way the world was going on, I asked them if there was one Sweeny an informer taken, who was bringing in a great many people, Delany said he did not know whether he was taken or not. Maher handed me a summons, and he told me he was the man was along with Delany that night, when I asked my daughters who was the man that came with Delany that night, they said it was a man of the name of Michael Maher, that was before I was served with a summons; I suppose it could not be more than half past 3 o'clock when they were going away in the morning, I did not see their faces, they were about fifteen perches from my house when I saw them first, I was not at Chapel that Sunday myself—I think my daughters, Catherine and Biddy, were at second Mass at Stradbally that day, my daughters eat their dinners at home that day, and then went off. my own children and Sally Dooley dined with me, we all dined together that day, I have no doubt at all but it was after dinner my daughters went out, I thought it was to their sister they were going, until I heard say from themselves that they had been at the bridge of Vicar's Town, I heard on Monday evening that Delany was taken up.

CHIEF JUSTICE —How many of your own family sat down together with you to dinner that Sunday? I cannot say that they all dined with me, but to the best of my knowledge they did.

Mr. TICKELL —Did you not tell me positively that all your daughters dined with you? I think they did, but I am not certain of it, for you set my brains a wool-gathering.

Third Witness, *Catherine Moore*, examined by Mr. MURPHY.—I know Thomas Delany; I recollect Sunday, the 13th of May, I saw him between 9 and 10 o'clock on Sunday night, in my father's house, I know Bartholomew Malone, I saw him about six o'clock in the evening at the Cross of Vicar's Town, I was in a public house with him there, after that I returned home, my sister and Sally Dooley, and Bartholomew Malone were with me, it was between 9 and 10 o'clock when we got home; I found Tom Delany and Mick Maher there, my father was in bed, and my mother was sitting at the fire, and so were Maher and Delany when I came in, they all remained in the house that night until it was day light; I never left their company the whole time they were there, they never left the house the whole night. I never left them, except when I went into the room to get some milk

Cross-examined by Mr MARTLEY.—I knew these two men since last August, they were in the habit of going to my father's house, I am related to Bartholemew Malone, I did not see Tom Delany that evening until I met him in my father's house, John Connor's was the only public house I was in that evening, no man was in my company except Bartholomew Malone, I left home about 4 o'clock that evening, I was at Mass in the morning, my sister Biddy was with me, Sally Dooley was sleeping at our house some nights before that, she slept some nights at my aunt's house, and some nights at our's, she went to my aunt's on Sunday, and we went for her as we were going to Vicar's Town in the evening, it was a little before 4 o'clock when we came to my father's house, I remained at home only whilst I was eating my dinner, myself and Biddy dined together, my mother was in the house when we were eating our dinner, and nobody else, my brother was at the same Chapel with me at Stradbally, I did not see him there, but I saw him going there, Biddy and I called on Sally Dooley, and we went together to Vicar's Town, we expected to meet somebody there, Bartholomew Malone was one of the persons we expected to meet there, Tom. Delany made an agreement to meet me there that evening, the third man we expected to meet there was Michael Maher, I knew him before that, he had never been at my father's house before that, I eat my supper in my father's house, I had to dress it when I came back, my sister Margaret was in bed when I came home, Sally Dooley went to awaken her; she got up and joined us, and the four girls and the the three boys remained up all night, We did not let my mother sleep I went to bed in the morning when it was clear day light, it was after the boys went away when I went to bed, it was a good deal in the day light when they went away I went to bed immediately after they went away—all the girls went to bed after that, we remained a very short time in bed, I got up before Sally and Biddy, I had time to boil a pot of potatoes before they were up, my mother was up before Sally and Biddy, and my father my father got up long before I got up, he was not up at the time the boys were going away, I am sure that he did not see them, I saw him in bed after the boys went away, my mother was in bed when the boys were going away, neither of them was asleep, for I went into the room after the boys went away. I went into the room with clothes and things I had to take off me, I am sure they were both in bed at that time, my father did not get up 'till I went to bed, I did not hear him getting up, my brother James slept in the kitchen, he wanted the men to go to bed, they said they would go home, and my mother said she would not let them go home, that they would meet the police.

To Mr. MURPHY.—I went to bed that morning, the very minute they went away.

To a JUROR.—I went into my father's room before I went to bed, my father and mother were both in bed when I went into the room

Fourth Witness, *Bridget Moore*, examined by Mr. MARA.—I am sister to the last witness. I know Bartholomew Malone (points him out) my sisters, Catherine and Sally Dooly, and I were in Vicar's Town, on Sunday evening the 13th, and we saw Bartholomew Malone there, I returned to my father's house that evening, Bartholomew Malone was in my company till I returned home, between nine and ten o'clock when I returned, I found Maher and Delany in my father's house; I was in company with these men until day-light they were not one moment out of my company that night

Cross-examined by Mr. CLARKE.—I was not at Vicar's Town before that day, I was at Mass, at Stradbally, that day, my sister Catherine was not with me, I got home between three and four o'clock, when I went home, there was nobody at home but my mother; I dined when I got home, I dined in my father's house my mother gave the dinner to us, when we went home, after dinner we went up to my aunt's place for Sally Dooley, I was going to meet Bartholomew Malone, Sally Dooley went with us to Vicar's Town, we were to meet Tom Delany, Mich Maher, and Bartholomew Malone. after meeting Bartholomew Malone, we remained a couple of hours in Vicar's Town; when we came home, I saw Delany, and Malone and my mother. my father was in bed when we went home, Catherine and Sally Dooley got supper ready for us, the three men remained there until day-light, Malone fell asleep after supper, nobody else took a doze that I saw, not one of the party went to bed. I saw them going off when it was day-light, Margaret was up at that time, after they went away, every one of us went to bed, my father and mother went to bed, when we went to bed, I heard of these boys being taken up that same day, it was at nightfall I heard of it.

Fifth Witness, *James Moore*, examined by Mr DARCY—I am the brother of the last witness, I recollect Sunday evening, the 13th of this month, I saw Delany and Maher in my father's house that night I was in bed when they came in, I slept in the kitchen I think I was half an hour in bed when they came, it was about nine o'clock when they came in my father, and mother, and my sister Margaret were in bed when they came in. Catherine and Biddy were not at home at this time in about a quarter of an hour they came in with Bartholomew Malone, I did not get up, but they kept me awake all night Upon your oath, could these men be out of your house that night without your knowledge? I am not able to say that, I did not miss them out of the house, I saw them go out in the morning, I heard them talk often during the night I think I did not begin to sleep for two hours after they came into the house. I got up between five and six o'clock, I think it was only just day-light when they went.

Cross-examined by Mr ARABIN—I was at Mass that Sunday, Catherine and Biddy left the house with me to go to Mass, I left them on the road after me, I did not mind them at all, I was home about two o'clock, I found my father, and mother, and Margaret at home. I dined with them that day, we all sat down to dinner together as the men were going away 1 heard the women at the door with them to the best of my knowledge, my father was in bed at that time.

Sixth Witness. *Sally Dooley*, examined by Mr BRADY —
I know the prisoners Tom Delany and Bartholomew Malone, I saw them at William Moore's house last Sunday night fortnight, I saw Bartholomew Malone at the cross roads of Vicar's Town, Biddy and Catherine Moore were with me, it was about eight o'clock when we left it we then went to William Moore's house, we found Tom Delany and Michael Maher there, the three men remained there until day light.

Cross-examined by the ATTORNEY GENERAL.—I went to bed that morning shortly after the men went away, I think it was about ten minutes after they went away Margaret, Catherine, and Biddy Moore, went to bed with me I am sure the old people were in bed when we went to bed, I saw the boys clear off from the door

CHIEF JUSTICE —When the boys were going away in the morning how many of you were at the door together ? Biddy Moore was with me at the door when they were going away I can't exactly say where Catherine and Margaret were but they were in the house Was there any one up in the house but you four ? There was not

Seventh Witness, *Michael Maher*, examined by Mr MURPHY —I recollect Sunday the 13th of this month, I know Tom Delany, I recollect to have made an agreement with him to go on that day to   in the county of Kildare, I went to his own house for him that morning, I went with him to Kildangan to Mass, we dined that day at Mr Prendergast's, in the County of Kildare, we came

across to Vicar's Town, we went to John Connor's at
Vicar's Town to meet Bartholomew Malone in the evening
we had agreed between us three to meet at Vicar's town
that evening, Delany and Malone expected to meet their
sweethearts there, we enquired at John Connell's, if
Bartholomew Malone had been there, he told us he had
gone away about ten minutes before that with some
women we came towards Inch expecting to overtake them,
we did not overtake them, we crossed the fields to William
Moore's house, they had not arrived when we got there
Delany Malone and I, remained at William Moore's until
day light in the morning, it was not long in day light, till
we went away.

Cross-examined by Mr TICKELL —I know Thomas Terrot, I live better than a mile from his house, the men in the
dock live in that neighbourhood, we stopped in John Connor's
in Vicar's Town only while we were drinking two pints of
beer, we were there about ten minutes we were at William
Moore's about a quarter of an hour before Malone came it
was about nine o'clock when we got to Moore's, I had not
gone to meet any of the girls there, I was turning my back on
my own place when I was going to Moore's, these girls were
old acquaintances of mine, I knew Catherine Moore, and I
knew Sally Dooley, I did not know Margaret any farther
than by name I never spoke to Biddy before I don't recollect whether the old woman was up when we came in I did
not offer to go home but Delany insisted on going home
shortly after we got there, Delany lives a little below Mr
Miller's he lives about a mile and a half from me his
place is about three or four miles from William Moore's,
(the witness hesitated a good while before he gave this

answer,) in about an hour after Malone came there Delany insisted upon going away, Margaret Moore was up at that time, Sally Dooley went in to make her get up to keep company I suppose with the rest, I made no offer to go home because I knew it would be dangerous to go home at that hour of the night, we all went away together in the morning. we said nothing to the old man when we were going away, nor to the old woman, It was not sunrise when we went away.

CHIEF JUSTICE.—Was it a moonlight night? It was.

To Mr. TICKELL.—It was day-light when we were going away, Delany, Malone and I went together as far Fisherstown, we got there at twelve o'clock, we went to John Connor's house in Vicar's Town, Vicar's Town is about a mile and a half from William Moore's, they were not up at Connor's public house when we reached it, we called them up and they let us in; I cannot tell how long we staid at Connor's, when we left it we went to Michael Whelan's in Vicar's Town, I cannot tell the hour that we got to Whelan's, we stopped there while we were eating our breakfast, I should think we stopped three hours at Whelan's, we did not go straight home, we went down a piece of the road towards Inch again, I did not go to any house there What was your object in going back again to Inch? We laid it out to go back to William Moore's to pass a bit of the day there. Did you go back to Moore's? No. Why? We took another notion and turned back, I believe we went a mile towards Moore's and then turned back, Delany and Malone were with me, we then went home through Vicar's Town, we parted at Fisherstown at the cross roads, it was about one o'clock when I got home to the best of my knowledge, I did not pass by Tom Delany's house to go home, after shaking hands with the girls we went on straight towards Vicars Town After leaving William Moore's we took a short cut across the fields, we did not enter the fields coming back at all.

CHIEF JUSTICE —How far is it from William Moore's to Thomas Terrot's the shortest way it can be gone? I don't know. Is it three miles? I don't know What is the birds flight from one place to the other, can you answer that question? I cannot Is there a river between them? There is a small river Is it a river a man could jump? It is not, I crossed a wall that was over it

Eighth Witness, *Margaret Moore*, examined by Mr MARA —I know Tom Delany and Bartholomew Malone, I recollect Sunday night fortnight, they were at my father's house that night, I was in bed when they came, my sisters were out, I did not remain in bed the entire night, Sally Dooly came for me and bid me get up, when I got up I saw Delany, Malone and Maher in the house they remained there all night they left it at day light.

Cross-examined by Mr. MARTIFY —Sally Dooly slept there on Saturday night she came with a pair of stockings to her brother that was to meet her, he came for the stockings before I was up that morning, I went to prayers that Sunday to Stradbally my two sisters went with me there, my father went to mass, my mother did not my brother went before us, it was to the same chapel we all went, I went with my sisters my father left home first I am sure he was at the chapel, I did not see him at the chapel, I saw him coming in to his dinner and he said he was at the chapel

BARON SMITH —Are you sure of all that? I am You are sure it is that Sunday, and that you are not confusing one Sunday with another? I am sure that he was at mass the

Sunday Sally Dooly came for the stockings, my father came home first that day, my father and mother and brother and I took dinner together, and my other two sisters came in afterwards, I was not at mass that day

CHIEF JUSTICE—Did you come in with your sisters? I was not at mass that day

Mr. MARTLEY—What do you mean by saying that your father left home that day before you to go to Mass? I saw him go out, do you say that when your father came into dinner he said he was at Mass? I do. Are you certain that your father said he was there? He did say it Why did you say that you were at Mass with your sisters that day? I did not recollect, my mother and I staid at home that Sunday, I am sure my sisters dined at home that day, they came in between two and three o'clock to the best of my opinion, that was about an hour and a half after we dined, my sisters left home after they got their dinner, they got their supper ready when they came home I knew Michael Maher a short time before that, I saw him once before that night I never saw him at my father's house till I saw him that night, I just lay in the bed when the boys went away but I did not sleep, they had clear day light to go away, my sisters and Sally Dooly went to bed, I got up when I heard my father getting up, that was in about an hour after the boys went away the sun was risen when I got up, the other girls did not get up at the same time, I got up and put down the potatoes, and Sally and Biddy got up when they were going to be teemed

Re-examined by Mr BRADY.—My father was coming down out of the room when I got up he went out to the field, I heard him open the door and I got up, I saw him go out to the field, and he went to work immediately, I was

in bed about an hour   Could your father have gone out
during that hour you were in bed, without your knowing
it?   He could not

CHIEF JUSTICE.—When the boys were going away did
you go to the door?   I did, and I shook hands with them
when they were going away, I stood at the door and handed
Tom Delany his hat, I looked out after them and saw no
nother persons but them

EVIDENCE FOR DEFENCE OF
JEREMIAH WEIRE

Andrew Weire examined by Mr D'ARCY.—I live in Kil-
legush, Mr Smith is my landlord, I am the father of the
prisoner Jeremiah Weire, he is a single man he lives with
me, I have another son, his name is Andy, I recollect
Sunday the 13th of this month.   My son Jeremiah slept in
his own bed that night in my house, I slept at home myself,
I went to bed at about 11 o'clock, my son Jeremiah, went
to bed at about 8 o'clock or thereabouts, my son Andy went
to bed about 9 o'clock, I was the last up in the house that
night myself, my sons slept together, there are three rooms
and a kitchen in my house, my sons slept in the room next
the canal, streetwards I slept in the room backward to the
fire I have a daughter of the name of Biddy, she was living
with me on the 13th, there is a bolt to the door of my
house, I am sure the door was bolted that night, I bolted
it myself, I got up about six o'clock in the morning, my
son Jeremiah and I were up about the same time, I don't
think he could go out that night, til' morning, unknown to
me, Andy did not get up for an hour after Jeremiah

Cross-examined by the ATTORNEY-GENERAL.—I live about three quarters of a mile from Terrot's the short way across the fields, there is only one outer door to the house, there was no lock on it, there are three windows to the house, they are small windows of four little panes each, the street door opens into the kitchen, I slept in the room to the left, no one but my wife slept in that room, my daughter slept in the room to the right that looks to the back, my son was at home the whole day, except that he went to Mass to Monasterereven at eight o'clock, he staid at home reading all day, Andy went to second Mass, and did not come home till two o'clock, we all dined together, I have a grand-daughter, she slept with my daughter, she is here, no other person slept in the house that night, I was awake till about twelve o'clock. I was not absent from the house the whole night, except about five minutes, when I went to turn a cow off the land, my wife got up earlier than me, I got up before my daughter, just as I was getting up, Jeremiah was getting up to go to Monasterereven to buy some medicines, he was not well; he used to swell sometimes after eating any thing, I don't know why he did not buy the physic on Sunday, I don't know that he took the physic that morning, he came home about eight o'clock, we all took breakfast except Jeremiah, we were done breakfast before he came home. Andy and I were working together after breakfast, and Jeremiah came out to help us, he was complaining of illness when he came out, between eight and nine o'clock is his general hour for going to bed, my daughter had been asleep part of the day, and she was not able to sleep during the night, when she went to bed she could not sleep she said, I heard her up in the house after I went to bed. I was in bed about an hour when I heard her stirring, I heard the boys desiring her to go to bed she had not lit a candle, I don't know that she did go to bed, I don't know whether she dressed herself, Jeremiah called out to her and desired her to go to bed. I heard that quite distinctly, she was sleeping for some hours during the Sunday, she did not go to Mass, she was alone, and she went to sleep What time did she go to sleep? I don't know Was it before or after dinner? I don't know that she went to sleep only as I heard her say she was at dinner with me, she went to bed about eight o'clock she is not in the habit of going to sleep in the day, I never knew her to do it before, I suppose it was while we were away at prayers she went to sleep I believe she went to sleep about two o'clock

CHIEF JUSTICE —When did she tell you she was asleep, was it on Sunday or Monday? I don't know When you went to bed that night did you know that she had been asleep? I did not know any thing about it. Did she tell you that she had been asleep in the middle of the day? I don't know rightly. When was your son arrested? On Monday night Was it after or before his arrest that she told you that? I did not mind—it was after my son was arrested.

ATTORNEY-GENERAL.—Tell me exactly what she said to you? I heard her say that she was drowsy, and that she went to bed at one o'clock and slept for about two hours, and that she could not sleep at night on that account Was any body by when she said that to you? She said it two or three times. How did you happen to talk to your daughter about it at all? I asked her what made her be up that night Which was it because she was drowsy or lonesome that she said she went to sleep? Not having any company When did you return from Mass that day? At one o'clock. When did you dine that day? About two o'clock. Did your daughter dine with you? She did

To Mr D'ARCY.—The size of the window was four small panes fastened in the wall I observed no alteration in the window that morning

To the CHIEF JUSTICE.—After I came home from prayers on Sunday, I was at home from eleven o'clock in the morning, until eleven o'clock at night, when I came home I did not see my daughter till dinner time

Andrew Weire, jun examined by Mr BRADY.—I am brother to the prisoner, I recollect the day he was taken · it was a Tuesday morning about three o'clock in our own house, he was in bed when he was arrested. I was in bed with him, I slept along with him on the Sunday night before, I went to bed about nine o'clock that night, he told me that he was in bed an hour, he had been unwell, he was complaining since Easter before, we slept together the whole night; it was after six o'clock when I got up, he got up before me he got up about six o'clock, I took a little sleep after him, I heard the six o'clock bell ringing when he was getting up

Cross-examined by Mr TICKELL.—We awoke in the night-time when my sister got up, we desired her to go to bed and she did, the door of the room was a little open, I did not see my sister at this time I saw no light in the kitchen I heard a step in the kitchen and I asked who was that, I did not fall asleep 'till I heard the coach coming, I cannot swear that it was not the four o'clock coach that was passing, I was at the chapel on Sunday, my sister remained at home; I returned from Mass about two o'clock, my brother and mother and sister and niece were in the house when I came back, we were all at dinner that day, when my brother got up he went to Monastereven

To the CHIEF JUSTICE.—I was always acquainted with Mr Miller we were always very thick he is a man we liked very well, and we thought he liked us the same

Bridget Heme, examined by Mr MARA—I am the sister of the prisoner, I recollect Sunday fortnight I saw my brother at my father's house that day he was very bad with a pain in his belly he went to bed that night at eight o'clock, I slept in the room next to him I went to bed at about half past nine o'clock, I got up in the morning about half past six, we were both getting up together, he was not out of the house that night after he went to bed

Cross-examined by Mr MARTIN—He could not be out of the house unknown to me, I never slept a wink all night till it was clear day there was a partition between us about seven feet high my brother Andy went to bed after me, my niece slept with me she slept very well I got up in the night and looked out through the window and my brother Jeremiah asked me who was that I told him it was me, and he asked me what I was doing there, he then told me to go to bed, I was in the kitchen looking out of the window the dogs were barking I was about two hours and a half in bed I did not go to Mass that day, my brother was reading to me I went to bed at three o'clock and I slept till five o'clock I was lonesome and drowsy we dined about two o'clock that day the whole family went out after dinner, I am not in the habit of going to sleep in the day time Jeremiah was in the house when I was asleep my father did not know that day that I was asleep, nor till the monday my brother was taken my brother was taken about three o'clock on Monday night, I got up when my brother was taken How did it happen that you told your father that you had been asleep on Sunday? I cannot rightly tell when I told him Tell how did the conversation begin between you and your father? I told it to Mr. Mara the agent Did you ever tell your father before the time you were telling Mr. Mara about it? I don't know

CHIEF JUSTICE.—At the time when you told it to Mr Mara was your father bye? He was

Mr MARILEY —Where did you tell it to Mr Mara? at his own house at Portarlington, I went there with my father, he was present when I told it to Mr Mara, was it then you told Mr Mara you were asleep on Sunday, and that that was the reason you could not sleep at night? It was Were you the first person that mentioned the matter to Mr Mara? No, it was my father Had you been speaking before about it to any body? I forget How did it happen that you spoke to Mr Mara about it? When I was giving in my evidence, I told Mr. Mara that my brother Jeremiah had got up in the course of the night What time was it? I think past twelve o'clock, he was up only a few minutes I was in bed at the time he got up, that was the time the dogs were barking, I told Mr. Mara that he was very bad, that he brought home salts, and that he handed me the salts, my brother had been complaining since Easter, he had been very bad some nights, he tried medicine before that, he got no medical advice but what I gave him, on monday morning he thought to apply to Mr Cassidy for a ticket, that was the first time he though of applying to him, he was very bad on sunday evening and on monday morning he was at work the whole of Monday from the time he came from Monasterevan

CHIEF JUSTICE —Did your father ever at any time ask you why you had gone to bed in the middle of the day? I don't know whether he did or not. Whether he asked you or not, did you ever tell him why you went to bed in the middle of the day? I don't know whether I did or not. Did you ever tell any body at all that you went to bed in consequence of lonesomeness or drowsiness? I don't think I did until my brother was taken. Did you ever tell it to any body? I did, after my brother was taken. To whom? To the neighbours. Do you recollect telling it to your father? I don't know. Did he ever hear it from your lips? I don't know. Did you ever tell any body at any time that it was at one o'clock in the day before dinner that you went to bed? No, I did not.

EVIDENCE FOR DEFENCE OF
MICHAEL MALONE.

Bartholomew Malone examined by Mr D'Arcy —I am the father of the prisoner Michael Malone; I have another son whose name is Bartel, they are both unmarried, they both live with me. I remember Sunday the 13th of May, my son Michael went to Mr Kilbride's that day; he brought a horse with him to bring his brother to the Doctor, he did not return that day till between nine and ten o'clock at night, he slept at home with his brother Bartel, they both went to bed between nine and ten o'clock, he waited no time but while a sup of milk was boiling, he eat no supper, I called up Bartel in the morning, Michael was then in bed, Mr Adair came to the house in the morning, he called me first and asked me was Bartel within, he desired me to tell Bartel to come to him, Bartel went to him, he then desired me to send Michael up to Mr. Trench's, Mr Trench lives about a mile from my house, I walked up with Michael to Mr Trench's, this was on Monday morning, Bartel went along with Mr Adair, and Michael and I followed them immediately, as soon as he put on his clothes, he was kept there

Cross-examined by the ATTORNEY-GENERAL.—Terrot's house is better than a mile from my house, Michael's uncle slept in the one room with him, his name is Paddy Beahan, there are two rooms and a kitchen in the house I slept in the other room, my wife and my two daughters slept with me in the other room, one of my daughters is twenty, and the other about fifteen, neither of them is here, John, the sick man came home to his own house, I don't sleep well generally, and especially when I was fretting for this boy that was sick, there is no lock to the door, there is a glass window in each room, I heard no noise in the room that night, it was early when Mr Adair came to the house, there was a policeman behind the house, Mr Adair never told me of the attack on Terrot's house, when I went out I saw the policeman that was standing behind my house Michael and I went up of ourselves without a policeman Mr Adair did not tell me what he wanted my son for, I had not heard at that time any thing about Terrot's attack, I saw Michael go to bed that evening, he went to bed before me, Paddy Behan and Michael went to bed at the same time, Bartel went to feed the horse, we had all done supper before Michael came home

Bartholomew Malone, jun examined by Mr. BRADY.—I recollect the morning Mr Adair called at my father's house, I went with him to Mr Trench, I slept at home the night before, my brother Michael slept with me he went to bed before me, I got up before him in the morning

Cross-examined by Mr CLARKE.—I went to Mass that Sunday, to Emo. I was at the funeral of an aunt of mine that day, she died in Emo, my brother only got some boiled milk when he came home

Patrick Behan examined by Mr MURPHY.—The prisoner, Michael Molone, went to bed between 9 and 10 o'clock, I went to bed the same time he remained in the same room with me the whole night he never left that room to my knowledge the whole night

Cross-examined by Mr. ALABIN.—I slept that night, and any time I awoke I got him in bed I awoke very often. he did not sleep in the same bed with me I can't tell how often I awoke that night, I awoke before day light several times, to the best of my knowledge he got up at 5 o'clock that morning he was in his bed when his father called him up to go to Mr Trench's I was in the house when Mr Adair came, I can't tell what time he was called up to go to Mr Trench's, I was at home on Sunday; I was at Mass at Emo that day, that is about a mile from where I live I did not immediately come home from Mass that day, because I was at a funeral

EVIDENCE FOR DEFENCE OF JAMES DEEGAN

Michael Key, examined by Mr D'ARCY.—I know the prisoner, James Deegan, I live in James Town I recollect Sunday the 13th May, he slept in my house that night, he is a common labourer, he slept with me I got up between 6 and 7 o'clock upon my oath he slept with me from 11 o'clock, until between 6 and 7 o'clock in the morning

Cross-examined by Mr TICKELL.—I saw him on Sunday morning, he and I slept together on the Thursday night before that; I saw him in my own house on Sunday morning, I know Terrot's house, it is about half-a-mile from my house. The prisoner did not breakfast with me on Sunday, he came there for linen, my sister washed for him, I remained within but a few minutes when he came, I remained out about two hours, when I came back Deegan was gone, I did not see him again 'till he came to me that night, This was the Sunday before the Thursday I speak of   When did you see him in the morning of the Sunday that Terrot's house was attacked?   I did not see him that morning at all, he came into my house about 11 o'clock at night, I had no watch, the Coach goes convenient to the road, two Coaches pass by in the course of the night   I am about forty perches from the road, my mother, my sister, and myself, were in bed when the prisoner came to my house that night, I had been asleep before he came, I had not been long asleep, I went to bed about 8 o'clock I think, my mother and sister did not get up when he came in, I went to the door to open it for him, and I bolted it again.   How do you form an opinion that it was at 11 o'clock he came?   In an hour after he came in I heard the coach, I did not hear the horn sound, but I heard the noise of the coach, the late coach passes at 2 o'clock   How do you know it was not the 2 o'clock coach you heard?   From the time that he came and told me, I knew that   What did he tell you?   He told me that the first coach did not pass.   Was that the only way you knew that it was the first coach?   Certainly   Did you say to him, that is the second coach?   I did not   How did he happen to say it was the first coach?   I could not think that it was the second coach from the time I went to bed myself

CHIEF JUSTICE —After you went to bed, and before he came, had you not been asleep? I had. After he came in, and before you heard the coach go by, had you not been asleep? From the time he came to bed 'till the coach passed by, I did not sleep.

BARON SMITH —Could the first coach have passed by before you awoke? It could not. How can you tell that when you were asleep? I can tell how much time passed from the time I went to bed.

CHIEF JUSTICE.—That man told you that the first coach had not passed by? He did. When? After he lay down, and before the coach passed by. How did the conversation begin? I asked him what time of the night it was.

MR TICKELL —Did he tell you how he knew that the first coach had not passed? He did—he said that he had been at the cross-roads, at Malone's public-house, that is about forty or fifty perches from me.

Robert Cassidy, Esq, examined by Mr D'ARCY —I know the prisoners Thomas Delany, Bartholomew Malone, and Jeremiah Weire, Thomas Delany was told by me that he was accused of this offence, and in my presence he gave himself up to Mr Hobbes, he has worked for me for some years, the first intimate acquaintance I had with his character, was upon an occasion of going security for a debt which his father owed, and to which he was not liable. His general character is, that of an honest and industrious man; but I will not say that he is altogether a very steady man. I have heard and I believe what I have heard, that he occasionally drinks, he is a man of very industrious habits. I do not know so much of Weire, his general character is most respectable and industrious Bartholomew Malone's general character is regular and industrious, he is not now in my employment, for I discharged him for neglecting a horse

Cross-examined by the ATTORNEY-GENERAL.—I believe you take a particular interest in this trial? I do.

Do you defray any part of the expenses? Yes, for any of them I know well I have partly paid, and partly made myself responsible for the expenses of Weire, Delany, and Malone

When did you first interest yourself for them, did you not on Monday the 14th, take up their cause? I did.—Mr Adair rode into my yard on Monday morning, and asked me, if my labourers were all at their employment as usual I told him I should enquire, and I accompanied him to where they were at work, and I found that two of them were absent. Tom Delany was absent, and Maher, who was examined here to-day as a witness Mr. Adair asked old Delany where his son was the father said, " I left my son getting up, when I was quitting the house," I turned round to Mr. Adair and said, " I will ride down to Delany's house, and ascertain the fact," I rode down to the house, and the house was locked, when I came back to my own place, Delany's father requested to speak to me, he told me that his son was absent. that he was afraid to tell, and that his son had gone into the County Kildare, in company with Maher, as fast as I could ride I went to Maher's house, I saw Maher's father, and he told me the same as Delany

CHIEF JUSTICE.—Did the investigation you made that

morning satisfy you as to the innocence of the party?
A I did

ATTORNEY-GENERAL.—Had you then read the informations of Mr. Miller? A I had not

Q Did you disbelieve the charge against the men?
A I disbelieved that these men were in it

Q Did you not hear that he swore positively to these men? A I did.

Q Did you believe that? A I did not believe that Mr Miller was correct in that

Q You came to the conclusion that Mr Miller was mistaken? A I did

Q And that without reading his evidence and the informations which he had made? A Yes

Q Now, have you not heard Delany to have been charged with rioting? A I know him to have been charged with being a party to a riot on the fair-day of Portarlington

Q And charged as being a party to an attack on the police? A Rather the reverse of that.

Q Several of the police were wounded in that scuffle? A Yes, I believe so

Q And several of the country people were convicted? A Yes

Q And this Delany was engaged in that? A He was in the house where the police were wounded

Q What did you say about Delany's having gone into the County Kildare? A The father of the prisoner Delany told me that his son and Maher had gone to a place called Clonabeg, to see a nurse Braughall

Q Did you on that morning hear that Delany had gone into the County Kildare? A I did

Q You were told that on Monday morning the 14th?
A Yes

Q Did you ever make any enquiries from the Moore family about him? A I did not, I had heard from Maher and Delany that they spent Sunday night at Moore's

Q Did you endeavour to use any influence to induce the Moore's to attend here? A Neither directly, nor indirectly I learned that they are people of a most respectable character

Thomas Lee Kenny, examined by Mr BRADY —1 know Thomas Delany the prisoner, I never heard any thing bad of him, only a riot in Portarlington I think if he was a bad character, I would hear something of it

Henry Smith, Esq examined by Mr MURPHY —Mr. Smith do you know the prisoner at the bar, Jeremiah Weire? Perfectly well, I have known him since a child. Then of course you have had a perfect opportunity of knowing his character? Most certainly

Now Mr Smith I want his character from you, I don't mean his character for industry, for honesty, or general morality, but I speak of his character in reference to those dispositions which either favour or repudiate the presumption of his being implicated in a transaction of this nature? If previous good character can avail a man standing in his situation, the prisoner, Jeremiah Weire, is entitled to the benefit of a very good character from me, I always considered his family decent and well conducted people

Cross-examined by the ATTORNEY GENERAL —I am afraid that a great many people of good character are now engaged in bad practices I never heard any thing bad of this man until this occasion, he has always had the reputation of being a peaceable man

Do you not believe that persons of heretofore peaceable character have unfortunately been engaged in insurrectionary crimes ? (Prisoner's Counsel objected to this question)

BARON SMITH —I have frequently known the question to be asked without objection In fact there seems some reason for allowing it to be asked For let us consider how evidence of character avails a person upon trial Only by rendering it more or less improbable that a person of good character should commit the offence with which the indictment charges him It is more or less improbable that a man of peaceable character should commit a violent assault, or that a man of honest character should commit a robbery. If upon the rest of the evidence the Jury be satisfied of guilt, character cannot avail But if other portions of the evidence produce doubts, good character may increase those doubts, so as to make them sufficient foundation for an acquittal. Now, experience informs us, that persons of previously good character are often betrayed into insurrectionary transgression. This experience, therefore encounters, and within certain limits, weakens the effect of character in such cases, for we cannot pronounce that to be very improbable, which we find frequently to occur But still, if the insurrectionary offence charged be one, in its circumstances of great cruelty and depravity, a good character, a character of peaceful and humane conduct, will be strong evidence to show the impossibility that such an offence has been perpetrated by a person of such reputation In truth, I have sometimes found the practical effect of what I consider to be a reasonable rule, pushed too far, I have found evidence of character too lightly treated, too much disregarded, where

L

the charge was of the insurgent kind, and I have cautioned Juries against refusing its due and proper weight

ATTORNEY-GENERAL.—Do you believe that that part of the country in which Weire resides, is disturbed? I believe it is considerably disturbed. Do you believe it is infected by the spirit of insurrection and illegal confederacy? I do, and I believe it is notorious, that persons of the best characters, from intimidation, have joined these associations I do not think from my knowledge of Weire, that he is capable of committing an act of wanton cruelty, I am sure he would not, and if he has joined these associations, I am satisfied it is from intimidation and that he has kept out of them as long as he could.

George Adair, Esq examined by Mr DARCY —I am a magistrate, I recollect calling at the house of Michael Malone, I saw the old man on that occasion, I had one constable with me, I think it was about half past five in the morning, I asked him if his son Bartle was within, he said he was, I told him to come out to me, he did come out to me, I asked him if his son Michael was at home, he said he was, and that he was very much fatigued from being at Luggacurry the day before, I was afterwards surprised to find that Michael Malone was the person charged, and not Bartle, I was surprised to hear it from his previous good character, Bartle Malone surrendered himself to me, he said that this charge was made against him, and that as soon as he heard it he was ready to go with me any where I wished

William Tynan examined by Mr. BRADY.—I know James Deegan, he has been in my employment since last November, his general character I cannot tell, for I am on my oath, but I will give him a good character as long as he was with me, I never heard any thing bad of him, the gentlemen that attend the Court at Ballybrittas, could give a character of him better than I can

William Carroll examined by Mr Murphy —I am not much acquainted with Deegan, I never heard any thing improper of him, though I know him these five years, I think him an honest industrious labouring boy

CHARGE

Chief Justice —The assaulting and breaking in the dwelling house of Thomas Terrot, charged by this indictment, are fully proved, if you believe his evidence, who saw the beginning of the transaction, his wife's, who saw it all and that of Thomas Miller, who saw the conclusion of it, but the question to be tried by you is, whether the prisoners, or any, and which of them committed that offence, and that depends altogether upon the credit which you shall give to Miller, for he alone has identified the prisoners, who have not been sworn to by Terrot, who knew them all before—In weighing his credit, you will not merely consider his integrity, which does not seem to be questioned, but his accuracy, in doing which you will remember, on the one hand, his long habitual acquaintance with the prisoners, his familiar knowledge with their persons, and the brightness of the night and you will judge of the character of his mind and nerves as far as they can be collected by the manner of giving his evidence, but, on the other, you will recollect the momentary opportunity of recognizing so many persons, however well known to him previously, and that in those few moments of conflict and battle, a scene of perturbation and confusion was acted, sufficient not only to try the courage, but to shake the self-possession of the bravest and firmest man

His evidence was encountered by many witnesses swearing to an *alibi* defence, and by others giving evidence of the good character of some of the prisoners I shall first discuss the latter because some confusion and inaccuracy seem to prevail upon the subject We must all lament that any man of good character should forfeit it by a crime, but if he has done so, he is not to be acquitted by reason of his former character, which can only, consistently with law and common sense, be available to him on his trial, as suggesting or strengthening a doubt of his guilt by the improbability that a good man should commit that crime —That part of a prisoner's defence well understood is always important, and is entitled to much consideration, but unless understood within reasonable limits, it will lead to conclusions at once erroneous in principle, and dangerous to justice —The character, upon which a man relies, must be always applicable to the offence with which he is charged, a character for humanity in answer to a charge of murder, of honesty to a charge of theft, of loyalty to a charge of treason, of peaceableness to a charge of riot are all intelligible applications of such a defence, but if those distinctions be confounded, consequences of an anomalous nature may be conceived which can scarcely be stated with seriousness, such as proving for a man, accused of a violent outrage upon a woman, that he was a man strict in all his money dealings, and punctual in the payment of his debts, or if, when another should be on trial for forgery or larceny, evidence should be offered that he was a good domestic man, of chaste life, and modest decent conversation. But even in the most indiscriminate latitude in which this species of defence can be permitted, I lament to say that there is a large class of offences to which it is seldom applicable at all such as treason and the crimes which may be called political in the several degrees, in which they endanger the public safety I find it necessary shortly to discuss this topic, in consequence of the objection made to a question, put by the Attorney-General to a gentleman, who had sworn to the good character of some of these prisoners, now charged with a Whiteboy offence —His question was, " *Don t you know and believe that many persons of good cha-* " *racter have been induced to join these associations ?"* To our surprise it was strenuously contended that the question was altogether illegal, we were surprised, because our experience has made us familiar with that question and we have no recollection that it was ever objected to before I see indeed one objection to it, and that is, its inutility, because it seeks to obtain the opinion of a witness as to an abstract moral truth deplored by every one, and to deduce a conclusion to which every Judge, without such a question or any answer to it, would direct the attention of the Jury, and which every rational Juryman's own good sense would anticipate Offences of this class from the highest to the lowest, flow from many sources through different channels, and unite in one common direction ---Sometimes, they may be traced to malignant passions---to envy and intolerance of the restraints of society, to turbulence of temper and restlessness of character---sometimes to ambition and cupidity, often to silly vanity and love of popularity---frequently, as was said truly by a witness yesterday, to the influence of others, operating by seduction or intimidation . —The man, unfortunately seduced or intimidated to join such a confederacy, is to be pitied, but unless he can esta-blish a case of actual compulsion, which when fully esta-blished is a defence, we can only pity him —It is not only to vices or weaknesses, but too often to the best qualities of mankind, that such crimes are to be traced, and from the traitor to the whiteboy, history and experience both tell us, that men delude themselves by the belief that those acts are praiseworthy, which the law calls criminal Youthful enthusiasm, misguided zeal for the public good, and per-verted talent have led many a man into acts, the paths of which, as he at last discovers when too late, lead to sedition, tumult, rebellion, and anarchy, and our very virtues become the ingredients of crime

A distinction yesterday was humanely suggested by a gentleman, who gave evidence as to the character of one of the prisoners, in saying, that the young man was of such a peaceable disposition, that he must consider it improbable that he could participate in the brutal and cruel outrage that was proved. The observation and inference are very just, but that gentleman, upon better reflection, will see how his opinion must be qualified with reference to the nature of such offences, as we are now dealing with In almost all those offences, and certainly in that before us, cruelty and blood-thirstiness are the consequences and not the objects of the confederacy,—In this case no man pre-meditated the murder of Mr Miller—indeed it appears that mere accident threw Mr Miller into their hands. and I am convinced that if, at the beginning of that evening, it had been proposed to the assembled conspirators to pro-ceed to butcher that man, many of them would have re-volted with horror from the idea. But it cannot be too often repeated, that whatever be the object of the Whiteboy system, its tendency is crime and that the object of the Whiteboy laws is to prevent crime, by putting down combination I am sure therefore, you all see that, when such is the character of this insurrection, a man's participation in it is not made improbable by showing that his nature is averse to those greater enormities, which he never anticipated as the necessary consequences of his joining in it. If the Attorney-General had never asked that question, I should have made these observations, and have always done so in similar cases, as it is my duty to protect jurors from being misled by confounding principles, that ought to be kept distinct

As a preliminary to reading my notes of the evidence, I shall make a few general remarks upon its application to the important defence, made by all the prisoners, called an *alibi*, which, when well established, is the best answer that can be offered to any accusation. In this case, if that defence be established by all the prisoners, it follows that Thomas Miller must be mistaken as to every man he has sworn against. But, Gentlemen, it may be that the defence has been established in favour of some prisoners and not of others, which would certainly justify a verdict, convicting some, and acquitting others of the prisoners, but although there would be no legal objection to such a finding, yet, I must leave it to your understandings to judge whether you could safely act upon the testimony of a single witness against some, who has been detected in inaccuracy as to others, that is, whether such inaccuracy is not a sufficient foundation for that reasonable doubt, which would make it your duty to acquit That observation would, however, be subject to this qualification, that the prosecutor may have had better opportunities

of identifying one prisoner than another, but even so it is
hazardous to convict upon evidence so exposed to doubt.
On the other hand, if one of those defences should fail, or
prove to be fabricated, you will not allow the defence of
the other prisoners to be disparaged, but you will consider
each case as if it alone were upon trial Your first enquiry
will be, whether the witnesses intend to swear truly, and
secondly, whether they are accurate, and not mistaken,
and in one part of this case, one of the means afforded for
that inquiry, consists of the comparison of the evidence of
all the witnesses to one fact, with a view to their consist-
ency or inconsistency Even in very recent transactions,
it is our general experience that very few witnesses of
whatever rank, are minutely consistent with each other as
to a transaction, which they have all witnessed within a few
days, and therefore you ought not to decide against the credit
of witnesses on account of those minute discrepancies,
which, all those, who have treated of the degrees of probability and the laws of evidence, consider as not only
consistent with a substantial coincidence, but as very often
amounting to corroboration of their common testimony by
rebutting the suspicion of previous concert and contriv-
ance —It may be, that all the evidence of *alibi* witnesses
may be unquestionably true with this qualification, that
the witness may have sworn falsely or inaccurately as to
the time at which they represent the transaction to have
occurred, and in the principal defence now before you, that
distinction is to be particularly attended to The eight witnesses of the Moore family may all have sworn truly, and it
is not easy to doubt that they have done so, as to the principal facts but unless they have been accurate, as to the
hours they have stated, their evidence will be unavailing

to the prisoners who produced them, for it will not be inconsistent with their guilt. That evidence represents them
as being at a distance of three miles from the scene of the
crime for three hours before and three hours after it was
committed, and you must, therefore, examine cautiously
as to the time attributed to the crime by the prosecutor,
and to that fixed by the Alibi witnesses, always recollecting the difficulty of dealing with the mere unassisted com-
putation of time, even by well educated by persons
There is, however, in this case, little difficulty to the witnesses at either side or embarrassment to you, arising
from the obliteration of long past transactions from the
memory, because it is but a fortnight since the transaction
occurred, and the next morning the prosecutor swore
informations, and the prisoners were apprehended, and
thus the attention of both parties was immediately called
to their respective cases

It sometimes happens that in weighing an alibi defence,
those who listen to it are inclined to visit upon the prisoner
a degree of suspicion, if the whole or any part of that
defence has been rendered questionable or exposed and it
is not always easy to protect our own minds from the influence of a confusion prejudicial to the prisoner, which such
a view might occasion It is not by any means true that
the prisoner is always answerable for the fabrication which
may be put forward in his defence Frequently the in
discreet zeal of officious friends leads to the exercise of a
depraved ingenuity, and to the ruin of a case otherwise not
free from doubt, but, Gentlemen, that observation is particularly applicable to offences such as you are trying, because
it frequently happens that factious partizans interfere in
those cases connected with public disturbance and bring
forward a mass of well conceited perjury for the double

purpose of furthering the objects of the confederacy, and obstructing the administration of justice, while the wretched being upon trial may be ignorant of the fraud contrived during his imprisonment, possibly deplores it—and perhaps one of the most awful consequences of our present situation is, that those confederacies thus familiarize the people to an indifference to truth, and the obligations of oaths

I have nothing further to state, except to repeat the observation you often hear from this place, which, though it may become familiar, can never be trite or common place, and it is this, that if after patiently considering the evidence, you have a reasonable and honest doubt of the guilt of the prisoners, although you may not be assured of their innocence, you ought to acquit them, and can only justify a conviction by your being morally certain of their guilt without any fair doubt

The Jury found all the prisoners—GUILTY

TRIAL OF JAMES DOWLING,

For Burglary in the House of William Jacob

Friday, 1st June, 1832

First Witness, *John Magee*, examined by the ATTORNEY GENERAL.—I remember the night of Good Friday last, I was then living with my uncle, William Jacob at Mayo my uncle was living there about a month before that his family were my mother, my sister, and myself Dr Carter was living there before that when I was in bed on that night I heard a knocking at the window about one o'clock there was a parlour in the house and two rooms at each side of it there is a porch door which is the entrance of the house that porch is about seven yards long I slept in the room at the left hand side as you come in there was a window to the room I slept in which looks to the front the window is about four feet high, and about a yard wide it was at that window I heard the knocking the people outside bid me open the door, I asked them who they were, they said, " your friends, open the door " I asked them what friends they were to come at that hour of the night they said nothing to that, but bid me open the door I bid them come by day and I would let them in then they knocked in the lower frame of the window, when I was getting out of bed they got in and caught hold of me before I could dress myself there were about thirty men altogether some of them were armed, they laid hold of me and beat me with sticks, and desired me to go on my knees, they did this when they brought me into the parlour, they asked me for fire arms, and made me go on my knees, and they then swore me if I had a gun or a bayonet in the house they beat me bravely, I got up off my knees, and the man that swore me went to another part of the house I was walking about the room looking about me and they came again in a very short time after and put me on my knees it was a different man put me on my knees the second time, they swore me a second time they made me repeat the words each time when I was on my knees a second time a man stabbed me with a bayonet on a gun in the right breast I said *yous* killed me, I walked about for some time after that I told them not to tell my mother or my uncle that I was killed, one of them struck me on the side of the neck with the breech of a gun and knocked me down, that was after I was stabbed when I got up I left the parlour and went to the door that led into the porch, I unlatched it and went out into the porch, there was a fire and two candles lighting in the parlour there was a large window in the parlour, and the light was shining in, it was the door between the porch and the parlour I unlatched it did not put me into the open air, it only put me into the porch, my sister lit one of the candles and I cannot tell who lit the other they were both over the chimney piece my sister lit one of them while they were fetching me out of the bed room I saw a man holding a candle behind me during the time they were swearing me after I got into the porch and opened the porch door, I looked out into the yard and I saw a good deal of people there, I found myself getting weak I said to myself that I might as well share the one fate with my uncle, my mother, and sister, and I closed the door and I bolted it again, after I closed the door I leant against the wall behind the door, I sat down easy and leant my back against the wall and stretched out my legs, I came to myself a little when I sat on the ground, I was bleeding all along, I could not stop the blood, it came over my hand and under my hand, the door of the porch if it was open would strike my legs, when I was in that place and posture, a man of the name of Dowling came up and stood over me with a gun, and pointed it at me, I looked at him earnestly, and he said, " boys he's only foxing, he is not dead, I will shoot him," he had the gun pointed towards my breast, he said something about killing us all, there were three or four along with him at the time, he was at the door of the parlour, one step would fetch a man into the porch, my sister just came in, she was near enough to hear these words, she was within about three yards of him, she came and knocked up the gun with a short stick she had in her hand, and jostled him, he wheeled a little from the position he was in and made an offer to stab her, when the gun was knocked up it burned priming, that was at the very time she knocked it up, there was a bayonet on that gun, when he offered to stab her she fell back into the corner, and another man came up and bid him not to kill these people, that we were strangers and we did not know them, I think the name of the man that desired them not to kill us is Leonard, I saw him in Maryborough jail after, I did not know his name at that time, he argued a great deal with them, he said that if they would kill the girl they should kill him, he did a great deal of good that night, I did not care whether they shot me or not, there was so much blood from me that I did not expect to live, and I thought from the way that my sister went on that she would positively be killed, and that they would be all killed, fear left me. and I was not a bit afraid at that time I could see very well what they were doing, for about ten minutes after I sat down I was able to see what was going on after that I found myself in my bed, and I do not know how I got there I very often before saw the man that said he would shoot me, he lives in the next house to us, his name is James Dowling, his house is about ten or fifteen perches from our house, I did not see him that night before I saw him in the porch, (here the witness identified the prisoner as being the man that attempted to fire at him) at the time he was going to fire at me there was a candle lighting in the porch, and my sister had another candle in her hand when she came in, that is the time she knocked up the stick, it was in her left hand she held the candle, she held a short white stick in her right hand, the candle that she held was the last that was brought into the porch.

CHIEF JUSTICE —Where was the other candle? A man stood just backward of me holding it.

ATTORNEY-GENERAL —From the time they came into the house until you lost your senses, how long was it?

About a quarter of an hour or twenty minutes, as near as I can guess

Cross-examined by Mr BRADY —I don't know the man that held the candle, I had an opportunity of seeing him I would not know him if I saw him since, there were three or four men in the porch when the man pointed the gun at me, but more came afterwards, those who came in afterwards came in after my sister, they came in while she was there there was a man standing at the parlour door that had a gun in his hand at this time How many of the three or four that were there at first did you know? I knew Leonard, I never saw him before that I could know him, one of the three men that came in on the Sunday night before Good Friday, was a tall man like Leonard, I could not know him as I did not see his face on the Sunday night, my sister said that one of the men that were there on Sunday night, was there that night, but she did not tell me which of them it was the time she told me this was after the Doctor came, and before any man was taken, it was after Dr Edge was with me, before Dr Byrne came, I think that was on Saturday, it was early in the morning that Dr Edge visited me. I might have some conversation with my sister before the Doctor came, she told me that she knew a good deal of them, and desired me to say nothing as I was not able to speak, in one of those conversations she told me that there was one of the men who had been with me on Sunday, at the attack, the tall man who was on the chair with my sister was the person whose face I did not see

CHIEF JUSTICE —There was a man at the visit on the Sunday, which man was tall, and which man you thought resembled the person who took your part? Yes

CHIEF JUSTICE —Was that the man which sat on the chair with your sister? I cannot say whether it was or not

Mr BRADY —You saw that night in the porch, a tall man who took your part, did he resemble any one that you saw at your house on Sunday? I cannot say that he resembled him according to his face, but he resembled him in stature, he was a tall man That tall man that you saw in the porch you have since identified? Yes. What is his name? I think Leonard is the name, to the best of my opinion that was the name he answered when he was in Maryborough gaol yard Did your sister tell you in that conversation whether she had seen any one at the attack that was in the house on Sunday? She did. That she had seen that man that was sitting on the chair? Yes. That man who was sitting with her on the chair is the man that called himself Leonard? I can't say that at all. Did she ever tell you that Leonard was that man? No, she did not tell me what his name was, she was taken away from me very shortly after that, my mother would not let her speak to me. Did she tell you whether she had seen any one in the porch that night, who had been there on Sunday? She did not.

CHIEF JUSTICE.—What she told you of the man who had been on the chair with her having been also at the attack, was it by her applied to seeing him in the porch? She did not say that she saw him in the porch or not, she only said that he was there that night.

Mr BRADY.—Do you say that one of the men who interfered for you in the porch was like one of the men you saw in your house on Sunday night? Any farther than that he was a very tall man, I cannot say that he resembled him. Am I to understand that when your sister told you that there was one man at the attack who was in the house on Sunday, that she meant that man who was sitting on the chair with her? Yes. Now thinking that the man who interfered for you in the porch, was like the person who was sitting on the chair with your sister, did you ask her whether that man who interfered in your favor was the man who was sitting on the chair? I did not ask her that question. Did you ask her whether any other of the persons who had been there on Sunday night, was at the attack? I did not ask her any questions, she told me that she knew a great deal of them, and that she would have all that she knew of them taken, I do not recollect that she mentioned any *name*. Did you ask her any of their names? I did not say any thing

to her, for I was not able to speak a full word scarcely
Then all she told you as to any individual in particular was,
that the man who was sitting on the chair with her was
there? That is all

CHIEF JUSTICE —In short she said to you, one of the
men that was here on Sunday night last, was here, and that
is the man that was sitting on the chair with me? That
is it

To Mr BRADY —My sister had spent more of her time
at Mayo than I did I think she was more than a year in it,
if the different times she was there were all put together,
she used to be there on visits with Mrs Carter, who was a
relation of hers, I came there at Christmas last, James
Dowling, the prisoner, was our next door neighbour, and
we found him a good neighbour I was frequently in his
house I recollect being in his garden some time before the
attack, assisting him. I was sowing a bed of parsnip seed
for him, I believe it was seven or eight days before that,
my sister was in the habit of going in and out there when
we wanted to borrow any thing, she knew him as well as
I did

When you enter the door of the porch you may go either
right or left, there were about three minutes between my
being sworn the first and the second time when I was
stabbed a man struck me. I was knocked down near the
parlour door, they were very thick about me, and I got
through them, and got out of the parlour, I shut the door
after me, my sister was not in the parlour when I went out,
she was in the parlour when I was sworn the first time, and the
second time; when I got up after being knocked down, I
looked about and I did not observe her in the parlour, she
stood opposite to me on my right hand, when they were

M

swearing me the second time, I was facing the fire place when I was kneeling, she had a candle in her hand about that time, they made me repeat the whole oath over again my sister was not standing quiet, she was saying something to them one thing she said was, that Father Kelly told her that none of us would be killed, I cannot tell whether it was before or after I was stabbed, but I heard it passing much about that time when I went out into the porch I cannot say positively that she was not in the parlour, for they were very thick about me on each occasion that I was sworn she had a candle in her hand I was a little while alone in the porch James Dowling was the first person that approached me he had a gun How long was he there with you before your sister came in? Only while he was saying those words Did you know him before your sister came in? I did. Did you address him by his name? No, I said nothing at all to him Did your sister? Not in my hearing How long was your sister there before the man who held the candle? He followed her in lively, she was only a step or two before him

Chief Justice.—Do you mean in the porch? Yes

Mr Brady.—But before she came in you knew that the man in the porch was James Dowling? Yes. Was it when she struck the gun with the stick that the powder in the pan burned? It was. I think they said they took you into the parlour in your shirt? They did Did you remain in that state until you were stabbed? I did Had you nothing on you but your shirt while you were sitting in the porch? Nothing else.

Chief Justice.—No cloathes on any part of your body except your shirt? No my Lord Which candle did you first see in the porch? It was a candle that a man was

holding who came out of the kitchen with James Dowling.
On the Sunday night did any more than one man sit on
the chair with your sister? I don't recollect that there did,
the chairs were scarce. I believe there were only two in the
parlour And that man that you saw sit on the same chair
with her you say was tall? Yes, he was the tallest man
that was there on that Sunday night And that is the man
that you thought somebody else was like? Yes Was
that the man, that interfered in favor of your sister, the
night of the attack? It was You afterwards saw a
man in the gaol that called himself Leonard, is that the
man that you thought you saw at the visit, and interceded
for her? That is the man that interceded for her When
you first saw that man in the gaol did you knew him to be
the man that so interceded? I did.

Juror.—Did you see his face the night of the visit? I
did not. Did you see his face when he interceded for
your sister? I did Was it by his face that you knew
him? Yes, and by his stature.

Chief Justice —What was your object in opening the
door and looking out? To see if there was any body outside After sitting down against the wall how soon did a
candle make its appearance? Very soon Who brought
it in? A man Was he the first who came into the passage? James Dowling came first, and the man with the
candle after him at his back Where did your sister come
from? Out of the parlour Did any body come out of
the parlour with your sister? A man came out after her
from the parlour Did you say any thing to Dowling when
Dowling was going to shoot you? I did not, I would not
thank them whether they shot me or not, because I thought
I could not live

Mr BRADY —What did you mean by saying that the man with the candle followed your sister into the porch ? The man I mean that was protecting her   Was it the man with the candle ?   No   What did you mean by saying that the man with the candle followed your sister in lively ?

CHIEF JUSTICE —Did you say the man with the candle or not ?   That is not it   What is it ?   One man came with Dowling, and my sister came with the candle out of the parlour, and another man followed her lively

Mr BRADY —Did you see the man with the candle or Dowling first ?   I saw Dowling first

CHIEF JUSTICE —Where did you see Dowling and the man with the candle come from ?   They came from behind me, but they came to me

Mr BRADY —Then you never saw them until they faced you in the same direction in which your sister came ? I saw them come up by my side   when they came Dowling stood and looked at me, and I looked at him   when they were looking at me my sister came in at their back ,   Did you not say that a man with a candle followed your sister lively ?   The man that protected her, followed her, but he had no candle   Then it is not true, that a man with a candle followed your sister lively into the porch ?   It is not

Second Witness, *William Jacob*—Examined by Mr TICKELL   I remember the 20th of April last , I was living at Mayo , I came there about the 5th of April   I am the uncle of the last witness , on that night a great parcel of people came to my house and rapped at the door; I was awake when they came , I heard the conversation between them and my nephew , when they knocked and broke in the window, I saw three of them come in on their bellies , I slept in the room where they came in   my nephew and I slept in the room where they came in , one of them took a little sword I had from me, and they took my nephew and put him on his knees, and were swearing him they knocked me down several times, and were striking me, they gave no reason for using me in that way, the man that took my sword pointed it at my breast and said that he would kill me with it there was no light when they came in, but I saw two candles lighting afterwards I cannot say that I knew any of the persons there that night because when I would be looking at any of them, they would strike me, and knock me down, I left my bed-room, and came into the room where John Magee was put on his knees, I am 74 years old

Cross-examined by Mr Brady I was present when they swore Magee, I saw them swearing him only once for they used to knock me down I was there when he was stabbed, that was about the time when they were swearing him, I got up before any one came into the house I saw the first three that came in, I remained in the parlour till my Nephew was stabbed, his sister was there at the time he was stabbed, I cannot tell whether it was before or after me the left the parlour, because I would be knocked down they tossed up a bed in the room I slept in to look for arms I think that was after the stabbing I saw my nephew when they were gone I found him in a kind of an entry that was there, we lifted him and brought him in the best manner we could, into the room he was not able to speak, he spoke some words to me after we brought him into the room, we were altogether then, he told us that he thought he was killed he said that Nash stabbed him with a bayonet on a gun he said he knew a good deal of the people that were there, he told me that James Dowling was there, and that he was going to shoot him with a gun, and that he snapped his gun, and that it burned priming, he told me that, in about ten minutes after he was put to bed, his sister was bye when he said that. Did she say anything? Yes, she said that she saw James Dowling, that she saw him snap a gun, and that it flashed and burned priming, she said, that he pointed the gun at Magee, and that she struck off the gun with a stick, and that the flash went off from the pan and burned priming, it was John Magee that first mentioned Dowling's name, Magee said that Dowling looked at him, and was going to shoot him, they both mentioned the name of Dowling, and that they knew him perfectly well, I desired them not to be talking about them for fear some of them would be waiting outside the door, and would return back and kill us, I don't know that they mentioned any other names but Nash's and Dowling's, but they said they would know a good many of them, I think they mentioned other names, but I cannot tell them, John Magee asked me did I know any of the men I told him I did not, I think my sister, as near as I can recollect, was present at those conversations.

Third Witness, *Ellen Magee*, examined by Mr. MARTLEY.—I am the niece of the last witness, I am acquainted with Magee about twelve months, I remember the attack made on my uncle's house on Good-Friday night, I was in the house at that time; I heard knocking at the door, the people got in through the window, I was not long in bed when they got into the house, they got in through the bed-room window where my brother slept, I got up when I heard the noise, the parlour was the first place I saw them in, they brought my brother out of the room where he slept, there was a good fire, and the light shining through the windows, and there were two candles lit, the people were in a moment before I lit the candle, one of the men lit another candle, I saw them strike and stab my brother, they gave him a book and made him swear about fire-arms they asked him whether he had any fire-arms in the house, and he swore that he had not after he was stabbed, he walked about a little, and then he went into the porch after he left the parlour, the next place I saw him was in the porch I saw him lying down, partly sitting and looking up I saw a man with a gun presented at him he was near him, I had a candle in my hand, and a man stood below my brother with another candle I came out of the parlour into the porch, and the man with the candle came out of the kitchen I had a stick in my other hand when I saw the man with the gun presented, I ran to him, and I struck the gun, a little fire came out of it, the man with the gun drew back, and made a stab with a bayonet at me I fell back from the bayonet, I knew the man that I saw standing with the gun, and who made the thrust of the bayonet at me, his name is James Dowling, the prisoner at the bar is that man, I knew him twelve months before that, I am positive that that is the man who had the gun in his hand, and made the thrust at me I heard him say to another man, "that my brother would not die, that he was only foxing," he said he would shoot him, and that he would shoot them all that was the first place that I saw him that night, when they went away, we carried my brother into a room he appeared to have lost a good deal of blood, when we carried him into the room, I thought he was dying, when we had him a little while, he was able to speak; shortly after he could not speak at all he continued incapable of speaking until morning we laid him on a bed on the floor, because we were unable to take him to his own room,

James Dowling lived next door to us, I saw him next morning about ten o'clock, he was taking his breakfast in his own house I went there because one of the women that came in bid me go for buttermilk to make whey to wet my brother's mouth, she bid me go to Dowling's, and that I would get it, I did not like to refuse to go there, and I did go, when I went in, Dowling got up, and ran into the room, as he was going, he struck his head against a post, that was in his hurry, he was taken that night.

Cross-examined by Mr. MURPHY.—How many persons did you identify as having been there that night? I think it was twelve. Did you swear against twelve positively, as having been in that house? I went and picked them out, and as I picked them out, Mr Singleton reckoned them How soon after this occurred did you identify the twelve? The same morning I identified some of them, that is, the morning after my brother was stabbed, I identified three afterwards in Carlow What do you mean by the next morning you identified some people? I think there was one day after my brother was stabbed before the prisoner was got. Did you not tell me this moment, that the morning after your house was attacked you identified some of them? I reckoned the night and the day my brother was stabbed, it is on Sunday I mean that I identified them How many did you identify on Sunday? I believe nine. How soon after did you identify the other three? I cannot tell the time Do you happen to know a boy of the name of Owen Brennan? I know one of the prisoners is Owen Brennan. Did you know a man of that name before the house was attacked? I cannot recollect knowing a man of that name before the house was attacked Did you know the servant-boy of James Dow-

ling? Yes, I saw him. Had you not seen him frequently
before the house was attacked? I saw him once, but I
did not know he was servant-boy to James Dowling.
Have you not frequently been in Dowling's house? Yes,
I went very often of a message there. I knew his wife and
his servant-girl there; I did not know that Owen Brennan
lived in the house; I saw him in the house. When?
After the house was attacked. Did you ever see him in
the house of James Dowling before the attack? To the
best of my knowledge, I did. By the virtue of your oath,
did you not know that he lived in that house? To the
best of my knowledge, I did know that he lived in it.
Will you swear that he was not a servant in that house?
I do not know that he was. Will you swear you do not
know that he lived in that house? I do not know whether
he did or no. But you have seen him in the house? I
believe once before, and once after. Did you identify
Owen Brennan? I did not identify him. Am I to understand that that boy is one of the prisoners? He is not
one of the prisoners that I swore against. Do you recollect
the Sunday night before Good-Friday? I do. Do you
recollect the people that came to your house that day? I
do. Who were the persons that came there? One was
Nash, and the other called himself John Moore; I don't
know who was the third. Do you know that that man's
name is John Moore now? He gave his name Laurence
Leonard when he was taken prisoner. Did you see him
after he was taken prisoner? I did. Did you know him
then to be the man that was at your house on Sunday
night? I did. Did you swear against him? I did.
Did he behave badly to you? He saved me from James
Dowling. Did you ever tell that to any body? I told
some of the police. Did you ever tell any body else? I

did, when the gentleman bid me tell the truth. Did you tell your brother? I did not tell my brother any thing about it. Did you ever tell your brother any thing at all? He was too sick that night.

Chief Justice.—Did you at any time tell him about Leonard? I do not recollect that I did.

Mr. Murphy.—By the virtue of your oath had you or your brother any conversation about Leonard? No, we had not.

Chief Justice.—At any time do you mean? I do.

Mr. Murphy.—Now, had not you and he been comparing stories about the persons that were there? Never. Before the gentlemen came there did not you and he talk the matter over? He was too sick. And you never did speak to him before you went to Dublin about the persons that were there? No. Nor he to you? No, he was not able? What do you mean by saying he was not able? I would not ask him any questions for I did not think he was able to speak to me. When did you go to Dublin? I went to Stradbally first. Before you went to Stradbally had you any conversation with your brother about these people? No. Nor before the gentlemen came? No. Do you mean to say by his not being able to speak, that he was exhausted? He could speak very easy but I could not understand him well. How long did he remain in that state? He could not until morning speak well. Did you help to put him to bed? I did. Did you go to bed after this? No. How long did you remain with your brother? I remained up all night going backwards and forwards. And did he remain in that state during the night from the time he was put into bed? From a little time after we laid him on the bed he could not speak until morning. Before he was put to bed did you see him lying on the floor? I did. Did he appear then to be greatly exhausted? Yes, a little after that he was very bad, we thought he was dying, when he would attempt to speak, I could not rightly understand what he said. Did his mind appear to be wandering? He was getting cold, he was laid as if he was dead. Did his eyes seem dizzy? He shut his eyes. At what time? After the men went out. Before the men went out did he appear to be dizzy? He seemed very well before they went out. Was it before or after he was put to bed you thought he was dying? This was when we were carrying him—when we put him on the bed we thought he was dying. We were watching his breath. Did he attempt to speak at all? When we were carrying him in I asked him if he was alive, he stirred his lips, but I could not hear what he said. Did you speak to him when you put him on the bed? I did not, I thought there was no use in speaking to him, a few minutes before the gentlemen came I recollect he spoke a few words. Do you recollect what it was he said? The first word I recollect was, that he said he was not killed. Did he say any thing else? He asked if any of us was killed, I recollect my mother bid him not to speak any, or else he would never recover. Did he speak any more after that? No, I did not hear him speak any more for a long time.

CHIEF JUSTICE.—What did you mean by saying that he was very well before they went out? I went to him when the man saved me, and there was a man twisting a gun. After he was wounded you got an opportunity of going into him, and standing with him? Yes, and when I looked at him, he was looking about, that is what I mean by saying, he was very well. I bid him shut his eyes, and he desired me not to be looking sharp at those men.

Mr MURPHY.—When did he say that? Before the men went out. You were examined in a former trial, on that trial did you not swear that Nash was the man that sat on the chair with you? Yes, and I told you that Leonard sat on the chair with me. You knew Leonard very well the night of the attack? Yes. And he knew you very well? I suppose he did. And did not he know James Dowling very well? I do not know, he did not mention his name. Leonard said you were strangers, and that you would not know them? He did. If Leonard knew, that you knew him, why would he say that, how do you account for that? Leonard asked me before that, did I know any one in the house, and if I knew him, and I said I did not. Where did he ask you that? In the parlour. Had you the candle in your hand then? I had. I was sworn and put on my knees, they swore me about fire arms, they gave me a book, and they struck me while I was on my knees, and they said they would shoot me if I did not tell them where the fire arms were. when they said that, I desired them to shoot me through the back, and they said that they would not, that they would shoot me in the face. Did you tell that to the Magistrates? I did, and the gentlemen said there was no occasion to put that in. Leonard acted very friendly to you? He did not act very friendly to me, when he brought me into the room, and gave me up to the men, and bid them kill me.

CHIEF JUSTICE.—Can you account for his bringing you up to the room in that way? For not telling where the fire arms were, he gave me up to the men, and said I should never be killed if I told where they were. When was that? When I was on my knees, when I bid them shoot me through the back.

Mr. MURPHY.—Then he did not act friendly to you? He saved me from being killed, and he saved my uncle too from being killed, it was after my brother was stabbed that he gave me up to the men, and it was before Dowling presented the gun at my brother Did he desire them to shoot you? He did Did he leave you there with them to shoot you? He staid there himself, I asked him not to let the men kill me Why did you ask him? He was civil to me, and told me that no one would be killed but my brother Had any of the men in the room that he brought you to fire arms? Yes, some of them had guns, and more of them had pistols, Leonard said I would be shot if I did not tell if I knew the men or not Did you then think that he meant to do you any harm? I thought it then Can you account why Leonard was so friendly to your family? I do not know, he came to deceive us, not to have the windows made up Do you think that the object of the visit on Sunday night, was to deceive you? I do And that Leonard was a party to that deception? I do Can you account why he was so friendly to you that night, if he came in to deceive you on Sunday? A man knocked my uncle down and kicked him, and made a stab of a bayonet at him, I struck the bayonet, and the man drew out and said he would kill me, and he bid Leonard stand back, and Leonard said, the old man should not be killed But how do you account for his being treacherous on Sunday, and being so friendly on Friday? I cannot account for it Did he take you aside when he asked you if you knew the people? I was standing beside him Don't you think he knew that you knew him? I think he he did, he was telling me that I did know him, and I said that I did not

Now who was the first person you told that James Dowling was there? I told it to a police-man of the name of Cole, and I bid him not tell any body else When did you tell him that? The morning after my brother was stabbed, about 12 o'clock on Saturday Was he the first you told it to? Yes Was this before or after you were

in at Dowling's to get the buttermilk ? I think it was after
—my mother told me not to tell I knew any of the people
Did you tell your mother that James Dowling was there ?
No—when I told her that I knew some of them, she struck
at me and desired me not to tell any body, and she bid me
tell if any one would ask me, that I did not know any of
them   Did you tell your uncle that you knew any of
them ? I did, a little after my mother was settled in the
bed, I told him that I knew a great deal of the men, and I
told them that I knew James Dowling. What did your
uncle say ?   He bid me to speak loud and to tell him what
I was saying, that he did not hear me, I did not speak then
for I did not like to speak loud my uncle did not hear me,
and in a few minutes after he bid me not mention their
names if I did know them   Then your uncle did not hear
from you the name of James Dowling ? He did not   Nor
the name of any other person ? No   What state was
your brother in when you told that to your uncle ? At
that time it was day light, and shortly after he spoke. Was
it at that time your brother said he was alive ? Not at that
time, he spoke after that   At the time you had this conversation with your uncle and that he desired you not to
speak, in what state was your brother ? In a very bad
state   Could he speak ? It was a good while after
when he spoke   Where did this conversation between
you and your uncle take place ? In the parlour

CHIEF JUSTICE —What conversation are you speaking
of? The conversation with my uncle and mother, when
they told me not to mention to any body that I knew any
of them, I told them that I would tell all I knew to the
gentlemen. and then my uncle told me that he would turn
me out of the house if I would.

Mr MURPHY —When you told your uncle that James

Dowling was there, and that he desired you to say nothing about it, was it in the parlour or the room that your brother was in? In the parlour. Your uncle told you that he would turn you out of the house if you told the gentlemen? Yes, but not at that time, it was half an hour after that. Was it in the parlour he told you that? No, it was down in the kitchen. Did you tell the gentlemen? Two Officers came first, and my mother bid me go out of the room and not to tell them, and then Captain Wright came and I told him I would tell the truth if he would bring police men to take care of my brother. Did you tell Captain Wright that you knew James Dowling? I did, because he told me he would bring the police-men there to take care of my brother. Did you not say that the first man you told it to was the police-man? I say it still. Where did you see the police-man? I went to the barrack where he was. How long was that before Captain Wright came? It was day light when I went to Cole, and Captain Wright came about twelve. Where did you tell Cole? In a room in my own house, where neither my mother nor my uncle heard me. Where was your mother? With my brother. Where was your uncle? With my brother too. Did they not know that the police man was in the house? They did, it was my mother that sent me for the police-man to go for the Doctor. Did you see Cole when you went up to the barrack first? I did. Did you then tell him about James Dowling? I did not. I bid him to come as fast as ever he could that my brother was bleeding to death. Was it before or after your mother told you not to tell that you told Cole? I don't recollect whether it was before or after. Why did you not obey your mother's directions? I intended to tell it as soon as I could get a few police-men, I thought it a pity to hide it, and Cole promised to get a few police-men to protect us that night. How came you to tell the police-man and not the officers? he was a Protestant, and a friend that I thought I could depend upon. Was it because he was a Protestant that you depended on him? There is many a Protestant that I would not depend on. Then why did you say a Protestant? I would not tell a Catholic. You have no dependence on Catholics? I have not. Would you believe a Catholic on his oath? I would be hard set. They must be shocking bad fellows when you would not believe them on their oaths? So they are bad. Now, I thought you were a Catholic? I am not. Nor never were? I only went to Chapel a few times, and would that make a Catholic of me? Did you ever tell any body that you had a conversation with the priest that you were not to be killed? I did. Who was the priest? Father Kelly in that country. I told in Dublin that Father Kelly said we would not be killed. What did you tell about Father Kelly? Father Tyrrell, a friend of mine said the place was full of whitefeet, and he desired me to go to Father Kelly, and in consequence of that I did go to Father Kelly.

CHIEF JUSTICE.—What was it you told the gentleman passed between you and Father Kelly? I told him that I came to live to the parish, and that Father Tyrrell would wish I would be acquainted with him, and Father Kelly said he did not like my family.

Mr. MURPHY.—Is that all that passed? No. What else passed? He said that he heard my grandfather killed a priest. he told me that Protestants were devils in the shape of men, he said it was not lucky to have me in the house with Protestants as I went to mass. he asked me where did I go the Sunday before, I told him I went to church, he asked me what took me to church when I went before that to mass, he asked me which would I rather go to church or to chapel, I told him I would like the chapel as well, but I did not though I told him so he asked me had we any fire arms in the house, I told him we had, I told him we had no powder but what was in the pistols, he asked me had we any thing else to fight with, I told him we had nothing else in the house to fight with, then he said he would make a pitchfork mind the house without any fire-arms, he said he did not like any one in the house only myself, and that he expected he would make a christian of me, he bid me often to go see him to his house, I said that I would go home to Carlow, that I did not like to be up where there were so many Whitefeet, he said that I need not be afraid of the Whitefeet, that he had them at his command, and that they would not meddle with me, he told me how Luther and Calvin beat them out when their religion was established, and that he intended to get his rights again Do you think he is one of the party? I think he is one of the party by the way he spoke.

Chief Justice —This topic unfortunately broke out the very moment I was congratulating myself that we had nothing about it

Mr Murphy —What took you to Father Tyrrell? When I would go to the chapel he would shake hands with me when I was going out What took you to Father Tyrrell's chapel? The reason was, that when I was going to church the blackguards threw stones at me and I summoned them to the court at Carlow, and they would not do me justice Were you living in the town of Carlow? I was living about a mile from it, it was in the town of

Carlow the church was   How long were you going to chapel?   I went about eight Sundays in all   but between some of the Sundays I used to go to church   Was it through spite that you went to mass?   It was because I could not go to church   Then it was not through religion you went to mass?   I used to say my own prayers   Have you any religion?   I am a Protestant   And you went to mass?   I expected to be killed if I went to church   How did you happen not to get law from the magistrates at Carlow?   I don't know   Were you sworn?   The people I swore against were bailed, and they threw at me the next day again?   And you were not satisfied with that?   Why should I be satisfied with it?   What did they say to you?   They said it would be the best way to settle it easy   And you were not satisfied?   I was not   Did you go to mass after that?   I did, but I did not go to church or chapel for a long time after that   How did Mr. Tyrrell know that you were coming to live in Mayo?   My uncle sent me to his house to tell him about the people that threw stones at me, and he said he would punish them, it was after I went to the Magistrates that I went to him   Did you ever go to confession to Father Tyrrell as a Catholic?   I do not know what confession is   Do you know what I mean by going to confession?   I do not rightly   Did you ever confess your sins to Father Tyrrell?   I do not recollect ever to do that   Did you ever receive the sacrament according to the Catholic Church?   I do not recollect any sacraments unless they would shake water on me   Do you know what communion means?   I can't rightly say

CHIEF JUSTICE ---Did you ever receive the Sacrament in Church as a Protestant?   I did   Did you receive a Sacrament like that in the Chapel, or any thing of the kind?   I did not.

Mr Murphy —Did Cole seem to be very much surprised when you mentioned the name of Dowling? He did, and he bid me not to mention it to any one until my brother would be settled, and the policemen would come Did he express his surprise when you mentioned the name of James Dowling? He wondered greatly at it Why? He said because he was a neighbour Did he say any thing else? I do not recollect Did he not express his astonishment that a man of such excellent character in the neighbourhood should be there? I heard him cursing, and he said he believed they were all Whitefeet Did he not express surprise that a man of such excellent character should be there? He said nothing about his character Is there in all the neighbourhood a man of better character than James Dowling? I would not give him a character

Chief Justice —Before this business, would you have given him a good character? I would

Mr Murphy —Would you not have said before this business, that he was a man of excellent character? I would as long as I knew him Upon your oath is it not the reputation of the whole neighbourhood that he is a man of the very best character, and was it not in consequence of that excellent character that Cole expressed his surprise? Cole did not talk of his character at all When he said, I believe they are all Whitefeet, was it not an expression of astonishment that such a man as that could be a party to such business? I think that was the meaning of it.

Mr Martley —Were you on your knees when they asked you for the fire arms? I was Were you on your knees when they asked you whether you knew any of them? I was When did you first hear the name of Leonard? After he was taken prisoner Had you ever heard that he was called by that name before? No Do you recollect whether after the attack you spoke to your brother of the man who was at your uncle's house on Sunday, sitting on the chair with you? I did not say that to him. Do you recollect having had any conversation at all with your brother about it? I do not

Fourth Witness. *Mary Magee*, produced

ATTORNEY-GENERAL.—We produce Mary Magee for the prisoner's Counsel to examine her if they please (Prisoner's Counsel declined to examine her)

Here closed the evidence for the prosecution

EVIDENCE FOR THE DEFENCE

First Witness, *Michael Dowling*, examined by Mr D'Arcy —The prisoner at the bar is my son, I slept no where on the night of Good-Friday last, I spent that night in the kitchen of my own house, I remained up all night watching my cows, because there was a cow stolen from me on Thursday night, and in the morning I pursued her : my son was out with coals, and when he came home, he went in pursuit of the cow to Ballyragget, his boy was with him this was on the morning of Good Friday, it was not unusual with him to be out at night with coals, that is his common occupation, there was a fair at Ballyragget that day, and it was in the hope of finding the cow at the fair that I was going there, the boy that took the cow was a grandson of my own, he came home and said he would take more, the two girls staid up with me that night, I saw my son come home about seven o'clock on Friday evening, he went to bed at sunset, for he was fatigued, he did not get up 'till after sunrise next morning, there were only two rooms in my house besides the kitchen, I spent the night in the kitchen, the door of the room my son slept in, opens into the kitchen, and it has no other door, from the time he went to bed about sunset on Good-Friday night, he never came out of the room until sunrise, the day following

Cross-examined by the ATTORNEY-GENERAL.—There is a room at each side of the kitchen, my son slept on the right hand side room as you go into the kitchen, two children of his slept with him   the servant-boy went to bed, that boy is Owen Brennan a prisoner, he slept in the other room, I saw both of them go to bed, my son went to bed about half an hour before the boy   the boy went to rub the horses, and he went to bed about night-fall, I could see them both, and I saw them in bed the whole night, Were the doors open?   No, they were latched but if they were open I could see them   Were the doors opened that night?   The doors were not opened the whole night; there was a servant-maid in the house, she staid up with me watching the cows, Mary Conran also sat up that night. she came to the house to look for a pail of milk, and my son's wife desired her to wait until morning, that she would churn early on Saturday, at the singing of the lark she went to bed with the child in the settle-bed, she laid down because the child was crying, they had a good coal fire, and rushes occasionally when they wanted them, it was the child crying that made Mary Conran go to bed, she did not remain long in the settle-bed   when the day opened a little she got up, and put down water to churn the milk, it was the servant-girl who put down the water to prepare for the churning, Mary Conran could not

be above half an hour in the settlebed, not one of us went
out during the night to look at the cows, there was a split
in the door, and there was a lock on the cow-house door,
if any thing touched the lock we would hear it from the
kitchen fire the cow was stolen the night before out of
the cow-shed they drew the staple and they left the staple
and lock under the door, I did not speak to my son the
whole night he was in bed before Mary Conran came in
from the rosary, she saw him in bed he could see her
from where his bed lay I don't know that the door of his
room was shut before she came back What were you
doing during the night? Smoking tobacco, and walking
about the floor What light had you? A good fire.
Had you any rushes lighting? They did not light rushes
at all, but if they wanted them, they had them to light.
Did the women fall asleep at all? They did not not one
in the kitchen lay down in the kitchen till the lark sung.
Would not one of you be enough to watch? I would not
be up, but I was in dread the girls would fall asleep.
Would it not be enough for you to stay up, and allow the
girls to go to bed? I would like to have company.
Where was your son on Thursday night? He went to
Stratford-on-Slaney with coals When I was going in
pursuit of the cow, I was about a mile and a half from my
own house when my son overtook me, I was riding bare-
backed when I left home, I sent Owen Brennan for a
saddle, and I desired him to meet me with it, my son and
he came to me nearly at the same time, I then came home,
my son took the horse to Ballyragget, that was my own
horse, Owen Brennan followed my son to the fair on foot,
he was home before my son nearly half an hour, they

supped together on Friday morning, when the boy got up, he came in and told me that the cow was gone, I heard no noise during Good-Friday night when Mary Conran came there first in the evening, my son's wife was in the house it was about four o'clock when she came there. Did you see any person of the name of Magee in your house on Saturday morning? No What time did you go out? I went out early to fodder the cows Did your son breakfast with you on Saturday morning? He did At what hour? About seven or eight o'clock What time did your son get up that morning? He was up as early as me that morning What time did you get up on Saturday morning? It was after sunrise About what hour did you get up on Saturday morning? About five o'clock, or earlier

CHIEF JUSTICE.—Who was present when you got up? All that were in the house, but the children that did not get up my son, and the servant-girl, and the girl that was with me, were present Where was your son when you got up? He was in the kitchen What bed had you been in? I had been in no bed at all that night What do you mean by getting up? I got up to get my big coat out of the room

ATTORNEY-GENERAL.—Did not your son know that the cows were to be watched that night? I suppose he did Did he not know the next morning that you had sat up to watch them? He did Did he know that the girls had sat up all night? I dispute if he did know it Did your son know, that you and the girls were to sit up that night to watch the cows? I do not know but I believe he did know it Did not your son know the next morning that you were sitting up all the night? He did know it And that the girls had sat up with you? Yes

CHIEF JUSTICE —How do you know that your son knew the next morning that you sat up all night? When he was told it Who told it to him? We all told him

Second Witness, *Mary Blanchfield* examined by Mr MURPHY.—I recollect last Good-Friday night I was living that night at Michael Dowling's the father of the prisoner, I was servant girl in the house, I saw the prisoner that evening, he went to bed at nightfall, he came home from selling a load of coals on Good-Friday morning, he was up the night before and travelling all day on Friday, and went to bed at nightfall, on Good-Friday night I sat up all that night, the boy that stole the cow did not give in that he took the cow, and he said that if he had not taken a cow he would Patt Daly was that boy he is gone to America, he was at the house on Friday and he was charged with taking the cow, and he said that if he did not take her, that he would I sat up to watch for fear he would come to take another cow. Mary Conran and my old master staid up she laid her head upon the bed at the singing of the lark. James Dowling could not go out of the house without my knowledge, he never left it the whole night until he got up in the next morning after sunrise

Cross-examined by Mr TICKELL — Patt Daly lived more than a mile from my master's house I can't tell how far it is from my master's house, I can't say whether it is two miles, or three miles, or four miles I cannot give a guess, I was not acquainted with Patt Daly, but I saw him passing the road he lived with the widow Brennan I dont know the widow Brennan, I was not in my master's house when Patt Daly came in, when I came in he was talking to Mrs Dowling, he said at that time that last night was a fine day, that was the first thing I heard him say, my mistress said to him " you know that for you were travelling "

He gave the flax wheel a kick and knocked it down, and I took it up, and he gave it another kick, and broke the fliers of it, he went out a short time after that that is the whole of what I heard, as he was going out on the road he met Owen Brennan, and he welcomed him home and he asked him if he had the cow, my master did not come in at that time, it was between five and six o'clock when my master came in Patt Daly went away and I did not see him any more that day, I saw him again on Laster Sunday at my master's house he wanted some help from his grandfather to go to America. Instead of going to Ballyragget why did not your master go to Patt Daly to look for the cow? I don't know Did you hear that your master went to Patt Daly's on Good-Friday? I did not. I sat up the whole of Good-Friday night, I never opened the door from the time that I put the bolt on at night, until I took it off in the morning. The cow-house was not locked only the night that he took the cow Why was it not locked that Friday night? Because he had taken it off the night he stole the cow, and then there was no use in locking it again He did not take the lock away with him? The lock and staple were in the house the cows were in If you were afraid the cows would be stolen why was not the cow-house door locked? Sure when it was locked it did not save the cow. Had you candle light? No. Nor rushes? No. The old man took a horse with him on Friday morning to go look for the cow Owen Brenan went before him to look for a saddle some where, I saw the old man coming home, I saw him coming into the house, and I dont know whether he came on horseback or not How did Owen Brenan come home? He came home on his two feet Mary Conran sat up with you that night? Indeed she did until the singing of the lark Did you hear the lark sing? We

did by dad Did you hear any noise at all that night?
No No Windows broken? No How far is Jacob's
house from your master's house? Eighteen perches.
Did you see Ellen Magee on Saturday morning? I saw
her before dinner time when she came to our house
What brought her to your house? She came for a ha'porth
of buttermilk to make whey for her brother

JUROR —Who was the first person who left the house on
Saturday morning? I was Do you remember the old
man going into his room that morning? I do not Had
he his big coat on all the night he sat up? He had two
coats on all night What child slept in the settle-bed that
night? It was the little girl Was she cross? She was
frightened in her sleep once, and the girl lay on the bed
with her, that was when the lark sung

CHIEF JUSTICE —You say that the old man wore two
coats that night? He did Have you any particular
reason for remembering that? He was at the fire with me
all night. I have no particular reason for remembering it

Third Witness. *Mary Conran* examined by Mr. BRADY
—I know Michael Dowling, he is my uncle, I was in his
house on Good Friday night, I spent the night at the
kitchen fire, James Dowling was in bed when I came in
from Chapel, he slept in the room at the right hand side as
you come on, I saw him in bed. I remained there all
night, I am quite sure he did not leave his room that night,
I was there when he got up, it was after sunrise when he
got up

Cross-examined by Mr MARTLEY —I live within a mile
of the prisoner, it was between four and five o'clock that I
left my own house that evening, to go to my uncle's for
milk, James Dowling's wife was there when I went in,
I left her in the house when I was going to Chapel, and

she was not there when I came back. I saw Patt Daley at the house that evening. he came in after me. I left the house before him he had been suspected for stealing the cow before I left my own house I heard that the cow was stolen, but I did not hear that he was suspected till I came to my uncle's, if I got the milk I would not stay all night, when I came in from the Chapel James Dowling was in bed, and Owen Brenan had his shoes and stockings off at the fire none of the children were in bed at that time. Owen Brenan soon went to bed after that I saw James Dowling in the room in bed I went to the room for clothes, I told him that he was almost all alone that night, as his wife was away the girl told me that James's wife had gone away, he said nothing but that he had company enough, the girl put the children asleep, the young one was asleep before she took him to bed, and the eldest was not asleep, I saw Mary Blanchfield putting them into their father's bed this was before I went up for the clothes that the children were put to bed, I did not see James Dowling any other time during that night the door was shut all night, he was looking for the cow on Good Friday, I had no conversation with him about the cow being stolen, I don't know that he knew I was to sit up to watch the old man did not go to bed all night, he had his big coat on, and his other coat, I did not see him take any of them off all night, I did not go to bed till the singing of the lark, I fell asleep for a very short time, the old man was sitting at the fire when I got up, his big coat was on him still, James Dowling got up at that time, I remained in the house till after breakfast, his wife was sitting at the fire when I got up, because she came home to make the churning, it was very early when I got up, I saw his wife dressing the children at the fire, I did not tell her I was sitting up all night it was a long time after I got up that James Dowling got up, it was after sun-rise when he got up, they were not talking about the cow that was stolen, nor about his being at the fair of Ballyragett

Fourth Witness, *Doctor Carter*, examined by Mr MURPHY —I have been proprietor of the house in which William Jacob lives, I resided for seven years and upwards in that house, I have had ample opportunities of knowing the character of James Dowling, the prisoner at the bar, he was a man of the very best character, quite of a character that would lead a man to suppose that he would not be connected with such a charge as this, I think him to be a man of a very firm character, from what I know of him, I think it impossible for him to be corrupted so as to join in those wicked acts, he was a most exemplary man.

Cross-examined by Mr MARTLEY.—You saw John Magee after this occurrence? I think I saw him the third day after What state did you find him in? Excessively debilated, and in a very dangerous state, he evinced having lost an immensity of blood, he was bruised all over, independently of the stab. This man lived near the place where you formerly lived? The houses are about a hundred and thirty paces asunder You know Ellen Magee? I do She had been in the habit of visiting you? She had, for twelve months previous to that She had opportunities of seeing the prisoner? She had. And of knowing him? I should suppose so I have been away about six months from Mayo, I went away when that neighbourhood became troublesome, I was cautioned to take care of myself on account of testimony I gave here at the last Assizes.

Mr Murphy —There was an attack some time ago upon your house do you remember that the prisoner acted any particular part on that occasion?

Mr Martley —You cannot prove character through the medium of a particular fact

Chief Justice —The strict rule is this, that you cannot upon your direct examination as to character, go into particulars Mr Martley might have given you an opportunity of doing so, if he brought any particular fact in evidence to take away your evidence as to general reputation I wish it to be understood not to be a decision, but I will allow the question to be asked

Mr Murphy —Now, Doctor Carter, will you tell us about that attack on your house? My house was attacked on the 26th of December, 1829; there were several White Boy acts at that time in that neighbourhood, and there were several persons arrested at that time by the Dowling family, and they prosecuted them, and sent them to jail for three months.

Chief Justice —Was it an outrage of this character, or a robbery? It was an attack on my dwelling house, it was a White-Boy outrage; the attack was made half an hour before night

Mr Murphy —Was it not a White-Boy act? Indeed it was; and that very family brought them to justice

Fifth Witness, *Mr William Dunn*, examined by Mr Brady.—I live convenient to Carlow; I know the prisoner these ten or twelve years; I am his landlord, and his father's landlord; his character is that of a peaceable and quiet man, and well behaved; I never before this heard any thing laid to his charge; I always took James Dowling to be above connecting himself with such business, he holds sixteen acres of land.

Juror —Have you known any persons having as much land connected with such practices? I don't know

Sixth Witness, *Mr Thomas Wilson*, examined by Mr Murphy —I have lived at Tolerton, I have known James Dowling upwards of ten years, I have resided in that neighbourhood, I had opportunities in abundance to know his character I never knew him to have any character but a good one, I never knew him to be rioting, or a drunkard, nor do I believe he was ever connected with any improper conduct

Cross-examined by the Attorney General —Do you know that there is a good deal of alarm prevailing amongst the peaceable inhabitants of this county from these Whitefeet? There is These Whitefeet have proceeded to great extremety? They have There is a good deal of intimidation? I believe there is, among the peaceable part

Seventh Witness, *John Willoughly*, examined by Mr. Brady —I am a landholder in this county, I know James Dowling, he is a very good character, his character is that of a peaceable man, I live within a couple of fields of him, I heard of his losing a cow, to the best of my knowledge, it was on Good Friday I heard of it

Eighth Witness, *Captain Wright*, examined by Mr Murphy —I know James Dowling, the prisoner, by character, very well, I have been stationed near where he resides I am there for the last nine years, I have had opportunities of knowing what his character is, I do not know him personally, I know from his neighbours, and people whom I can rely upon that he is a man of a very superior character, it is rather subsequent to his being taken that I have heard this

CHARGE

CHIEF JUSTICE —Gentlemen of the Jury, In this case the prisoner is charged with burglary, a capital felony, and if the evidence be believed, the charge in point of law is supported The testimony in support of the prosecution is in one part of it altogether unquestioned for it has been corroborated by the witnesses for the prisoner, and not disputed, and that is, that the outrage in question was committed at the time stated, and in the manner described And the question is, whether the guilt is brought home to the prisoner by John and Ellen Magee, the only witnesses who have identified him You will in considering their evidence, first form an estimate, as far as the evidence enables you to make it, of their moral character, and you will consider from what has been laid before you whether they are persons who would wilfully commit perjury, you will secondly consider even if they are moral persons who wish to speak the truth, whether they may, or may not have made a mistake, you will recollect upon the one hand, that the sister has been acquainted with the prisoner for more than a year, living in his neighbourhood, with opportunities of seeing him constantly, her brother had an opportunity of knowing him for four months those were their opportunities of knowing him before the outrage, you are next to consider their opportunities of recognizing him at the moment of the outrage

Gentlemen, it was a short space of time occupied by transactions very unfavourable to accurate observation I think fifteen or twenty minutes is the time stated, during which the assailants were in that house, and you will recollect that the persons who had that opportunity had been awakened out of their sleep by a dreadful outrage, that they were put into a state of great danger, and that there were some moments of that time that they were exposed to the most imminent peril of their lives, you will recollect that both were cruelly beaten; and that some portion of that time must be allowed for the time which elapsed after the young man had received a disabling, and nearly deadly wound.

You will therefore have to consider whether those circumstances go at all to detract, or in what degree they go to detract from the inference against the prisoner, arising from the previous acquaintance between the prosecutors, and the prisoner Gentlemen, you will also consider whether or not in the cross-examination of those witnesses there have been extracted from them, admissions, or contradictions sufficient to impeach their credit, either as to their moral character, or to raise a reasonable doubt of their accuracy. If such admissions or contradictions have been established in this case as would lead you to believe that these two witnesses have wilfully fabricated from any motive a false charge, I need not tell you how you are to deal with the case —But if these admissions or contradictions go to raise an inference in your minds short of that imputation of perjury, but representing to you these persons as inaccurate in their statements you will judge whether such inaccuracy is sufficient to raise a doubt in your minds on the subject of identification

Gentlemen, the contradictions or admissions, if any, arise out of a comparison of the testimonies of John and Ellen Magee with each other, and of both with the evidence of their Uncle as to which you will recollect that small circumstances of contradiction may, and almost must exist between several narratives of the same transaction, but the question for you is, whether they are sufficiently important to affect the credit or accuracy of the witness, so as to raise a reasonable doubt of their truth

You have all had experience of various instances in which it is next to impossible even for persons of enlightened minds to concur minutely in giving an account of a recent transaction, and it is for you to say, whether there are in this case contradictions that imply falsehood or gross inaccuracy sufficient to raise a doubt in your minds as to the truth of the charge As to the falsehood, if you are satisfied that they have sworn falsely, it will not be upon the principle of doubt you will act, but upon the principle that you have not heard any credible evidence to support the charge But if you are of opinion that the accuracy of the witnesses is brought into doubt, you will consider whether that doubt is sufficient to overbear the positive testimony in the case

Gentlemen, I cannot too often recall your attention to this, that if you have any fair doubt on your minds of the prisoner's guilt you ought to acquit him, and your having some doubt of his innocence will not justify a conviction

Gentlemen, his principal defence is an *alibi*, but he is supported also by evidence as to character in way that in my experience is, I will say unexampled It is not the trite, loose, and common place defence of character There is something peculiar in it It is pointed to the nature of the charge on which he is tried, it comes from a

o

great many witnesses. No one of them has spoken even in what may be called moderate language, of the character of the prisoner. They have not only stated that he is a man of exemplary character, and of a peaceable disposition, but they have gone farther, they have proved that about two years ago that prisoner and his family distinguished themselves not in resisting an attack upon their own property, but in volunteering to turn out against combinators and insurgents, and in bringing them to justice. If the prisoner continued to deserve that character up to the day before Good-Friday, it ought to go very far indeed to rebut the probability of his having participated in the outrage of that night. Gentlemen, it is farther in evidence that since he has been apprehended, Captain Wright has made enquiries into his character from the most respectable persons, and that he has found the same good character remaining behind him in his neighbourhood, and that it does not appear to be qualified in any way except by the pendency of this charge.

I think there is another circumstance very deserving of your attention, and that is, that character in this case is brought forward to rebut not merely the charge of a common participation in this outrage, but to rebut the charge of a blood thirsty and savage pre-eminence in the dreadful crimes of that night, manifesting a murderous disposition quite inconsistent with the former nature of the prisoner. It is to be deplored that the influence of those diabolical associations every day makes inroads not only on the peace of the country, not only on property and life, but on the morals of the people and if it shall appear that the soundness of that man's heart has been broken down by that influence, we shall have to lament the loss of perhaps as valuable a member of society in any rank as ever had to repent of having yielded to temptation, and forfeited his integrity

Gentlemen as to the *alibi* defence you will examine it by the usual tests If you had never attended an Assizes before, your constant attendance here for the last ten days would be sufficient to instruct you in some of the principles of the criminal law You will judge whether the witnesses in support of the *alibi* have sworn truly You will judge whether, if they are accurate as to facts, they are accurate as to the times as to the day whether they are accurate as to the hours and by all those tests you will come to an opinion whether they have disproved the charge, or whether concurrently with the evidence of character they have brought it into a reasonable and honest doubt It is scarcely possible that they can be inaccurate as to the day First of all, the fact is not a stale one secondly, the day is a notorious one and thirdly, attention had been called to it the morning after the transaction occurred If therefore they have annexed true facts to a false date as to the day, that cannot in this case be mistake, it must be perjury As to the hour, you will recollect that persons of their rank are not so much to be depended upon as persons in a higher rank might You will deal with this very difficult part of the case with a recollection of that polar principle which Juries ought to steer by, that an honest, a conscientious, and a reasonable doubt ought to stand in the place of a demonstration of innocence, and you will have to apply that principle in analyzing the evidence and in finding your way through very great difficulties It is hard to understand from what we have heard what could transform that man of whom his prosecutors speak with respect, not merely into a Bandit but into a demon and on the other hand it is most difficult indeed to understand what could be the motives for fabricating this charge against that man in selecting him, beyond others, by persons who have no feelings towards him which could account for such a fabrication.

Gentlemen, that is a view of the case, which if you be put to the election between truth and perjury, will press upon one party or the other, and therefore consider well whether the case affords the means of reconciling those difficulties by supposing the prosecutors to be mistaken

Mr BRADY here suggested to his Lordship that although the witnesses had known the prisoner before, they had on that night only a view of him whilst in the porch.

CHIEF JUSTICE —That is a most important observation if borne out, as I believe it is by the testimony, and we shall see how that is in the course of my getting through the evidence

His Lordship then proceeded to read to the Jury his notes of the evidence, observing on it as he went along, when he came to that part of the evidence of Ellen Magee where she said that she mentioned the name of the prisoner to the police-man because he was a Protestant, his Lordship said

Gentlemen, the using the word Protestant in that answer, has led to the introduction of all that afflicting matter, some of which was brought before us on a former trial against another prisoner Before 1 read to you my notes of the evidence upon that subject, I think it right to make an observation upon it; a distressing subject, God knows it is, nothing can be more painful If she has not actually fabricated, if she has not invented what she has stated upon this part of the case, she represents a spirit of bigotry and persecution quite unheard of, and the tendency of her evidence would lead us to deplore that a new character has been, at least in this instance given to the Whiteboy confederacy, and that religious discord has been thrown into a bitter cup already too full, and now overflowing Her statement is that she was exposed to personal insult, and was actually pursued and pelted by crowds in going to, and returning from Church partly on account of her religion, and partly of a tradition that her grandfather had persecuted a Roman Catholic Priest, and that in consequence of her thinking that Magistrates to whom she had complained of this ill treatment, had not done her justice, she had been induced to pretend a change of religion, and with the concurrence of her family to attend Roman Catholic worship as a protection against outrage, and that she has since had those extraordinary communications with Father Kelly, to which she has sworn If this be true. I fear that some of what has appeared mysterious in this extraordinary case is accounted for by a disclosure not only to be regretted, but calculated to excite much well-founded alarm, for if this additional virus has been communicated to the minds of our people, already too deeply infected, the disease becomes formidable indeed This extraordinary young woman appears to have a very excited mind on the subject of religious controversy, and to entertain some bigotted and uncharitable opinions derived from real or imaginary danger, or perhaps to be attributed to the prejudices of a narrow and illiberal education , and you must consider, Gentlemen, whether a person of that description is not likely at least to colour, and exaggerate facts, which if communicated by one of cooler character, would appear to be of a harmless nature, or capable of satisfactory explanation, at least all parts of her evidence which consists of opinions and inferences must be attended to with this qualification, for it is very plain that the sentiments she avows, as well as those which she imputes to Father Kelly, are in their opposite directions so violent and unchristianlike, that very little dependence could be placed upon persons influenced by either, and must be regarded as the extravagancies of two individuals, and not, I trust, as fair specimens of the principles of the Protestant or Roman Catholic religion. You will also consider, whether she does not represent Mr. Kelly in his communications with her, as acting with an imprudence not easily accounted for, in making her the depository of those sentiments, which one would think, he would not be likely to confide to her, and whether that, and the whole character of her narrative, as to her intercourse with him, do not amount to an improbability sufficient to overbear her testimony, however positive. If you should be of opinion that she has fabricated this charge from any motives, then you ought not to act upon her testimony, and must discharge from your minds altogether so much of the evidence as came from her lips, but her credit is for you—you have heard what she has sworn, and observed her manner, and it is your province, and not mine, to decide upon it. It is, however, my duty in justice to the prisoner, to observe, that all we have heard of this witness's communication with Mr. Kelly on controversial subjects, so unfortunately introduced, is not only quite foreign to the question you are to try, but I must remind you that no participation in any of those bigotted opinions, or in any previous ill treatment of Ellen Magee, has been traced to James Dowling, but that on the contrary, she and her brother admit, that up to the moment of Good Friday he had been their kind and good neighbour, and was respected by them.

The CHIEF JUSTICE then read the remainder of the evidence from his notes, and after a deliberation of two hours, the Jury found the prisoner Guilty, but strongly recommended him to Mercy on account of his excellent character

Baron Smith.—James Dowling, in finding you guilty of the offence for which you stood indicted, a humane and intelligent Jury recommended you to mercy. They were induced to do so, by the excellent—I had almost said—the admirable character, which was given you upon your trial, by witnesses eminently competent to form a judgment, both of your conduct and reputation: witnesses highly faith-worthy and respectable themselves.

Nay, what did they further disclose on your behalf? That little more than two years have elapsed, since you opposed insurgent outrage, and assisted to make transgressors amenable to law.

Though it be impossible that severe punishment should not ensue, upon an offence so grievous as that of which you have been convicted,—though this would be impossible, even in a state of far less disturbance than that with which we are so distressingly hemmed in, I, however, cannot but indulge a hope, that the recommendation of the Jury will avail to spare your life, and that those who instigated you to crime, will be but answerable for your banishment: not covered with your blood.

Scarcely ever have I heard, from the Bench of a Crown Court, a character so excellent as that which you have received.

We find a spotless reputation accompanying you to the eve of enormous outrage, and placing you immaculate on the threshhold of William Jacob's house.

What a frightful picture have we here, of the effect of those instigations, which have plunged this county into crime, and drawn down this commission to call sternly for expiation!

In almost the twinkling of an eye, we find innocence put on corruption and the purity which we had been admiring, at once shroud itself in black and criminal pollution.

Let us hope, that the innocent inmates of William Jacob's house were not the only victims on that sanguinary night

Let us hope, on your behalf, that you also were a victim, devoted to crime and punishment, by that secret power, to which so many bear mysterious and diabolical allegiance

In contemplation of law, you, heretofore esteemed, stabbed the unoffending and unarmed Magee for you abetted that nightly outrage, which produced the shedding of his blood

When you made one of a party armed with instruments of death, and joined in this burglarious attack upon your neighbour's house, you must have known, that you risked the aiding in the infliction of wounds or death.

But you are charged with having been yet more criminal than this

The Jury have found you guilty They must therefore have believed (indeed how could they disbelieve?) the ingenuous testimony of John Magee

And what did he prove against you? That when, in his own opinion, and to all appearance, he was expiring, you exclaimed, "he is but foxing, I will shoot him," and made a bayonet thrust at his sister, who interposed to save him

Let us suppose that what is possible may be true Let us hope that this was bluster and bravado that you did not entertain the cruel purposes which you professed

You did not stab the girl, you did not shoot her brother You might have done both If the Jury considered you to have cruelly aggravated your offence, by intending to do either, they would never have recommended you You made the push at her, but, though unparried, it did not strike her Your gun burned priming, but even this may have been without your pulling the trigger, and at all events the muzzle was not then pointed against John Magee

These sanguinary demonstrations may thus have been an ostentatious but a sham display of obedience to the orders under which you were acting, and may have been intended at once to intimidate the inmates of the house, and prevent your incurring the vengeance of your more criminal associates, or inducing them at least to denounce you to the higher powers of misrule, as slack and lukewarm in the execution of their atrocious wishes and commands.

Something mitigatory of this kind is the more conceivable in your case, because it seems to have occurred in the case of another of the party

John Magee swore that Laurence Leonard had done a great deal of good, evidently meaning that he had contributed to the protection of the inhabitants of the house Yet, from the testimony of Ellen, we collect, that he too uttered some ferocious threats and denunciations

You and he, reluctant, but intimidated and coerced, may, for the protection of your own Lives, have been acting a murderous part and counterfeiting a malignity with which you were not inspired Towards promoting a humane object, you may have been obliged cautiously to conceal it to cloak it under the garb of fierce and ruffianly intention of a counterfeit participation in the fury of these less merciful banditti, amongst whom you were enrolled

The indictment originally preferred against you, was one which did not affect your life But some circumstances which transpired upon a former trial, seemed to impose upon the Attorney-General, the irksome duty of a more rigorous course

Upon those circumstances however, perhaps equivocal in their nature, the recommendation of the Jury has impliedly put a favourable and benign construction, which will again, I trust, let in the clemency of the Crown.

It would have been better, if you had confined yourself to making character your defence For the verdict which has been returned, has stigmatized your *alibi* evidence as false But perhaps this defence did not originate in your instructions, but in the error of your relatives and friends, or in a less innocent sacrifice, by them, of their consciences to your safety.

Be this as it may, the Jury have not found it an insurmountable obstacle, in the way of their recommendation, nor shall it impede our wish that their recommendation may prove effectual In truth, as I said in another case, we ought not to visit with too much strictness, the false swearing of a witness, upon him for whose supposed benefit such witness has been forsworn The perjury may not have been committed at his desire, and if not, it should not prejudice his other claims to mitigation At all events we ought not to punish perjury with death, still less by the death of one man, to expiate the perjury of another.

I dwell with satisfaction on whatever justifies the recommendation of your Jury, and those hopes of mercy to which their interference has given birth

I therefore remind myself, that you had no share in that treacherous and preliminary visit, which was paid on the Sunday evening that preceded this outrage

For the same reason it gratifies me to recollect, that when the recommendation was announced, you at once dropped humbly upon your knees and returned thanks to the fountain of all mercy, to your God

This very piety leads to a hope that their recommendation was deserved When a feeling of religion has struck deep root, we cannot be utterly depraved

Upon the whole, I hope and trust that the mercy of the Crown will avert the execution of that awful sentence, which it becomes my duty to pronounce

The secret movers of that disturbance which this Commission seeks to quell, have stripped you of innocence and reputation have plunged you in infamy and guilt They have banished you from a country which, but for them, you would not have disgraced, they have torn you from your mourning friends and destitute family, for your life But, I trust, they will have failed to bring you to an ignominious death

As it is, let them reflect penitently on the evil which they have accomplished and diligently amend their lives, according to God's Holy Word

The sentence of the law, which I trust will be intercepted by the mercy of the Crown, is ——here the

Attorney-General rose, and said, that as well from the recommendation of the Jury, as from what had just fallen from the Bench, he, on the part of the Crown, would be contented that the judgment should be recorded, if their lordships should approve of such a course

The Lord Chief Justice and Baron Smith expressed their entire concurrence and approbation, and judgment of death was thereupon not pronounced, but merely recorded against James Dowling

COUNSEL FOR THE CROWN

Mr Attorney General. | Mr. Clarke.
Mr Tickell | Mr Arabin
Mr. Martley |

COUNSEL FOR THE PRISONER

Mr Brady | Mr Murphy.

Agent—Mr. Delany

ELEVENTH DAY

Monday, 4th June, 1832

THE KING,	Mr BRADY.—My Lords, in
v	this case, on the part of the pri-
FRANCIS ADAMS, and	soner Francis Adams, I have to
THOMAS LANGTON	put in a Challenge to the array

of the panel

Mr D'ARCY said, that on the part of the prisoner Thomas Langton, he had to put in the same challenge

THE CHALLENGE TO THE ARRAY

THE KING,	Court of Commission of
against	Oyer and Terminer, and Jail de-
FRANCIS ADAMS, and	livery, in and for the Queen's
THOMAS LANGTON.	County

And upon this the said Francis Adams, and Thomas Langton, the prisoners at the bar, challenge the array of the said panel, because they say the panel was arrayed by one

Arthur Moore Mosse, and not by the High Sheriff, or Sub-Sheriff of the Queen's County, and because the panel, by whomsoever arrayed, has been arrayed in a manner more favourable to the prosecutors than the prisoners. And because Thomas Kemmis, Esq. Sheriff of said county, did permit said Arthur Moore Mosse to array said panel, and did return thereon certain persons, and omit to return certain other persons, at the instance of the said Arthur Moore Mosse, and among the rest did return thereon the said Arthur Moore Mosse himself. And because the said Arthur Moore Mosse, or the said Sheriff or Sub-Sheriff, at the instance of the said Arthur Moore Mosse, did, in arraying said panel, omit the names of certain persons, because he, the said Arthur Moore Mosse, deemed them more likely to acquit than to convict the prisoners, and inserted thereon, the names of certain other persons, because he, the said Arthur Moore Mosse, deemed them more likely to convict than to acquit the prisoners. And because the said Arthur Moore Mosse, or the said Sheriff or Sub-Sheriff, at the instance of the said Arthur Moore Mosse, did, in arraying said panel, dispose the names of certain persons whom he the said Arthur Moore Mosse deemed more likely to convict the prisoners, above the names of other persons whom he, the said Arthur Moore Mosse, deemed more likely to acquit the prisoners, to the manifest wrong and injury of the prisoners. and this, he the said Francis Adams and Thomas Langton are ready to verify. wherefore they pray judgment, and that the said panel may be quashed, and soforth.

The ATTORNEY-GENERAL joins issue. First, that the panel was arrayed by the High Sheriff, or for him by the Sub-Sheriff, and not by Arthur Moore Mosse, and secondly, that the panel is an impartial one.

ATTORNEY-GENERAL.—I join issue to this challenge to the array.

CHIEF JUSTICE.—Our course at present is to appoint Triors.

Mr. D'ARCY here suggested the propriety of having two of the Grand Jury sworn as Triors, to which the Attorney-General assented.

CHIEF JUSTICE.—We appoint the Hon. Thomas Vesey and Henry Smyth, Esq. both of the Grand Jury, to be the Triors to try this challenge.

It was then arranged that two *issues* should be sent to the Triors.

First Issue.—Whether the panel was arrayed by the Sheriff or not.

Second Issue.—Whether the array was an impartial one or not.

The Triors were then sworn.

Mr. D'ARCY.—We will first examine the High Sheriff and we have to request that Mr. Beere, the Under-Sheriff, Mr. Arthur Moore Mosse, and James Molloy, be out of Court. We will examine the High Sheriff for mere form, as we are perfectly satisfied that he has not done any thing but what is honorable and proper.

Thomas Kemmis, Esq. High Sheriff, sworn and examined by Mr. D'ARCY.—You are the High Sheriff of this county? I am. Did you return this panel yourself? I did. Did you draw it up yourself? No. Did you put the names or any of them on the panel? No. but I ordered certain names to be put on, that I believe were not hitherto returned on that panel, and I believe I made it a larger panel than it generally is? To whom did you give the directions to do that? To Mr. Beere, my Sub-Sheriff. Had you any communication with Mr. Arthur Moore Mosse on this

subject? Not one single word Did you give any particular names to your Sub-Sheriff? 1 do not recollect the
names now

Cross-examined by the ATTORNEY-GENERAL.—Does
the panel returned by you contain the names directed by
you, and in the order directed by you? The order 1 gave
no direction about You saw the order before you signed
the panel? 1 saw the panel, but 1 cannot exactly say that
1 examined the order In giving the names were you
directed or controlled by any body? As far as 1 gave
directions about them 1 certainly was not In directing
the additional names, and in enlarging the panel, did you
act fairly according to your own judgment and discretion?
1 did, but 1 advised with Mr Beere my Sub-Sheriff Did
you in returning that panel advise with any body but your
Sub-Sheriff? 1 did not positively

Edward Beere, Esq sworn and examined by Mr
BRADY —You are the Sub-Sheriff of this county? 1 am
How often have you been so? Two years Do you mean
two years successively?

ATTORNEY-GENERAL.—You cannot ask him that question.

CHIEF JUSTICE —Surely Mr Brady that does not bear
upon the issue to be tried.

Mr BRADY —It was not at all with the expectation of
getting an unfavourable answer that 1 asked him the question, but to see how long he is connected with the county

Mr BEERE —1 have been two years Sub-Sheriff, but
not successively

Mr. BRADY.—How often have you returned the panel
to the Crown Court? 1 believe this is the fourth time
When did you commence preparing the panel for this
commission? The day that 1 got the precept from Mr
Gibbs the Clerk of the Crown, I commenced preparing the

panel immediately. Had you any conference with the High Sheriff upon the subject? I had Before you took any steps? Not before I took any steps, but as soon as I could I looked over my former panels, and sent to the High Sheriff How soon afterwards did you see him? I cannot exactly say Did you meet him and converse with him upon the subject before you took any steps? I had many conversations with him before I commenced arranging the panel, and before it was returned to Mr Gibbs Was this panel prepared from the former panel? I do not think it was, man for man, but every man upon the former panels was summoned, and every respectable man in the county was summoned Do you mean to say that the panel for this commission was prepared in the ordinary way that you prepared other panels? Certainly I do not mean to ask you whether there are individuals on this panel that might not have been on former panels, but I ask you is there a considerable class of persons upon this panel of a different description from the class of persons upon former panels? Not at all, from the time that I came into the country until this moment I have been anxious to make the Jury panel respectable Did you select from any particular class a number of persons not usually placed on the crown panel? I did not select from any particular class, good, bad, or indifferent, I put them on indiscriminately, looking to nothing but their respectability. Do you mean to say that you put more respectable persons on this panel than upon other panels? I do not think I did Did you receive from any person whatever any names with directions to have them inserted on that panel? I received names from many persons, I asked and made enquiries, and did every thing in my power to get persons to send me the names of respectable Jurors, but I

P

got no directions, good, bad, or indifferent I took directions from nobody, and I conceived that nobody had any right to give me directions Do you not think that the High Sheriff would have a right to give you directions? I don't conceive he would In point of fact, did he, or did he not? He did not, further than to do what was proper and correct, and without favor or affection He mentioned no names? Not a name, he never told me to put down a name, with the exception of Mr Joshua Kemmis I think he was the only person he spoke to me about, that was left off the panel, he desired me to take care and summon every proper man that I could make out in the country Are you quite sure that in none of those conversations he suggested any particular names? To the best of my knowledge he did not suggest any name at all, he asked me was such and such a man summoned, but I do not recollect the names of those persons I am now speaking of the panel returned to Mr Gibbs Were they persons usually summoned, or persons that were not before on the crown panel? I believe they were persons that I had summoned before at other times, but there was nothing but general conversation between me and Mr Kemmis, except about the Grand Jury panel

BARON SMITH.—The enquiry upon which the triors are now engaged. I apprehend to be merely this, whether the panel be returned by the High or Under Sheriff, or by some other person

Mr. BRADY —It was with a view to the second issue that I asked those questions. Would not this be the proper time to swear the triors upon the second issue?

ATTORNEY GENERAL —I would rather they were not mixed up.

Mr BRADY, (To Witness,)—Are you able to recollect

that he made any suggestion to you to this effect that there ought to be persons upon the crown panel that were not usually on? He never made use of any such expression, all he told me was to summon Jurors indiscriminately, which I did and returned them to Mr Gibbs —I made enquiries from several as to proper persons to return on the panel, and I have done that ever since I came into the county. Are you speaking as to former times, or with respect to this Commission? I did so generally, I always took it as a compliment when any person would send me a number of names. Were you sent a list of names to have them put upon this panel? I think I was not. I think I had them all before my clerk had always instructions from me to make out as many names as he could, to put them on the Bailiffs' lists. Do you recollect that you received any names with a view to this particular panel? Any body that told me he had any names, I sent him to my clerk. So far as you recollect the formation of this particular panel, it was made without a suggestion of any names? I think every man that was on this panel, was on the last panel —I think that this panel, and the panel of the last Assizes are very nearly the same; I believe every name upon the last panel, is upon the present panel, with the exception of one name. When did you actually set about making out this panel? I think it was on the Monday before the Commission. Where was it made out? In my office. Did you get any body to assist you in making out the panel in its present form? I got it regulated by my clerk, and one or two others that I got to assist me, because I was very ill myself, and while they were regulating it, I never left the room, unless for a few moments, when I was backward and forward. In what manner did those two other persons assist you? I considered them to be assisting me as clerks, and I directed these assistants not to mention to any body the particulars of the panel, nor to give any copies of it. I had the Bailiff's lists about me, when the panel was regulated. What are these Bailiffs' lists? They are regulated by districts, each Bailiff has a list of Jurors to summon in a particular district. I presume you put no person's name on the panel who had not been summoned? I think I did, because I met people whom I spoke to, and they said they would attend. Did you meet many such persons? I do not think I did. Do you recollect the name of any person whom you spoke to? I thought Mr Warburton might not wish to attend as a Petty Juror, as he was high on the Grand Jury panel. I spoke to his father, and he told me that his son would attend, if I put him on the list, and I accordingly did put him on the list. Then with the exception of Mr Warburton, there is no person on the panel, whose name is not on the Bailiffs' lists? I am not able to say, at this moment—yes, I recollect, Mr Lawrenson's name is not on any Bailiff's list, I saw him in town and I put down his name. Do you or not recollect any other names put upon the panel that were not in the Bailiffs' lists? I do not. When did you make out those Bailiffs' lists? I made them out for this Commission, because at the last Assizes some person came behind me when I was in the Sheriff's box, and stole the Bailiffs' lists out of my pocket, that is the reason why I was obliged to make out new Bailiffs' lists. Had you any assistant besides your clerk in making out the Bailiffs' lists? I had. Whom else had you besides your clerk? Mr Arthur Moore Moss assisted me, and some other young man who came in with my clerk, and Mr Handsborough, that lives next door to me.—They assisted me, to save me the expense of hiring clerks and they did exactly as I desired them. Did you receive any assistance from those persons as to what names you would put on? They suggested to me several names in the county that I might summon if I liked, but if I did not like, I need not summon them. Did you, in point of fact, put on the Bailiff's lists those names that were suggested to you? I believe I put on every name that was suggested to me since I came into the county, I never considered what any man was, provided he was respectable. I swear that I know nothing at all of the feelings of any man on that panel. Upon my oath I never studied nor considered what their politics were. Did Molloy suggest any names to you? No. Did Mr. Handsborough suggest any names? I dare say in the course of conversation he might have asked me is such a man summoned. What assistance did you get from Mr. Moss? The principal assistance that I wanted from Mr. Moss, was as to the districts. The assistance I got from him was for the purpose of distributing the Bailiffs in their proper districts. Did nobody suggest to you whether it was right or wrong to put down certain names? Oh! no my Lords. Where were the Bailiffs lists made out? I think principally in my own house, as Molloy brought me the lists they were not correct as to distribution, and I had to correct and regulate them in my own office with the assistance I have already described. I suppose you were not at Molloy's when he was making out these lists? I was not. I think they were all made up in my own office, to the best of my knowledge, I am not sure whether Molloy brought me the drafts of those lists, but I rather think he did not. I think they were all made out in my own office. If they were all made out in your office, were they made out during the time Mr. Moss was there? The summonses that Mr. Moss filled up were wrongly filled up, and I was obliged to have them again filled up by Mr Handsborough Mr Moss gave us as much trouble as if he had not been there, he was as anxious to do it rightly as any one, but he was wrong in the form   Is Mr Moss in the habit of attending your office ? Not my office, but he is in the habit of coming to my house   Did he give you any other assistance that day ? I think not, I am satisfied that he never interfered at all, any more than to fill up the summonses, nor did any one ever interfere with me, I told them what to do, and they did it   How long was he in your office ? I dare say four or five hours, and he filled up about four or five hundred summonses he assisted in filling them all, and the whole came to about that number I think I gave Molloy a large list of names, and told him to fill up summonses for all those names, Mr Moss was in the room, to the best of my knowledge, when the lists were making out If I understand you rightly, the lists and the summonses were all taken from some long list that you had made out previously ? I gave Molloy a large list that was made up of old panels Was that before you received the precept ? It was certainly I want to know whether subsequent to issuing the precept, you made additions to that long list ? I added to the Bailiffs lists the names that I found on the long panel, and I am satisfied that I put other names on it During the four or five hours that Mr Moss was with you, did you put on any names ? I do not recollect that I did Did Mr Moss suggest a single name ? I cannot recollect, if it struck him, I am sure he did. Had you any communication with him previous to that day with respect to the formation of the panels, or the issuing of summonses, or the making of lists ? I am satisfied that I made a request of him to send me as

many names as he could When did you make that request?
I made it two or three years ago But since the issuing of
the Commission? If I met him in the street I might say,
as I would to any other man "Mr Moss have you any
names that I ought to summon" Since you heard of the
issuing of the Special Commission, did you make any such
request of Mr Moss to furnish you with names proper to
be summoned as Petty Jurors? I do not think I did Do
you recollect whether in point of fact, since you heard of the
issuing of the present Commission, that he did himself furnish you with any names proper to be summoned as Petty
Jurors, or did he suggest them in any manner to you? I do
not think that he suggested any names that I had not before
on the panel Did he suggest any names that you had
before on the panel? I believe he did In writing or
otherwise? To the best of my knowledge it was in writing
By the virtue of your oath, how many names were contained
in that writing? I think there were twenty-three What
use did you make of that writing? I don't know what use
I made of it By the virtue of your oath were these twenty-three names on that old panel or list? By the virtue of
my oath I believe they were on some of the old panels in
my office When did Mr Moss give you that paper? I
cannot exactly say but he gave it to me in time to send out
the summonses I think it was after the day he spent four
or five hours in my office How long after I cannot tell,
but it was in time to send out the summonses there was
some confusion among the Bailiffs by the loss of the lists,
and I think I was obliged to send out summonses a second
time. Murphy was the Bailiff I sent them to I do not
recollect I sent them to any other Bailiff Did the second
set of summonses consist of those names that had been fur-

nished to you by Mr Moss? Indeed I do not recollect; I only swear to the best of my knowledge, that I sent a second list at all In what district was Murphy employed in, in summoning Jurors? Rathdowney Did the list furnished to you by Mr. Moss, consist of names in that district? Upon my oath I do not recollect a single name of the twenty-three, it made no impression at all upon me Did Mr Moss ever before furnish you with a list or not? I do not think he did, but I am sure he told Molloy several names on former lists Did any one besides Mr Moss ever give you a list? No one certainly for this Commission

CHIEF JUSTICE —I am to take it for granted, that all this is *de bene esse* for the second issue, because this does not apply to the first issue

Mr BRADY —I think it does, my Lord

CHIEF JUSTICE —Very well, take your own course

Mr. BRADY —From what documents did you make out the panel? From the bailiffs' lists that I had sent out on former times Did you transcribe each bailiff's list from the top to the bottom as they stood? Certainly not, I mixed them up as well as I could according to the respectability of the persons on those lists How many names on this panel? I believe upwards of four hundred Were you able from your personal knowledge of those four hundred persons to dispose of them in the order of their respectability. If I was perfectly well, I think I would be as well able to place them, as any man that I know, and I ultimately did so And by the virtue of my oath no body saw that panel from the time that I arranged it myself, until I gave it to Mr Gibbs the Clerk of the Crown Were you in perfect health this day fortnight? I was not What do you mean by saying that if you were in perfect health you would be as able to arrange them as any other man ? There was a great deal of labor in doing it, there were five or six lists It was the mere physical labor that you were unable to undergo but from your knowledge of the persons were you able to place them ' I could place them without favor or affection Did you in point of fact receive any assistance from any person in your office day in placing these persons on the panel ' To be sure I did, just the same as if Mr Moss had been my clerk Did any one assist you as to the place in which particular names should be put on the panel, high or low ' I desired Mr Moss and Molloy to make the list as they thought right, and to let me see it, and to take a respectable name from each panel and so to go on, I was standing by listening, except as far as I was not able to stand, and they did nothing except by my directions By the virtue of my oath the panel returned is not exactly what they made ont.

CHIEF JUSTICE —The verbal meaning of that last sentence is that they made out the panel I am not giving an opinion The Jurors will have to interpret those words, not according to the meaning of the letters or syllables, but according to the meaning of the person who spoke them.

Mr BRADY.—If I understand you rightly while you were present. Mr Moss and Molloy were making out the lists ? They were acting as my clerks I ask you whether in point of fact they were making out any list from the bailiff's lists ' They were And in that list they were putting persons in a certain order ? They were

BARON SMITH —My view is this, that a Sheriff or Sub-Sheriff who receives and even solicits assistance from various quarters as to the names proper to be put on the panel, if he afterwards exercises his own discretion and controul, and alters and revises that list impartially according to the best of his judgment, skill, and knowledge, and then returns it so revised as his panel, it is his panel, and it is impartially returned And I would say that to the selection of the names I would apply precisely the same principle

Mr BRADY —Whilst you were present in the room, and whilst you were out of the room, Mr Moss, and Molloy were engaged in making out a list of names from the Bailiffs' lists? They were and they continued employed till they transcribed on that list all the names on the Bailiffs' lists? They did I believe every single one of them. And when they had done so, they gave you that list? They left that list for me Am I to understand that at the time it was completed you were absent? I rather think Molloy was at his dinner when I got it, but I cannot exactly say, I read it over and over again, and I did my best, by the virtue of my oath, to return a fair panel What were the directions you gave them? To take names from each list, and to make out a fair list How many Bailiffs' lists were there? I think there were four, but I think one of them was not returned for some time after Murphy sent me a letter stating the number of names that he had summoned, and that there were eight that had not been summoned What became of these eight? They were added to the list Were you by when they were added? No, but I swear that I gave directions that it should be done I now recollect speaking to Molloy in my own office while he was doing it, they were put on the panel, and they were returned Was it in the discretion of Mr Moss or Molloy that you reposed confidence as to placing those names on the panel? In the first instance it was, but it does not follow that I was obliged to leave them there, nor did I leave them there I ask you simply this, with respect to making that list, which was made partly in your presence, and partly in your absence, to whom did you leave it to decide, as to the placing of the names according to their respectability was it to Molloy or to Mr Moss? Upon their consideration together. Molloy was writing the lists and Mr Moss was selecting the names out of the Bailiffs' lists. Then, as far as you recollect the names were placed according to the order read out by Mr Moss? I believe so And that list was afterwards left with you, and the panels were made out from that list? Yes How did they differ? By the virtue of my oath they are exactly made out as I would have made them out myself, if I had been well Do those panels contain all the names on that list? They do Are those names in the same order as they are in the list? No, I changed some of them myself How many did you change? I don't know how many

BARON SMITH —Where you did not change the collacation, was it because, upon examining the list, you approved of that as a just and proper collacation? Just so, upon my oath

Mr BRADY —Can you say that you altered the position of six names on that list? I do not think I did Can you say that you omitted six names that were on the list? I don't think I did

BARON SMITH —Do you believe that you altered more than three or four? I believe I did

Mr. BRADY —Do you think there are three names in the list that are not in the panel? There is not a name in the list, that is not on the panel Are there six names on the panel, that are not on the list? I cannot say Are you able to form a belief whether you altered the position of three persons on that panel? I did Can you form a belief that you altered the position of six names? I cannot say.

CHIEF JUSTICE.—Do you wish Mr Attorney-General to ask Mr Beere any questions?

ATTORNEY-GENERAL.—Oh no, my Lord.

Arthur Moore Moss, Esq examined by Mr MURPHY.—Have you seen the Clerk of the Crown's panel? I saw it in this Court when this Commission commenced. Where? With Mr. Gibbs the Clerk of the Crown. Did you read it over? Never, I heard it read over; I never had an opportunity of reading it myself. It was in Court I first saw it. When you say that the first time you saw that panel in Court, do you mean by that panel, that piece of parchment? I mean no such thing; I mean to say that as to the arrangement of the Jurors as called by the Clerk of the Crown, I did not see it until I saw it in Court. Did you know any thing of the arrangement of that panel until you saw it in the hands of the Clerk of the Crown? I did not. Then, am I to understand that you had nothing to do with the arrangement of the names of the Jurors who were to serve here at this Commission? I had. But you had nothing to do with the panel? Not with the panel that I heard called by the Clerk of the Crown. Then did you, in point of fact, take any part in the previous arrangement of the names before put into the panel? I was assisting the Sheriff in regulating them when the lists of the Bailiffs came in. the panel was never made up, but what I thought would be a panel was made up. the panel called in court, in point of the placing of the names, I think is quite different from that. Now, will you state what it was you thought to be the panel? There are gentlemen now on the Grand Jury whose names are not on that panel and were on the other one. Is there, in point of fact, a panel which you assisted in making out? There was a panel, but it was never put together Did you ever see the skeleton of a panel? I did, I suppose it was intended to be one

ATTORNEY-GENERAL —Was it upon paper? It was

Mr MURPHY—Did you see a list, which in point of fact, was to be a panel? I did

Mr MURPHY —Who prepared that list? I assisted in preparing it the panels were referred to, and the names were taken down with reference to the Bailiff's lists, the impression upon my mind is, that every person who had been summoned was put down Who else assisted besides you? Mr Beere and his clerk Whom did you assist? Mr Beere What part did Mr Beere take in it? The placing of the jurors was submitted to him for his approval How did you manage when he was out of the room? To the best of my judgment, we went on, when Mr Beere was out of the room, I went on giving the names, and Molloy entered them down Do you recollect what day that was? I think it was the day before the Commission opened I suppose it was you managed the whole matter? No, Mr Beere was consulted in what was the principal part, the whole was submitted to his approval Did you remain in the room till the list was completed? I did not, there were some names not down in the list when I left it Did you at any time suggest any names that were not in that list? The impression upon my mind is, that I did suggest persons who were not summoned, although they were on the Bailiff's lists for summonses Who finished the list? Molloy Was Mr Beere there when you left the room? I don't think he was. Do you know of any names being added after that? I never saw the list since Did Mr Beere give you any directions as to the course you should pursue? I cannot recollect, as to the mode of doing it, I think there were two panels there What two panels were these? One was, I think, the panel of the year that Mr Kelly was Sheriff Did you pursue the order of those two panels in arranging the names on that list? I think I did very nearly Did you ever suggest to Mr Beere, or give him the names of any persons that were not on those lists, or those panels you speak of? Immediately after the Commission opened I assisted him in filling up the summonses Did you ever suggest to him any list besides those that were served with summonses? I recollect to have mentioned to him very many respectable names who were never on the Petty Jury panel, and, who, I thought, ought to be summoned Can you state how it was that you came to be concerned in that occupation? I thought there was no impropriety in doing it—and I am of the same opinion still. I thought I was doing a public service Then it was entirely with a view to a public service that you did this? It was, upon my oath, and to assist a man, who, in my judgment, did not know much of the county Do you mean to say that the Sub-Sheriff is so ignorant of the county, that he required your service? There were very many persons that had been repeatedly a cause of complaint for not being in the Jury-box, and, as far as lay in my power, I assisted to have every one of them summoned. Do you think Mr Beere ignorant of the county? He may know the county very well—but I think I know it better Then of those persons that Mr. Beere did not know, who suggested the order in which they ought to be on the panel? In a great degree they were guided by other panels

CHIEF JUSTICE—Did you in any degree assist as to the collocation? I did

Mr MURPHY—In making this list, did Mr Beere over-rule your judgment in any one instance? He did in several instances Can you name any one person as to whom he overruled you? I don't this moment recollect

BARON SMITH—Might he not have done so out of your presence? Certainly

Mr MURPHY—By what standard did you govern your judgment in the selection By two other panels Then you took no other test than the occular demonstration? I think that is all, I think the other panels were pretty fairly placed, the understanding between Mr. Beere and myself was, that the first men on the panel should be those taken from the Grand Jury panel, and after them, those who were Magistrates, and then Record Jurors, I am almost positive Mr Beere had them placed from the Grand Jury panel Did you at any time give Mr Beere a list, from your own private knowledge of parties, that you had not seen on either of those panels? I am not confident that I did, but I am positive that I had summonses filled up for persons that I did not see on those two panels Can you form any idea of the number of persons for whom you had summonses filled up, that you had not seen on those panels? There might be thirty or forty perhaps Were they persons that you never saw summoned in any Court here? No Do you mean to say that there were thirty or forty persons summoned who had not been summoned on former occasions? I know there were very respectable persons summoned, who had not been summoned before Do you recollect the names of any of them? I do, Colonel Price is one, Mr Joseph Fishbourne is another Do you recollect any more? Yes. Mr William Bulter Scott, Mr Edward Palmer Mr Humphrey, Mr Dames, Mr. Dawson French, Mr Franks, Mr James Short, jun, Mr Charles Hart, Mr Robert Roe, Mr. Joseph Palmer, Mr Owens, I don't at this moment recollect any more, I got a list of the persons who were not in the habit of attending, and I filled up summonses for them, I asked several persons to give me a list of persons who were not in the habit of being summoned, and I got names from several persons. Did these gentlemen volunteer to give you lists, or did you solicit them? There was a general feeling and a wish, that every man respectable enough to be a Juror, should attend. Now why did these gentlemen go to you, and not to the Sheriff or Sub-Sheriff? Because I declared my intention to have them all summoned. Had you made yourself very busy upon any other occasion, with respect to other Juries? Upon a former occasion I acted in the same way, I think it was at the Summer Assizes. Am I to understand, that you ever took so active a part upon any former occasion, as upon this Commission? I rather think I took more trouble upon this Commission than before. Did you consider it a very heavy labour? I felt it no labour

BARON SMITH —Do you recollect at the last Assizes, while you were discharging your duties as a Juror, that several Jurors complained that a great deal of duty had been thrown upon them? Complaints were then made, and that is what brought me forward, and even the Jurors themselves, had a notion of going forward in a body, for the purpose of complaining that too much of the duty was thrown upon them

Mr MURPHY —Can you call to mind what position those strangers filled? Some of them were high up, and some of them were not so   Do you happen to recollect that they hold the same position on the panel? They do not, the placing in the panel is quite different from what it was in the list made up in my presence   Do any of those persons who were strangers, hold high places on the panel? Some of them do   Can you mention the names of some of them? Mr William Scott   Mr Joseph Fishbourne   Mr Hutchinson, Mr Swan   Are all these persons that had not served before? They are   Did Mr Beere complain of the collocation you were making? He did   Did he complain that you were putting persons out of their proper places on the panel? He did

CHIEF JUSTICE.—You have enumerated a good many gentlemen whose names you sent in, either by a list or verbally, were those gentlemen among your intimate friends and acquaintances? Yes, there were some of them I knew, my idea was, that my most intimate friends should come in, as well as any other man   Were any of them strangers to you? At that time there were some of them but I have become acquainted with them since the Commission

BARON SMITH —And your feeling with respect to your friends, was, that you ought not to have them spared, but that they should undergo the same trouble as those who were strangers to you? Certainly, my Lord

James Molloy, examined by Mr D'ARCY —Were you employed by Mr Beere before this Commission? I was How many Bailiffs had he out previous to this Commission? I believe four or five   Did you make out the lists? I did. Where did you make them out? Some of them in my own house.   From what instructions did you make them out? By the Sub-Sheriffs' order   What did you take them from? From a return the Sub-Sheriff gave me.

Q

What did you do with that return? I returned it to the Sub-Sheriff When did you last see that return? Not since I gave it to the Sheriff Was it you wrote out the panel that is now calling by the Clerk of the Crown? I wish to see it. (the Clerk of the Crown hands the panel to witness) it was, that is in my hand-writing From what paper did you take that panel? Mr Moss read out the names, and I wrote them down What did he read them from? He had the Bailiff's lists before him, and I believe the old panels Was there any body else by when he read them out? The Sub-Sheriff was in the room a part of the time, and a son of mine Did you hear any dispute between Mr Moss and the Sub-Sheriff as to the place particular persons should hold on the panel? I don't recollect that I did Upon your oath, the names that you put down there, did you put them down from Moss or Mr Beere? From Mr Moss, I have no recollection that I took them from any body else

Mr SMITH, (one of the Triors,)—What directions did Mr Beere give? He left it all to Mr Moss, I believe.

ATTORNEY-GENERAL—Mr. Beere at this time was not well, I believe? He appeared not to be well How long were you making out this list? The best part of a day Was Mr Moss there the whole day? He was not Where was Mr Beere during the day? He was in and out of the room. What was before Mr. Moss, was it the Bailiff's lists? Yes Besides that, there were old panels on the table? Yes Now, was it not by the assistance of the old panels, and with the lists, that Mr Moss read the names? I believe some of them Look at that paper, (handing witness a paper) is that one of the papers or not? I can't be positive. Was not one of the papers which he had, the Lent panel of the present year? I cannot say, I did not read it. Did you see Mr Moss making use of it? I did

---

CHARGE TO THE TRIORS ON THE FIRST ISSUE

CHIEF JUSTICE —Gentlemen. there has been an entire day lost in this enquiry, but it is by no means thrown away. It is a most important enquiry —Nothing can be more fatal to the interests of justice than that the slightest suspicion should be thrown upon its administration. and if this challenge be well founded, we shall have to deplore an occurrence that will bring the character of the administration of the laws into disrepute, and you will therefore carefully enquire whether, or not, such an imputation be well founded upon the evidence which you have heard

Gentlemen, your issue is to try whether that panel has been arrayed by the Sheriff, or not —If a stranger has been allowed to array it from any improper motives, it is a most reprehensible. mischievous, and alarming practice

I do not think though, if either the Sheriff or the Sub-Sheriff received assistance from those who are better informed than himself in arraying this panel, that it can be justly said that it is the panel of those who assisted him, provided he exercised his own judgment upon it, and either adopted it altogether, or altered it according to his own judgment. It mostly happens that the High Sheriff is a gentleman who knows very little more of the county than his own neighbourhood, and must depend upon the better information of his Sub-Sheriff, and if his Sub-Sheriff received such assistance as I have mentioned, the panel made with such assistance is his panel, and also the panel of his High Sheriff, and the best informed Sub-Sheriff may stand in need of such assistance, and every Sub-Sheriff must have a first year of office in which he cannot do without it, on the other hand, if the Sub-Sheriff in this case permitted any officious man to meddle with his panel and to put names upon it, and to dictate to him what was to be his panel, without exercising his own judgment upon it,—in short, if he from any motive, corrupt or otherwise, adopted a pannel made by another man, and merely lent his official name to another man's panel, in the whole or in part, then this challenge is supported, otherwise not.

VERDICT

TRIORS, we find that the panel has been arrayed by the Sheriff.

SECOND ISSUE

CLERK OF THE CROWN.--Gentlemen, your next issue is to try whether the panel is an impartial one or not.

George Gibbs, Esq (Clerk of the Crown,) examined by Mr MURPHY.—Is that panel in your hand, the panel upon which you have called the Juries during this Commission? It is Every Jury that has been sworn during this Commission, has been sworn out of this panel Do you see the name of Arthur Moore Moss on that panel? I do What place does he hold on that panel? The twenty-second Do you see the name of Captain Moss? I see the name of Thomas Moss What number does he hold? The fifteenth Do you see the name of Robert Belton? I do. What number? Twenty Do you see the name of John Southern? Yes, it is on the sixth page, his name is about the hundredth Do you see the name of William Clarke? Yes, William Clarke, of Green Grove Mills What place does he hold on the panel? His name is on the fifth page Do you see the name of Christopher Bailey? Yes Where is he placed? On the the third page Do you see the name of Rice Meredyth? Yes, on the third page Robert Greenham? On the fifth page Robert Doyne, of Castletown? On the third page Edward L Swan? On the second page Humphrey Palmer? On the second page William Bell? On the third page Maunsell Dames? On the third page William Wall Grey? On the fourth page James Hutchinson? On the first page, fifth man William Butler Scott? On the first page, seventh man Emor Hart? On the second page, thirty-sixth man John Butler, of Castletown? On the second page Edward Seale? On the seventh page Henry Brereton? On the second page, about the twenty-seventh man Lodge Philips? On the third page Gilbert Greaves? On the fourth page George Galbraith? On the fifth page James Edward Scott? On the first page, the sixth man Pierce Robinson? On the fifth page.

John Abbott? On the seventh page —He was excused, being a county cess collector

Mr MURPHY.—That is the end of that class, we will now go to another. Do you see the name of Thomas N Kenny on the panel? Yes. What place does he hold? He is on the eighth page George Anderson of Fisherstown? On the fourth page. John Butler, of Ballinakill? On the ninth page Robert Cassidy? He is not on the panel

CHIEF JUSTICE —What did you ask his name for?

Mr. MURPHY —He is a freeholder of the county

CHIEF JUSTICE —I am quite incapable of understanding the course that is taking, but I give Mr Murphy credit—which every body who knows him must give him, for having an object of a proper kind in taking this course

Mr MURPHY —Do you see the name of Joseph Lyons, of Moyally, on the panel? He is not on the panel Daniel Egan of Mountrath? His name is on the fifth page —He is excused by an affidavit. Edward Willmot? He is not on the panel John Harvey, of Ballyroan? On the ninth page Patrick Lawlor, of Timnikill? On the fourth page John Lawlor? On the ninth page Patrick Lawlor? On the ninth page Bernard Fitzpatrick of Portarlington? Not on the panel John Kelly, of Stradbally? He is the Coroner John Dunn, of Rahanarone? Not on the panel Denis Kilbride? On the ninth page Edward Comerford, of Ballinakill? On the sixth page Michael Dillon? The first man on the fifth page Patrick Dillon, of Ross? On the sixth page. Andrew Ryan, of Ballyroan? On the ninth page Patrick Dillon Delany, of Oldtown Lodge? Not on the panel James Helsham Ryan? Not on the panel Peter Brenan, of Maryborough? On the fourth page Michael Delany? Not on the panel William Kelly? On the fourth page William Thornhill, of Ballynakill Not on the panel

Edward Beere, Esq Sub-Sheriff, examined by Mr BRADY —You said that you diligently inspected the panel, and made some alterations in it, and where you did not make any alteration, that you abstained from it because you coincided with Mr Moss, and that in fact you exercised your own judgment upon the whole panel? Yes. Let me ask you why the name of Robert Cassidy is not on the panel? When I came into the county I found that he was left off by Mr Lewis, my predecessor, who is his own relation, and if I did put him on I was afraid it might be supposed that I was doing any thing that was annoying to him

BARON SMITH —Is there any connection between Mr Lewis and Mr. Cassidy? I understand they are brothers-in-law Mr Lewis had filled the office of Sub-Sheriff for several years before I came there about two years ago I came down here, and I did not find the name of Mr Cassidy on the panel, and I understand it never was on the panel

Mr BRADY —How does it happen that the name of Joseph Lyons, of Movany, is not on the panel The reason is marked on the panel, a return was made to me that he was not in the country, and it was my belief that he was not in the country, and that was the only reason What was the bailiff's name who made that return? Abraham Dunn Have you seen him in this court since the commencement of the present commission? I think I have And yet you believed he was out of the country? I know nothing more about him than that that is the return of the bailiff You don't know whether he is a resident of the county? I know nothing more about him than that that is the return of the bailiff Do you know any reason why Bernard Fitzpatrick, of Portarlington is not on the panel? I never heard of the man before and that is the reason he is not on the panel. Why is not John Dunn, of Ballyroan, on the panel? He wrote me word that he was in the habit of giving Mr. Lewis a Guinea for leaving him off, and he requested me to leave off his name, and that he would give me a guinea. What did you say to that? I am very intimate with the man, and I said to him just in a joking way, " I will leave you off, and I'll send you a horse to grass." Do you know James Helsham Ryan? I never heard his name before. Do you know Patrick Dillon Delany? I never heard of him before. Do you know William Thornhill? I never heard of his being called on a panel in this county? Do you know Edward Willmot? I understood he was not a resident in the county, and he told me himself that he was extremely ill, and he pledged his honour that he could not sit in the jury-box if he was put into it. Do you know Thomas N. Kenny? I do. Can you tell whether according to his rank and respectability he ought to be above or below Thomas Moss? He ought to be below him. Do you think he ought to be below Arthur Moore Moss? It depends upon whether you put down a man for his respectability or his money, I believe Mr. Arthur Moore Moss to be of a very respectable family. Do you think Thomas N. Kenny ought to be below Arthur Moore Moss? I do. According to your notion of respectability do you think that Arthur Moore Moss ought to be so high on the panel as the twenty-second man? I think he ought as to his rank and respectability I do not see that he is placed wrong. Do you know John Southern? I do. Do you think he ought to be above Thomas N. Kenny? It depends upon circumstances, I do not think he ought indeed, but I do not think it signifies much where a man is placed on the panel? Do you know Robert Greenham? I do. Do you think he ought to be above Thomas N Kenny ' I don't know Do you think he ought to be above Denis Kilbride? I think one equally respectable as the other Will you undertake to say that your panel is arrayed according to the rank and respectability of the names it contains? It is arrayed according to the best of my knowledge where there are four hundred persons upon the panel it is impossible to place them exactly according to their rank and respectability Do you think that William Clarke, of Green Grove Mills, ought to be above Denis Kilbride? I do And above John Harden? Yes Do you think Edward Comerford is in his proper place? I believe he is placed in the same place he has always been Did you think it a proper thing to place Edward Scott and his son next to each other on the panel? I did

BARON SMITH —Are they both Magistrates? They are

Mr. BRADY — Do you know John Butler, of Ballinakill? I do Do you know whether he ought to be above Lodge Philips? I think Lodge Philips ought to be above him, I met Mr Butler walking here for he was obliged to walk, and he begged of me to leave him off, he is a poor man, and I met him walking on as wet a day as possible, at all events he is placed rightly Do you know George Galbraith? I do Ought he to be above Denis Kilbride? I think he ought, I think after the third or fourth page it does not signify where they are placed Do you say you were governed solely by the consideration of rank and respectability? No By what other consideration? By the custom of the country Had not Denis Kilbride consented to serve on Nisi Prius juries? He had And Edward Comerford? Yes Do either of those gentlemen hold a position on this panel such as they ought? I think they do What do you mean by the custom of the country?

Where I heard they were always stationed on the panel
You know most of the Jurors? I do Upon the whole,
how many Roman Catholics are upon the panel? Upon
my oath I don't know, on the general run, upon my oath
I don't know whether they are Roman Catholics or Protestants Upon your oath you are not able to say whether
any Roman Catholics have been upon these juries on this
Commission? Upon my oath I don't know whether there
have been or not I suppose you are equally ignorant of
the politics of Mr Kenny—do you happen to know what
his religion or politics are? Of my own knowledge I
don't know Or of Mr Anderson's? No Nor Mr Thornhill's? I never heard the man's name Nor Mr. John
Butler's? I know nothing at all about his politics.

Arthur Moore Moss, Esq, examined by Mr. MURPHY —
Do you recollect the summonses you sent out, that were not
on the list? I do not Do you recollect the nineteen
names you gave us a while ago? I recollect some of
them You know the people of this county pretty well?
I do Do you mean their persons or their property?
Their persons Do you know their politics? I know
the politics of some of them. How many of the nineteen
strangers that you sent out summonses to, are Roman
Catholics? If you tell me the names I'll tell you as
far as I can Will you, upon your oath, give the name
of any one? Michael Weldon is one John Lyons of
Moyanna is another. Mr Maher near Abeyleix is a third,
and I think, one of the Mr Lawler's, that is on the panel
Did you know Mr Fishburn's politics? Upon my oath,
I did not know his politics at the time that I had the summonses filled up for him Do you know Mr Swan's politics? I do not. Nor Mr Stannus's? No Nor Mr Franks's?
No Nor Mr Robert Roe's? No Nor Mr Charles Harte's?

No Nor Mr Joseph Palmer's ? No There are some of those names that I heard complaints against, for not being summoned, and I was anxious that they should be brought forward You have been an attentive observer of what has been going on at this Commission, can you tell how many Roman Catholics have served during this Commission ? Mr Dunne of Ballinakill served, and Mr Dunne of Ballymanus objected to himself In one case ? Yes Don't you think that Mr Joseph Lyons would be a proper Juror to serve here ? I think he would Do you know Mr Egan of Mountrath ? I rather think it a hardship to be called upon to give an opinion of these gentlemen

CHIEF JUSTICE —I was just waiting for you to say that, because it appears to me that unless perfectly indispensible it is a particularly invidious enquiry It may have bad consequences

Mr Moss —I will say this upon my solemn oath that I thought every man of every class and creed should be summoned without distinction, and I never have thought that any man should or should not be summoned on account of his particular feeling On the contrary, I think there are more summoned of that second class (as they are distinguished) than ever

Mr MURPHY —Do you happen to know what position they hold ? I am not saying as to that Was not the panel formed from the list that you arranged ? No such thing, it was not at all placed in that way Is not every man that is in the panel on the list that you had ? If you will mention the name of any man I will answer you in the best way that I can

CHARGE

Gentlemen—I must recall your attention at the end of this tedious and painful discussion to the question you have to try, whether this panel has been impartially arrayed so as to afford a fair trial to the prisoners who have challenged the array, and by their challenge have insisted that persons have been put on the panel in high places more likely to convict the prisoners than others who have been left off or put in lower places who would have been more likely to acquit the prisoners

That very plain question has led to the discussion of another, its connexion with which I am unable to discover, that is, whether the Roman Catholic freeholders of the Queen's County have been returned on that panel in such numbers and in such places as their fair pretensions on the score of rank and respectability entitle them to. If they think otherwise, it is not surprizing that they should feel sorely and jealously, but it is very much to be lamented that so inappropriate an opportunity should have been selected for bringing this complaint before the public, and to that complaint, and that alone, the evidence we have listened to, has been directed we have nothing to do with the question whether that complaint is well founded, or whether the evidence you have heard has not afforded a sufficient answer and explanation, but we must confine our attention to the single enquiry whether this is an impartial panel I might say that it has not appeared to this moment of what Religion the prisoners are, but it would be affectation not to assume that they are Roman Catholics, and we know from the Crown book that they are charged with an offence connected with the existing insurrection but when I look at the words of the challenge, I cannot imagine to myself, how the evidence we have heard, supposing all the inferences claimed from it to be well founded, can apply to the question before us, unless we are bound to identify that insurrection, and the crimes it has produced, with the Religion of the prisoners, an insult and calumny directed against my Roman Catholic fellow subjects, in which I cannot consent to participate. Certainly the time has been during the old civil wars out of which the penal code grew, in which offences against the state connected themselves with the religious persuasion of the parties, and more recently when the public mind was much agitated by the question of Emancipation, there might have been, and there did arise, questions in courts of justice that would excuse the jealous and angry feelings which have led to this challenge; but since the Catholic Relief Bill has passed, since all distinctions between the two religions have been abolished, and all the king's subjects of all persuasions have become equally entitled to all civil rights and privileges, since, as I had hoped, we had become one people, I am at a loss to discover any other grounds for this anomalous proceeding, except the assumption of that opinion which I have deprecated, that the wicked and dangerous conspiracy now infesting this county is identified with the profession of the Roman Catholic religion. To alledge that in the trial of ordinary offences, a Roman Catholic cannot be fairly tried by Protestants, would be extravagant and ridiculous; and to confine that assertion to the crimes of such insurgents, as upon this Commission, we deal with, implies a cruel aspersion upon both religions, the truth and justice of which my heart and understanding equally disclaim. It is the misfortune of this strange proceeding, that we all in our several departments, find it difficult to abstain from topics, which belong less to a court of justice than to a political assembly, but I cannot avoid suggesting, that a fair and candid mind might discover other causes than partiality and corruption in sworn public servants, for the construction of this panel in the instances complained of Property is generally, though not universally, adopted as the standard of rank and respectability, by those who have not more precise information, and it must be recollected, that for nearly a century before the year 1793, Roman Catholics were under the interdicts of the Penal Code, the dreadful policy of which was to lower their grade and influence in the country by the means of impoverishment Since that year the acquisition and enjoyment of property has been opened to Roman Catholics and I am unfeignedly happy to say, that all over Ireland, they have been rising to their natural and due position with that recuperative energy, which belongs to those from whom a pressure has been taken off, which had kept them down. But, we all know, that in fact, and according to the nature of things, that change takes place in different degrees, in different districts, and, my brother Smith and I, who have administered justice in all parts of Ireland, well know, that in several western and southern counties, such as Galway, Kerry, Mayo, Tipperary, Waterford, Kilkenny, and others I mention, gentlemen of the Roman Catholic religion crowd the Grand and Petty Jury boxes, not because they are Roman Catholics, but because their rank and property entitle them to those stations to which the wisdom of the legislature has restored them. In many other counties that has not as yet equally operated, and, perhaps, this county may be one of them Surely, if there be any reason for dissatisfaction, or, even for jealousy against this panel, it would have been wise, and generous, and charitable, to look to those other causes, rather than to adopt an invidious proceeding, calculated to bring justice into contempt, to impute corruption and perjury to a public officer, and to convey an unmerited censure upon jurors, both Protestant and Catholic. Other topics press upon my mind and feelings, which I must restrain, and I shall only add, that in my youth I witnessed the commencement, and in my advanced life, the progress and ultimate success of the public measure to which I have alluded, and never once changed my well-known opinions upon it, but, if it is to be followed by the revival and perpetuation of religious discord, I and many others must feel a disappointment proportioned to what had been our expectations. Gentlemen, your duty is to try, whether this is an impartial panel, or has it been so constructed as to deprive the prisoners of a fair trial. If persons have been left off that panel, or corruptly placed, or postponed in such a manner and to such an extent, as would deprive the prisoners of impartial jurors, or throw them into the power of jurors prejudiced against them, then this is not an impartial panel, and you will find accordingly, but, if otherwise, there is no pretence for this challenge.

BARON SMITH.—Gentlemen Triers, my Lord Chief Justice having done me the honor of enquiring whether I have any thing to add, my answer is, that I have not. In his Lordship's positions I entirely concur. On some matters not directly pertinent to the question, but which have in argument been introduced and mingled with it, I shall avow very briefly what my opinions are. I conceive that the legal rights and capacities of every man should be considered and allowed, without reference to his religion. If a person were a fit one to be returned upon the Grand Jury, or so circumstanced that his name ought to appear upon the Record or Petit Jury panel, I would not exclude him from either, because he happened to be a Roman Catholic

Neither, on the other hand, would I place him in a situation to which on other grounds he was not entitled, merely because he belonged to that religion   Though at the same time, if the situation were an honourable one, and it should seem difficult to ascertain which of two persons had the best pretensions to it, I might prefer the Catholic for the present, in order to put that class of my countrymen in possession of whatever distinctions they have lately recovered the capacity to enjoy   But I protest against the doctrine—I never can admit it—that a Catholic prisoner is not safe in the hands of a Protestant Jury   Such an opinion would be as false as it would be mischievous   By a parity of reasoning we should have to hold, that a Protestant prisoner would not be safe in the hands of a Catholic Jury   If a Roman Catholic cannot safely trust his case to a Protestant Juror, can he securely trust it to the decision of a Protestant Judge ? Or when Roman Catholics are appointed Judges, can the rights of Protestants be safely committed to their protection ? Such distrusts and jealousies are monstrous and pernicious   I have now been for many years upon the Bench, and I believe it is known of me—and I call God to witness, that the fact is so—that I have never bestowed a thought upon the question of what was the religion of the prisoner whom I was trying, or the suitor upon whose rights it became my duty to decide   In Church I am a Protestant—every where else I am but an Irishman and a Judge

VERDICT

Triors   We find that the panel has been impartially arrayed.

TRIAL OF FRANCIS ADAMS AND THOMAS LANGTON

For administering an Unlawful Oath

Tuesday, 15th June, 1832

The Clerk of the Crown was proceeding to swear the Jury, when Mr. White, Attorney for Adams, challenged Mr William Fishbourne peremptorily

CLERK OF THE CROWN —You can only challenge for cause

Mr BRADY —My Lords. in this case the prisoners stand charged with a felony, punishable by transportation The question as to the right of peremptory challenge in such a case, has arisen before in this Special Commission. and your Lordships have pronounced an opinion upon it It is not my wish to raise any discussion here all I desire is, to put the question in a train for the decision of the highest criminal tribunal in the country I submit, whether the challenge be well founded or not, that unless it be demurred to, your Lordships will have no alternative but to allow it to be received I mention it now merely with a view, if the Attorney-General be pleased to do so, that it may be put into a situation for solemn argument

CHIEF JUSTICE —According to my recollection, the decision that we came to, when this question arose before,

R

in the course of this Commission, was this, that having got the opinion of the twelve Judges upon a question which never arose until the last Spring Circuit, we ought not to receive the challenge If there be any thing in your opinion, inaccurate in that decision, or any way in which, out of this Court, you can get a solemn discussion of the question, I should be glad of it but we see no reason for changing the opinion we then formed, and we shall, in this case, abide by our decision in the former I shall take a note of your challenge

[The Trial then proceeded]

First Witness, *Robert Large*, examined by the ATTORNEY-GENERAL —I live with my brother John at Dromeen I remember the morning of Good Friday last, I was in his house that morning, between eight and nine o'clock that morning as my brother and I were sitting at our breakfast, I heard a noise in the kitchen I stood up, and as soon as I did a man met me at the parlour door, and bid me stand back, he had a detonating fowling-piece, four men came in, and one stood at the parlour door, the man with the gun ordered my brother to go on his knees, the four men were all armed, another man had a carbine, the rest had all pistols, and one of them had a bayonet; my brother went on his knees, and the man that had the detonating fowling-piece threw a book on the floor, and ordered my brother to take it up, he threw the book on the ground before my brother went on his knees the other three men were by at this my brother did take up the book, and the man desired him to repeat what he would say to him he swore him to give up land to the Widow Fennell, I know what land that was, it was about two acres of land and a house, that Sir Edward Walsh, when the lease was out, gave him, that land was not in my brother's own hands it was occupied by a cottier Fennell had been the former occupier, after the oath was taken, I stood up and I told them that it was to Sir Edward Walsh they should go about it, that we had nothing to do with it after that when they were going away one of them said to another, " we did not ask for the arms, serjeant " the serjeant, as they called him, turned back, and handed my brother the book before he handed the book the second time he asked him if he had any arms or ammunition in the house and he said, " we will search for them " then I told them to search away, they did not make any search for the arms they swore my brother whether he had any arms or ammunition or any thing belonging to his Majesty the four men were in the room all this time I could not identify the man that was at the door after that they went away, they were about ten minutes in the parlour (Here the witness pointed out the prisoner Langton, as the man who had the carbine) That man presented the carbine at me, and desired me to sit, and he cocked it afterwards, and swore he would shoot me if I did not sit down, I had never seen him before to my knowledge in about a fortnight after that I saw him, I think there were four men with him in custody

Cross-examined by Mr D'Arcy —It was John Carty that was in possession of the land at that time he was in possession of it for about three years, it was about three years since the lease had expired Sir Edward Walsh desired my brother to give it to him Carty never had these lands before I don't exactly know the rent he paid, I am sure that the oath was, that he should give up the land, but whether they mentioned the house or not, I cannot say, I don't recollect that I ever before saw any of those men, my sister and mother and sister-in-law came into the parlour shortly after these men came in. they are here, there were two little girls in the house, and, I believe, three servant men. there are none of the men here that were in the house, I am sure there were three of my brothers men in the house at that time

Second Witness, *Sarah Large*, examined by Mr Tickell —I remember the morning of Good Friday last. I was living that day in my son's house. I am the mother of the last witness. the dog made a noise when I was in the kitchen that morning. I went out to the hall-door. two men approached the door. and they rushed in, one man had a gun in his hand. and when I turned round in the hall there were three more at my back. they were all armed with pistols. the man with the gun rushed in first. my two sons were at the table in the parlour, I saw the man present the gun at my eldest son John, and he asked him to give up two acres of ground. he made him stand up and he threw down a book to swear him, that he would give up the ground. he said, that he wanted it for the widow Fennell. the man that had the gun presented it at my son Robert, and I made a snap at the gun, he pulled the gun out of my hand, they all drew up round me. and one of them pulled out a pistol, and struck me in the face. he made me sit, and he swore vehemently, that he would shoot me as soon as he would shoot a mad dog. I am satisfied that both the prisoners at the bar were there. I cannot state, that I saw them do any thing but just moving about the room, with the pistols in their hands, they did not offer any violence, further than to advance up towards me, when the other man struck me

Cross examined by Mr Brady —Are you quite certain about these men? I am. Are you quite certain as to the one and the other? I am. Were you always so? I was.

but I did not wish to have any thing to do with them, if I could avoid it. What do you mean by your wishing not to have any thing to do with them? Because I would rather have done with them at once. How soon after did you see them? I saw one of them that evening in Stradbally. I had heard of his arrest before I went there. I had some doubt on my mind when I saw him through a window; but when I saw him at the gate I knew him immediately. Mr Clancy and Mr Johnson I think, were with me. it was to these gentlemen I expressed some doubt; but when I met the man at Mr Clancy's gate, in a few moments after I knew him at once. I believe my daughter-in-law was with me. there were two or three of the police with him, when I met him. I was put to the window for the purpose of seeing him. he was in the yard. I thought I then knew the man —but I was not positive, there were two men with him in the yard. I did not know them, Adams is the man, I believe it was a fortnight after that I saw the other man. When you saw the man at the gate, did you not know that he was one of the three you saw in the yard? Certainly.

JUROR —Was the man's dress changed from the time you saw him from the window until you saw him at the gate. No.

CHIEF JUSTICE —Where did you see the prisoner Langton? At Sir Edward Walsh's. I saw him through a window. there were other persons with him. Did you know him when you saw him? I had some doubt; but when they brought him to the hall-door, I knew him. When he was brought to the hall door was he alone, or with others? There were two others with him. On the occasion of seeing the man at Mr Clancy's gate, did any person whatever give you any assistance to distinguish that man from the others? No When you saw the three from the window, what did you do? I pointed to the prisoner When looking through the window at Sir Edward Walsh's, did any body distinguish for you between the prisoner and others? Not one Between the time that you saw him at the window and his being brought round to the hall-door, did any body in that interval, say any thing to you about the man that you had a doubt about? Not one

JUROR—What removed the doubt off your mind? I knew him through the window, but I was better satisfied when I saw him at the hall-door

CHIEF JUSTICE—You said, that you wished to have nothing to do with him? Yes Did that wish at all induce you to say any thing about doubtings, when you said, that you had a doubt about him, were you sincere, or did you really doubt? Of the first man I had some doubt—but the doubt expressed as to the man at Sir Edward Walsh's, was not a sincere doubt

JUROR—If you had seen that man at Sir Edward Walsh's the first time in the open air, suppose you had not seen him through the window, would you identify him at once? I would, certainly

Third Witness, *Margaret Knowles*, examined by Mr MAHONY—I am servant to Mr John Large I was living with him on Good-Friday last, about eight o'clock that morning I saw some men at his house they had arms I saw five men in all I was in the scullery when they passed through the kitchen I saw one man come in by the back door, he had a gun and a pistol he went into the parlour where my master was, I opened the back door for him he was trying himself to open it, I saw him afterwards in the parlour I had an opportunity of seeing the men both the prisoners at the bar were there that day. I am positive that I saw them there that day.

Cross-examined by Mr. D'Arcy.—I let in one of the men, the others came in by the hall-door, I saw them running round as hard as they could to get into the hall-door there was one little window in the scullery the distance between the window and the back-door was about a yard and a half, I had never seen any of those men before. I think I would know others of them if I saw them. I saw one of the prisoners the day after at Stradbally. Had you been told before you saw them at Stradbally that one of the persons who had been at your master's house was taken? Yes. I heard it from a police-man when I went to Stradbally, to the barracks. Sir Edward Walsh, Mr. Hunt Johnson, and Mr. Singleton were there. Did Mr. Singleton say any thing to you about the man? He did. What did he bid you say? He bid me say nothing but the truth. Did he say any thing more to you? He asked me what sort of man was he that was before I saw the man. I was shown the man after that. he stood in the yard, and I stood at a window. Mr. Singleton was at the window with me. he said nothing but bid me look close at him. Had you said any thing before to him about the man? I told him that I saw him. Did you mean by that, that you saw him at your master's house? Yes. And then he said to you "look close at him?" Yes, there were two men standing with the prisoner at that time I never saw the other two men before. I did not know whether they were prisoners or no. How near was the prisoner standing to you when Mr. Singleton desired you to look close at him? He was not much farther than I am now from the Judge. Do you know what made Mr. Singleton desire you to look close at him? For fear I would wrong himself and myself. Had you not spoken to Mr Singleton before that, about that man? I had Did you ever see that man after that day that you saw him in Stradbally? I did in Maryborough gaol yard What brought you to the gaol yard? The day I was coming to Maryborough, I was brought up by some police men I don't know what made them bring me there Did you see Mr Singleton in the gaol? I did What day was that? Last Monday week Had you any conversation with Mr Singleton at the gaol about the prisoner? Not about that prisoner Upon your oath were you not brought there to look at those men that day? Upon my oath I was Did not Mr Single-ton bring you to look at them? He did Where did you see the other man? At Maryborough Was that the first time you saw him? It was Langton was brought in first a police man brought him in, he brought him in by himself.

CHIEF JUSTICE —You say that a police man brought Langton into the gaol, and brought him in by himself, was that the first time you saw him in the gaol? I saw him outside the window a few minutes before that How soon after you came into the gaol did you see Langton? About three quarters of a hour, I remained about three quarters of an hour in the gaol before I saw either of these priso-ners Were there any persons in company with you du-ring these three quarters of an hour? Yes, more wit-nesses and a police man. Upon your oath had any police man any conversation with you during that time about those prisoners? No. Did you say a word to any of them? I did. What was it? I was longing to get out of it —I had some talk with police men in Tolerton, they were some of the men I saw in the gaol, I cannot remember the conversation I had with them, I told them I was coming to the gaol to look at prisoners   they did not tell me that any of the men that attacked my master's house was there, I saw Mr Singleton at Maryborough gaol the day I was there, he was in the room where I was looking through the window   he was in the room when the two prisoners were brought into it   the two prisoners were brought in separately   whilst the first man was there, the second man was not brought in

JUROR.—Did you identify them before they were brought into the room?   I did

CHIEF JUSTICE.—Do you know why they were brought into the room to you?   I do not

JUROR.—How many did you see altogether when you looked out through the window?   Four men, besides the police   Had you seen any of the four men before?   I saw Langton

CHIEF JUSTICE.—Did you look through the window in the gaol at the man you had seen at Stradbally, or was it the other man you looked at through the window?   It was the other man

Mr D Arcy.—Were you not shewn through the window the man that you had seen at Stradbally?   I was

CHIEF JUSTICE.—Did any one point him out to you? No, I saw him out through the window, before any one told me who he was.   Were you brought into the yard to look at them?   I was not

Fourth Witness. *Eliza Fisher*, examined by Mr CLARKE —I recollect the morning of Good Friday last, I was in Mr Large's house that morning; I recollect persons coming into it, they were armed, I saw a person at the parlour-door, I had an opportunity of seeing his face   he was about a quarter of an hour in the house   (Witness lays the rod upon the head of the prisoner Adams) I am sure that man was there that morning, he is the person that was standing at the parlour door

Cross-examined by Mr MURPHY —I was standing in the kitchen whan I saw him I saw them all I did not mind any body but him I did not take particular notice of the others I saw him in Stradbally the day after that. When I was going to Stradbally I knew what I was going to do I see now the man that was taken I knew him when I saw him, I told the police that I knew two of the men, that man was dressed in Stradbally in the same way he is dressed now there were two or three more men with him in the yard when I saw him, I saw him through a window, Mr Singleton and Sir Edward Walsh were with me, and nobody else I saw him in the yard after that going into the cell, I was outside in the yard I was in the new gaol the first day the police-men brought us there I don't know for what purpose I did not see the prisoner that day

Fifth Witness, *Susan Large*, examined by Mr ARABIN —I am the wife of John Large, I was in the kitchen the morning our house was attacked, I think about three men entered the kitchen they went to the parlour, my husband was in the parlour at the time they were armed (Witness identifies the prisoner Adams as one of the persons who attacked the house)

Cross-examined by Mr BRADY —I saw him first in the kitchen, I think I saw the prisoner passing through the kitchen I was more sure of his face when I saw him at the gate, when I met him at the gate there was a police-man with him

Sixth Witness, *Sergeant Hooker*, examined by the ATTORNEY-GENERAL —I know both prisoners at the bar I arrested Langton he was searched by my order I arrested him in Lalor's house, I know where Langton lives, he lives about one hundred perches from Lalor's. I arrested him at 2 o'clock in the morning of the 10th of May when I arrested him he was hiding under a bed, he was lying on his face on the ground, he had his shirt and small-clothes on him. I had made a noise before I entered the house, the door was fastened and I rapped and demanded admittance. they asked me "who was in it," and I told them the police, and I told them my name and that I was the Constable of that district.

Seventh Witness, *John Suter* examined by Mr Tickell.—I am the gate-porter of the gaol, I know Langton the prisoner. I saw him the night he was brought in a prisoner, I searched him and found that upon him, (a detonating cap produced.)

Eighth Witness, *George Perry* examined by Mr Tickell.—I was on duty on Good-Friday last about ten o'clock in the morning we were following an armed party of men that were alleged to be going through the country. I observed five or six men in a lane, they were seemingly hiding and resting themselves, one man peeped out three times, at last they ran, some of them seemed fatigued. we pursued them. we did not overtake them there. I ran better than one hundred perches until I got into a field we went to search the next house we met thinking they might possibly be there. Shalloon's house is about fifty perches from where we saw them resting themselves in the lane. just as I went into that house the women were churning, and I saw a man take hold of the churn-dash. I saw him agitated, and I said "that is not the work you were at a few minutes ago," he said it was the work he was at, and that he belonged to that house. I told him that I thought he was one of the men that ran before me in the lane I asked the man of the house, and the man of the house told me that he did belong to that house, I told him that I would make a prisoner of him and the man of the house until I would ascertain whether he was or not I searched the cradle, and I found a coat, and a hat and stockings in it they were rolled in the clothes in the cradle, the clothes were warm after being taken off, he acknowledged they were his clothes, he had a riding coat that he said was his own, the man of the house told me afterwards that this man did not belong to the house, and that he thought the man was mad when he saw him strip off his clothes, he said that in his presence, I asked the prisoner was he not from Clough, and he said he was The prisoner Adams is the person I have been speaking of

Mr *John Large* produced

ATTORNEY-GENERAL—We will not ask this witness any questions we offer him for cross-examination

The evidence for the prosecution closed here

Mr BRADY —I submit that a serious question of law arises for your lordship's consideration The prisoners were indicted under the 27 Geo III ch 15 s 6 by which it had been made felony to " cause, induce, or procure to be taken, *an unlawful oath* " The 15th and 16th Geo III ch 21, s 21, had already provided against another species of offence familiar to the Whiteboy system, by making it a misdemeanor " by force, threats, or menaces, *unlawfully to impose* an oath " The 27th Geo III seemed to provide against the administration of *oaths which import something unlawful*, oaths which bind the party taking them to some illegal confederacy, to the commission or concealment of crime And accordingly, that statute has made it felony to *take* as well as to administer such an oath But the offence

created by the 15th and 16th Geo III consists in unlawfully, and by force, threats, or menaces, *imposing on another
an oath*, although that oath may import nothing unlawful,
but, on the contrary, bind the party taking it to the performance of some moral duty, or some indifferent act. The
offence consists in the " unlawful imposition of the oath "
and hence it is that this statute visits with no penalty the
party upon whom the oath is imposed. The case of the
prisoners falls within the latter description of offence. The
oath to restore the widow to her habitation, imports no
crime and your lordships cannot sanction the conviction
of the prisoners under this statute, without holding that
the prosecutor is liable to transportation for seven years

CHIEF JUSTICE.—The point shall be reserved for you

EVIDENCE FOR THE DEFENCE

John Carty, examined by Mr D'ARCY.—I live in Dromeen, I know where Mr Large lives. I recollect last
Good-Friday. I was brought to Mr Large's house that
day. two men came in to look for my father. my father
owns that house and land, there were five men in all. they
brought me prisoner with them to look for my father. they
took me to the house of a man of the name of Short and
from that to Mr Large's. these men were armed. when
they brought me to Mr Large's I did not enter the house,
some of them went to the back of the house and more of
them to the front. Upon your oath did you ever see the
two prisoners at the bar before, until you saw them in

Stradbally Upon my oath I did not to my knowledge The man that made me prisoner kept me on with the Captain of them before them Are you able to swear that these two men were not of that party? I am not able to swear that because they made me run on before them I saw James Fennell when I was coming out of my own house, he had an opportunity of seeing the five men that were with me Had you not an opportunity of seeing the men? Not I, for they would not let me look at them at all

Cross-examined by the ATTORNEY-GENERAL —What day did you come to Maryborough? Last Wednesday week Who brought you here? The boys that are in brought me here Look at that gentleman (pointing to the clerk of Mr Delany the prisoner's agent) do you remember his examining you? I do Did you not go home the Friday after you came? I did Why did you go home? Because that man told me my evidence was no good When did you come again to Maryborough? Last Thursday Who brought you there? The police You saw that these men were all armed that were bringing you to Mr Large's? I did What made you show them the way? I did not show them the way

CHIEF JUSTICE —Did they ask you the way? No, they made me go over the ditch, and they made me run to Short's house as fast as I could, for I was afraid they would shoot me, then they brought me to Mr Large's they put Short on his knees and swore him, they asked Short was my father in there, and he said he was not, when they came out of Short's they bid me run on again, as I was running on I looked over my shoulder and I got a blow in the jaw, they left me at the gate at Mr Large's Why did you not then run away? Because one of the men stood at the door to watch me

Second Witness *James Fennell*, examined by Mr Brady —I live near Mr Large's house, I was standing outside my own door when I saw five men come down the road, and I saw them go into Carty's I did not see them coming out, because they ordered me into my own house they came into my house after, They swore me to give up my house as tenant to Mr Large, they were all strangers to me

Third Witness, *Patrick Purcell*, examined by Mr Brady —I know the prisoner Adams for some years I reside near him I had an opportunity for knowing his character he is a quiet, sober, and industrious boy

Fourth Witness *Mr Denis M'Bride* examined by Mr D'Arcy —I know Langton nearly two years I always heard of him to be an honest and industrious boy

---

CHARGE

CHIEF JUSTICE —Gentlemen of the Jury, the opinion of the Court is that provided this case is supported to your satisfaction in point of fact it is supported in point of law But at the same time there has been an objection made in point of law which we think very well deserving of consideration, you have nothing to do with that you have only to consider the evidence before you, and if you have a reasonable doubt upon your minds as to the guilt of the prisoners, you will acquit them

The prisoners were found guilty

Mr Brady tendered, on the part of Adams, the following plea

And the said Francis Adams, in his own proper person having heard the judgment of the Court, saith that the same ought to be reversed Because he saith that he, the said Francis Adams. did peremptorily challenge the said William Fishbourne, one of the Jurors empanelled and returned, to recognize upon their oaths, whether he the said Francis Adams was guilty of the felonies aforesaid, or not guilty, as he the said William Fishbourne came to the book, and before he was sworn And the said Francis Adams further saith, that the Right Honourable Francis Blackburne, Attorney-General of our said Lord the King, who was present prosecuting for our said Lord the King, did not, nor did any other person on behalf of our said Sovereign Lord the King, demur to said challenge, nor plead thereto, nor join issue thereon, but on the contrary declined so to do nor did said Francis Adams withdraw his said challenge, but insisted on the same, yet was said William Fishbourne sworn to speak the truth, of and concerning the premises, and was one of the twelve, who upon their oath did say, that he the said Francis Adams was guilty of the said felonies aforesaid, and this the said Francis Adams is ready to verify

Therefore he prays that the said judgment be reversed

When this plea was read Mr Brady referred their lordships to 1 Chit. Crown law 743, and to the case of the Earl of Leicester v Hayden, Plowd 390, as giving an account of this plea Your lordships have decided against this right, and the decision of your lordships is sustained by what my Lord Chief Justice denominated the opinion of the twelve Judges still it is the right of my client to question the decision of your lordships, and it is my duty to assist him in bringing it under the cognizance of a still higher tribunal Nay more I do feel there is a higher obligation, by which I am bound to proceed I do conceive it to be the duty of an advocate when the vindication of a great constitutional right devolves on him, in the course of his profession. to take care it does not perish in his hands I have therefore endeavoured, decorously I trust, to put this question on the record in order that it may be fully discussed, and solemnly decided I regret to be obliged to say, that the Attorney-General has not given me any assistance

ATTORNEY-GENERAL.—I shall certainly afford no facilities to the agitation of a question which has been settled by the twelve Judges

The CHIEF JUSTICE then said that they would reserve the question for the twelve Judges, whether the plea should be received or not

TRIAL OF

LAURENCE LIONARD, HUGH SLATTERY, OWEN BRENAN, MARTIN BRENAN, WILLIAM DUNN, AND THOMAS DUNN

For appearing in Arms and assaulting the Dwelling House of William Jacob

———

Tuesday, 5th June, 1832.

First Witness, *Mary Magee*, examined by Mr TICKELL. I lived at Mayo on Good Friday last, in my brother, William Jacob's house people rapped at the door, when I was in bed that night, I had slept until then, I was awoke by the noise of those people, they broke a window, and a good many of them came into the house, I saw a man stab the dog there was light where he stabbed him, there was a candle lighting, I saw the man stabbing the dog (witness was here desired to turn round and point out the man she saw stabbing the dog, when she turned her face to the dock, she wept, and appeared very unwilling to identify the man

BARON SMITH —Do not point him out, unless you are perfectly sure of him

Mr TICKFII —If you are not quite sure of the man, say so

BARON SMITH —Do not let any advice or solicitation induce you to point him out, unless you are quite sure of him —Fear God more than man

WITNESS —I know the man, but I think it hard to tell on him for killing a dog, when he did not kill myself and I had no more defence to save myself than the dog had, (being again asked to point out the man, she laid the rod on the head of Thomas Dunn)

Cross-examined by Mr BRADY —The dog was stabbed in the hall there was a candle lit there, I was standing inside the parlour door the dog was stabbed just at the parlour door. I can't tell who held the candle the dog was making a noise before it was stabbed, the man that stabbed him came out of the parlour I was standing on the floor at the time he passed through the parlour and went into the hall, I could not see what happened in the hall from where I was standing, but what took place outside the parlour door he was the last man of the company that I saw go away, I saw no more of him that night, there was no person in the parlour but myself, when I saw him, as well as I recollect, when he killed the dog, he went down into the hall as if to go out. I came into the hall after that, and there I found my son lying, I had no candle myself, when I saw the man that stabbed the dog, there was a good fire of turf in the parlour I saw his face and himself clear enough his face was turned to me when he killed the dog

Where was the dog all the time these people were searching the house? Was it a dog I was minding when I saw my child bleeding to death Did you get up before they got in? I was getting up when I heard them breaking the window, I saw them dragging my son in his shirt from the bed-room into the parlour my daughter and I got up together my brother came out of the room that my son slept in, and they were kicking him about, when they were dragging in my son, my daughter lit a candle I remained from that time till the dog was killed in the parlour, I never left it during that time Did you see any one that night that you saw before? I took no notice of any of them but the man I saw stab the dog, I was in Carlow, and I saw prisoners there my daughter was with my son about a moment before I found him in the hall, he was so heavy that we could not raise him we dragged him as well as we could we got pillows, and he was cold, and I held him in my arms endeavouring to stop the blood, he was speechless I rubbed his feet, and the first word he said was, " Mother, there is life in me, I may live," that is the first word he said that was a good while after we carried him into the room he did not say any thing before we dragged him into the room, he was not able to speak when I saw him he was pale and quite cold we put warm bricks to his feet, I remained with him, endeavouring to stop the blood, and I could not stop the blood until I caught the wound in this way, (shews how she closed the wound), some gentlemen came there in the morning, I believe they asked me questions I saw serjeant Byrne of the police that morning, and I begged of him to go for the Doctor he came into the room where my son was my son was able to speak at that time Thomas Wilson, a man that lives in the neighbourhood came into the room Doctor Edge came there, I remember I sent my daughter Ellen for buttermilk to make whey for my son that morning, there was a young man of the name of Thomas Cole, a police man, who gave us every assistance he could, some women came in to see our situation but they did not assist me in any way I don't recollect who they were, but I used to see them laughing going off You must have thought that very inhuman? So I did think it very inhuman Had you ever seen these women before? I had Do you know who they were? No I did not see any of them smile but one and I thought they were not sorry for me Why? Because I saw such inhuman slaughter done, and they did not pity me I was not satisfied with them at all for killing my son The women did not kill him? Might not their sons, or their husbands You thought every one you saw was concerned in the attack on your son? I did not They came in to ask how your son was? They did not ask how he was they came to look about them, and walked out again Did you talk to your son about the killing of the dog? I don't recollect that I did Did you ask him any thing about what occurred the night before? I asked him nothing, for he was not able to speak much What were you doing from the time the people came in till the dog was killed? Doing indeed! Were you looking about you? I was Was your brother there? He was Was your daughter there? She was not there the whole time I cannot recollect particular things that way, I was so frightened How often did you see your son put on his knees? Twice—When he was first put upon his knees, his face was from the fire and when he was put upon his knees again, his face was towards the fire I asked my daughter once who saved her from being killed and she said his name was Leonard I disremember when she told me that my daughter went to Dublin after that I think it was before she went off that she told me that this man saved her from being killed she said that she thought

his name was Leonard, she did not tell me that she had
ever seen him before that night   Did you hear her say any
thing that night about Father Kelly ?   I do not remember   Did you hear her say any thing to this effect—that
Father Kelly said you should not be killed ?   I do not remember   You do not recollect to hear her mention Father
Kelly's name that night whilst the people were there ?   I
do not remember hearing his name that night from any one
Had you ever heard his name mentioned by your daughter
before that ?   I never heard Father Kelly's name mentioned
at all, except that I might have often heard his name mentioned in a common way, as, " there is Father Kelly passing by," or something that way   Did she ever tell you
that she was at his house ?   I think she was at his house
Whom did you hear that from ?   I do not recollect from
whom.   Do you know what brought her there ?   I cannot
tell if she did not go of a message   Did she ever tell you
whether she had been at Mass ?   She did not   Do you
know Father Tyrrell ?   I do   Was she acquainted with
him ?   Yes   he was a neighbour, and we were all acquainted with him   Did she go to Father Tyrrell's chapel ?   I thought that every one was left to a free consci-
ence   Did she ever leave off going to church for any reason ?   She did   How long ?   Some Sundays, she said
she would not go to church for some ill treatment they gave
her   Did you hear that she did go to Mass from some ill
treatment ?   I did

Second Witness, *Ellen Magee*, examined by the ATTOR-
NEY-GENERAL —I remember last Good Friday night, I
lived at Mayo at my uncle William Jacob's house at that
time   I was a year before that backward and forward there.
Dr Carter had lived there before my uncle, I am related

to Dr Carter when he was living there I would go there sometimes and stay a month, and return there again my home was a mile beyond Carlow I lived there with my uncle William Jacob I remember the Sunday evening before Good Friday I was at home all that evening my mother, and uncle, and brother were at home all that evening I remember some men coming to my uncle's house that evening it was about night-fall when they came in (witness turns round to the dock and lays the rod on the head of the prisoner Leonard) that young man saved our lives he was there the Sunday night he called himself John Moore that night I spoke to him that night I asked him in the day time before that what his name was, he said his name was John Moore it was about 12 o'clock on Sunday when I saw him I had some conversation with him when I saw him at 12 o'clock on Sunday I had an opportunity of seeing him in the course of that day almost until night I sat down for some of the time that the men were at the house on Sunday night Nash was the first that sat down with me then he got up and was talking, and asked my brother to shew him some leaps, they went a bit from the fire and my brother shewed him leaps, Leonard and I sat together afterwards he was sitting at the time he was speaking to me

BARON SMITH – On the same chair ? Yes

To the ATTORNEY-GENERAL — The chair was near the corner of the room I sat up late on Friday night I think the family went to bed at 9 o'clock I slept with my mother in the parlour I was disturbed that night by a knocking at the door I got up and dressed myself, the man broke in my brother's bed-room window I heard them say they would break the window a door comes into the parlour out of the room in which my brother slept I put on

my frock before any one came into the parlour, the first
thing I saw was the men bringing my brother in his shirt
into the parlour, they were striking him and bidding him
go on his knees there was a good fire in the parlour, and I
lit a candle, and one of the men that came in lit another,
that was before my brother was put on his knees, as near
as I can guess about thirty men came into the house some
of them were armed, they struck me and put me on my
knees and said they would shoot me, and they swore me
about fire-arms they made a search in the house, I went
with them, during that time I held a candle my brother
was stabbed and beaten, when he was stabbed he went
into the porch out of the parlour, I afterwards went into
that porch and brought the candle with me my brother
was sitting down lying against the wall there was a man
going to shoot him in that porch I struck the gun first,
and Leonard saved him afterwards the man made a stab
of a bayonet at me and I fell back, and Leonard came up
and took hold of the man and said he should not kill me,
and that he should not shoot my brother, I had a candle
lighting in the porch at that time, and another man had a
candle Before you saw Leonard in the porch had you
seen him that night? He went about with me looking for
the fire-arms I went into the room with him looking for
fire-arms, and he gave me up to the men and bid them kill
me if I did not tell them where the fire arms were. I do
not think he was in earnest because he saved me I think
it was on Easter Sunday morning I saw him after that he
was at that time at the school-house in Mayo there were
a good many men with him. (witness lays the rod upon the
head of the prisoner Hugh Slattery) that man broke a lock
that night (lays the rod on the head of another prisoner)
What is that man's name? (Witness does not know his

name the prisoner she points out is William Dunn)

WITNESS.—You ought to bring the rest of the prisoners not to be bringing wrong ones   Can you point out any other?   (Lays the rod on the head of Thomas Dunn)   I saw that man at the house that night   What did you see the prisoner Slattery do that night?   He broke the lock of a door that night   How did he break it off?   With a hammer, the hammer was in the house   How soon after did you see that man that broke the lock?   I think it was Easter Sunday, there is a man there that took the sword from my uncle   (points out Thomas Dunn as the man who took the sword from her uncle)   my uncle had the sword inside his shirt   I saw him give the sword to another man saying, " See what I got in the old devil's bosom '   I cannot safely say that I ever saw the man that broke the lock before that night   I cannot say that I saw the man that took the sword from my uncle before that night   I think it was at Carlow that I first saw him after that   I think it was more than a week after Good Friday that I saw him   How soon after Good Friday did you see that man that calls himself William Dunn?   I think he is one of the three prisoners that I picked out in Carlow   When did you see the man that took the sword?   I saw him in Carlow   I think there were more than ten or twelve with these three men when I picked them out   Did you see that man that calls himself William Dunn do any thing particular on Good Friday night?   He had a gun and he was putting me on my knees and he said he would shoot me and he was swearing me

Cross-examined by Mr MURPHY.—You say you never knew Thomas Dunn, the man who took the sword before Friday night?   I don't remember that I did   How often did you see him since? Once in Carlow, and now. Are you quite sure of him now? I am. And what did you mean by saying a while ago, "you put the wrong prisoners to me?" I ask you, why you did not lay the rod on him at once? I wished to be sure. Do you know that young boy (pointing to the prisoner, Owen Brennan)? I think I saw him at Dowling's. I don't know his name. Did you not see that boy before the night of the attack? I think I saw him once. Did you not see him the next morning? Yes I did. Did you say any thing to him? I think I asked him where I could see a doctor. Was he not Dowling's servant boy? I do not know that he was his servant. I don't recollect to have seen him in the house the night of the attack. Do you know what prisoners your brother is to identify? I cannot tell, but he is to identify some of my prisoners. How many have you picked out for yourself? Twelve, as near as I can guess. I will swear to the men I saw and picked out myself. Did you examine their countenances so accurately as to know them again? I think so. Had your brother been stabbed when you were making these marks of identification? Yes, before he was stabbed. I knew two, and I knew Dowling a year before that, but I did not see him until after my brother was stabbed. I knew two before that, Nash and Leonard, I knew Leonard perfectly, I knew him that night by the name of John Moore. You knew his figure? I did, and when I described him to the police-man, he said, he knew him from the description. When did you tell your mother that you knew him? I don't recollect telling her about him. Did you ever tell your mother that his name was Leonard? I might after I returned from Dublin, but I did not before I did not know his name. Have you any friendly feeling towards Leonard now? I think I ought, when he saved us? Had you a friendly disposition towards him on Sunday night, when he sat on the chair with you? The reason I sat on the same chair with him was, because we had only a few chairs He seemed to be very civil to you? He did but I had always a bad opinion of the Whitefeet Did you suspect this man to be a Whitefoot that Sunday? All the time they were there on the Sunday night my brother was minding the fire-arms Did you think they were Whitefeet on Sunday night? No Why were the fire-arms watched? We had no suspicion that they were Whitefeet Do you think Leonard knew you when he saw you on Friday night? I think he did and I knew him well Do you recollect Leonard saying, in the course of that night to anybody, " do not touch them—they are strangers, and will not know us?" Yes, and James Dowling bid me blow out the candle before I came up to him I was running up to him at the time he bid me blow out the candle, when he was going to stab my brother I had a short stick in my hand he took hold of it, and he let the stick go with me, it was when I was in the parlour a few minutes before my brother being stabbed that I got the stick from Leonard I cannot account why Leonard said we were strangers Dowling said, they will know us, and Leonard began to twist the gun from Dowling I saw Dowling the next day in his own house, and he ran in, and lay down on his face, on the bed Do you know whether any men were taken up on suspicion by the police, except those that were identified? I know that they had some men, and they let them home I examined them all very closely at the time if there were any that I partly guessed to, I would not say that I knew them, I did not partly guess to any, but those that I knew.

I went and picked them out. I had no suspicion of any that I let away, after James Dowling was identified he was brought a prisoner to Stradbally, I cannot tell what prisoners were brought to my brother Who were present when you identified those men at Stradbally? The men were put into the yard there, and a good many were mixed up and down Were they or not put into the dock, at Stradbally, and you put on the table to identify them? I think they were putting them into the dock Upon your oath, were they not put into the dock? I think I picked out some prisoners in the dock The men that you did identify in Stradbally, did you not identify every man of them before you saw them in the yard? I was beginning to pick them out from the dock, when they took them out to the yard they mixed them up among all the men in the yard, and then I had to take them out of them Who was with you when you were identifying them at Stradbally? Mr Singleton Did he say any thing to you? He bid me tell the truth, and not to make a mistake, and to pick out no man but the man I knew Where was Mr Single-ton when you were on the table, and the men in the dock? He was near the dock Was it not the men in front of the dock you picked out? I picked out some of the men that were in front of the dock, and had to pick them out again in the yard I cannot tell how many I picked out at the school-house of Mayo Did you or not identify more than twelve men at any time taking them altogether? I can-not tell the exact number I picked them out, and Mr Singleton put down their names Were there any of those you identified at the school-house let go afterwards? No what I picked out were prisoners, I have no reason to think they were let go I did not see at the school-house the man that put my brother on his knees. I do not know the particular man that put my brother on his knees. I do not recollect to charge any particular man for it: the man is not here that handed me the book to swear me. I cannot tell the man that swore my brother: there were several shouting at him to go on his knees. I do not recollect to charge any person for being the person to put my brother on his knees; I know there was one man in particular that took hold of him. Did you see the man stabbing the dog? No. Did you see any man stab the dog? I did, but I did not see the first man: he was stabbed twice. I saw the last man that stabbed. I did not see any of those men here stab him. Where was the dog stabbed? Outside the parlour-door in the porch; I was going outside the door, and the man made the stab: before that my mother told me, that a man stabbed the dog: she was not near me the last time the dog was stabbed. I could not see from the parlour to where the dog was stabbed; if I did not go to the door, my mother was after coming out of the porch a little before that. I know the man that stabbed the dog.

JUROR.—That was the second stab? It was: for he was bleeding before, and I heard him roaring before.

Mr. MURPHY.—When you saw the dog stabbed how many men were in the house? About thirty men, but they were cleared out of the parlour and were in another room; my mother was in the parlour when I saw the dog stabbed; I think I recollect my mother said at that time, that she believed they were all gone. Were they gone? They were gone into another room. But the thirty men were in the house? They were: that short-nosed fellow (pointing to the prisoner Thomas Dunn,) was the person my mother told me, stabbed the dog: the same night the man was passing me by, and my mother said, " Oh ! there is the man that stabbed the dog, I was afraid he would kill myself after " How soon after did they all go away ? Shortly after How soon after they left the house, did you see your brother ? I was in the porch while they were going out. Did you tell your brother that you knew any of the people in the house that night ? I do not recollect that I did Did your brother tell you? He could not speak Did you hear your uncle saying any thing about the men ? I recollect he bid me not to tell if I knew any of the men, but I do not rightly know whether he said that, until morning or not Do you recollect this conversation that you said you knew James Dowling was there, and that your uncle said, " take care that they do not hear you ?" I cannot exactly tell what words were said after they went, I did not tell my mother what I swore the last day I was examined here, but I told her it was a terrible place for any person to come up to Did you tell your mother what you said about Father Kelly ? I do not recollect that I did Did you tell her that you swore on the table that Father Kelly sent to murder you ? I do not think I said any thing about that Did you tell her any thing about his sending the people at all to your house ? I do not think I ever said that he sent the people to murder us Did you ever tell your mother any thing about Father Kelly ? I don't know, but I am sure that I said nothing about his sending people to murder us, I recollect my mother asked what made me be talking about the priest, and I said that I could not help it, that when you asked me the questions I should answer you, as I was on my oath Did you tell your mother what you swore about him? I might tell her an odd word, when I went out of this, I think she asked me what made me talk about the priest Was that the very first question she asked you when you went out? I think it was she said to me, "why should I be talking about the priests or about the chapels," and she said she did not think it was right to be talking about such things

I believe you told me the last day you were examined here, that you believed Father Kelly was one of the party? The way I mean is, that he is over them like a Captain, or something like that, that he advises them

Do you think that he has any controul over them? I know he has, and that they are all under his command, and I think if he did not advise them so much, there would not be so many Whitefeet

Do you mean to say that he knows every thing they do? I think they do nothing unknown to him

Do you think he knows when they are going to attack those houses? I don't like to be talking about him at all

Do you think that Father Kelly knew that they were about to make this attack on your uncle's house? The prisoners asked me about the pistols I knew there was no one by when I told the priest about them, and he must have told the Whitefeet

What did you tell the priest about the arms? That we had them hid, that we had no more powder, but that we had plenty of ball

Did you tell him then where the arms were? If I told him the spot, I think they would get them

He, you think, would have told them? He would

You told him no lies? I told him no lies, and I am sorry I told him the truth

He knew your secrets? He did, and the Whitefeet could get in the readier

When did you tell him about the pistols? I think it was three days before the attack

He seemed to have great ill-will towards your brother? I thought so from his conversation

Did you tell any body about what the priest said? I recollect my uncle sent me to the priest, and when I came home I told him what the priest said. I told him that the priest did not like him, because he was hindering me from going to Mass

Did Father Kelly say any thing more to you? He told me he did not like to have me in the house with my brother he wanted me to leave the house, and to go where he would send me.

Did you tell your brother that Father Kelly had ill-will towards him? I did

And your uncle? I think I did he spoke as if he had ill-will, for he said, "it was not lucky to leave me in it, because I would be made to go to Church," and he told me, "that I would be damned if I would go to Church, and that none of my breed would have any chance of being saved but myself.

What did he say about Luther and Calvin? He said, that the Protestants at the beginning robbed the Catholics, I think it was three hundred years ago, he said they robbed them, and he said, that the people were ready to lay down their lives, to have their rights again, he said, that Luther and Calvin began to preach against the whole world, and that he would shortly have his own religion established again

What brought you to Father Kelly that day? Another priest sent me there, my uncle was at me every day to go to Father Kelly, when I told him what Father Tyrrell said to me, that I could not live in the country unless I got acquainted with them; I do not recollect to go to his house more than once, but I met him on the road

Had you often conversations with Father Kelly? I think I often met him in the fields about the Chapel, I often had conversations with him before I got acquainted with him he came a great way with me from his own house, the day that I went there

Do you think that Father Tyrrell knew that Father Kelly had influence with the Whitefeet? I don't think he did.

What was your object in going to Father Kelly? I wanted to get acquainted with him, for I thought the people there would be civil to any body that the priest would like.

Was it for the purpose of protection that you went to him? That was the reason

You had no religious feeling that brought you to him? I would not go about religion to a priest

Baron Smith.—It appears to me that this evidence is not pertinent to the question that the Jury have to try, except so far as it affects the credit of the witness

Mr. Murphy —We will see that Had you any religious motive in going to Father Kelly? I would like to go when Father Tyrrell told me

Did you ask liberty from Father Kelly to go to confession? I think he asked me to come to confession in a couple of days, and I think I said I would, but I had no notion of it

Did he speak to you on the subject of confession before you spoke to him? He was telling me to tell every roguery that I knew, but I thought it not right to tell of my comrades, and I thought it a bad thing to tell of myself

T

Until Father Kelly had told you about confession, did you know any thing about it—were you ever at confession with a priest? No, I got until next day to consider whether I would go to confession

Did you ever go to confession to Father Tyrrell? I did not

Did you ever say you were at confession with Father Tyrrell? I think I said that I did

Did Father Kelly ever tell you any thing about your grandfather? He told me that my grandfather took a priest in the Whiteboy times, and that he was burned all, except his right hand, he told me he killed him in taking him, and that he was burned afterwards

Do you recollect the morning after your house was attacked to see women coming into your house? I recollect women coming in laughing, to ask how my brother was, (witness mentioned the names of four or five of the women)

Can you account for their barbarity in laughing? I cannot, in all the houses I went to after the morning of the attack the women laughed

Do you mean the neighbours houses? I do, the morning after the attack I went very early and rapped at the doors, and they seemed pleased that my brother was stabbed

Who went with you from Mayo to Stradbally when you went to identify the men? Mr Wright I identified all before I went to Stradbally, except the three that I identified at Carlow.

Did you identify nine before you went to Stradbally? I think it was nine

If you identified nine before you went there, what was the necessity of bringing you to Stradbally? They mixed them up 1 think to baffle me, I picked out the same men at Barrackmyler and at Carlow

By the virtue of your oath were not those persons on a car before you on the road to Stradbally? Yes

What was the meaning of putting them into the dock and you on the table? I think to baffle me worse

After you went to Stradbally and went to Dublin, did you ever see those prisoners until to day? There are some prisoners there that I saw in Carlow

Did you see the man that took the sword in Carlow I did

Did you see him in Stradbally? No

Did you see him ever since you saw him in Carlow until you saw him here to day? I do not recollect to see him since until to-day

Were you in the new gaol of Maryborough since you came here? I don't think I know where the new gaol is

Did you see any of the prisoners since you came to Maryborough up to this day? I think I saw two of them passing through the yard here, I was sitting down beside the wall

Were you brought there for the purpose of identifying them? I was not.

Did you tell Captain Wright you knew Dowling? I don't recollect that he asked me

Did you tell him that you knew Nash, Moore and Dowling? I think I did

You are quite sure that you told Cole about Dowling? I am. and I think I told about the names of Nash, and Moore

CHIEF JUSTICE—Can you give any explanation how it happened that the people were actually taken that day? I think from the way I described them

Do you mean to say that you gave marks and tokens of the nine men? I did.

ATTORNEY-GENERAL.—You described the sort of persons and the police knew whom you meant, is that it?

It is.

Third Witness, *John Magee*, examined by Mr MARTLEY —I am brother to Ellen Magee, and nephew to William Jacob, I was living with my uncle in April last, at Mayo, I came there to live the day after Christmas day, I believe my uncle was not there a month altogether before Good Friday last, There was an attack made on my uncle's house on Good Friday last, I was in bed when they rapped at the window, the first noise that I heard was at the window of my bed-room persons got in from the window of my bed-room, they broke in the under part of it, when they were coming in at the window I was out of bed, and I was going to put on my small-clothes when they got a hold of me, they brought me into the parlour in my shirt; after I got into the parlour there was a candle lit by my sister, there was another candle that I saw lighting afterwards, after they took me into the parlour they beat me bravely, and they swore me kneeling, they were asking me if there were fire arms in the house, and if I had any pistols, or gun, or bayonet in the house, the last time they had me on my knees, a man stabbed me with a bayonet he had on a gun, they got no arms, I had a case of pistols in the house, I had them hid, I would not hide them if I had powder to act with them, I had but one charge of powder, they swore me twice they put me on my knees twice; both the swearings occurred in the parlour the two candles were burning the whole time I was in the parlour with those men

Did you know any of the men who brought you from the

bed-room into the parlour — I did (Witness points out the prisoner, Martin Brenan) I had seen that man before that night, I saw him on the Sunday before Friday in the evening about duskish, there were two more with him there were about thirty people in my uncle's house that night, as long as I can remember any thing that happened in the house, they were in it about fifteen or twenty minutes, during that time I had an opportunity of seeing them, (here the witness identified all the prisoners) I had seen the prisoner Owen Brenan often before that night he lived with James Dowling, that is the man that saved our lives, (pointing out Leonard) after getting the stab I walked about, in a short time I was struck with the breech of a gun and knocked down, I got up soon after, and I opened the porch door, and went to look into the yard I bolted the door and I sat down and leant my back against the wall, I lay there until there came a man up behind me, and another man with a candle the man that came up behind me had a gun and a bayonet on it, and he put it towards me and said, "boys, he's only foxing, he's not dead, I will shoot him," my sister came out of the parlour, and the man came opposite to me out of the parlour, she had a candle in her hand, and she had a stick in her other hand: and she knocked up the gun with it, and jostled the man, he turned about, and was going to stab her, and this man interfered and said, " those people are strangers, and do not know us,"—he said they should kill himself sooner than kill the girl, in the parlour I saw him do another good turn my uncle was knocked down in the corner of the parlour, and a man came and held a gun over him, the way he did over me, and this man interfered and would not let him fire the shot, I did not know the tall man's name at that time, the prisoner, Martin Brenan, was the man that swore me I saw a great many of them with sticks about the house, I did not see a sword with any of the party, I saw three guns in all, in the parlour I had a good opportunity for seeing them I saw Owen Brenan, I believe the morning after, on Sunday morning he was brought into the room to me, and so was Slattery the next place I saw the other three prisoners was in the gaol yard of Carlow I saw Leonard in Maryborough, it was some days after I saw Leonard in Maryborough, that I saw the men at Carlow.

Cross-examined by Mr. Brady —How many persons have you sworn against altogether? About thirteen.

How many of these had you known previously? About four or five—I knew four of them by name, John Dowling, James Dowling Owen Brenan, and Patrick Nash.

As to the other nine, whose names you did not know, had you known their persons before the night of Good-Friday? The chapel was covenient to me, and I might have seen them there, but I did not take particular notice, to the best of my knowledge. I did see a great deal of them before that

How many persons did they bring you on Sunday morning? About twelve —I don't recollect how many I identified that morning, it was in the gaol-yard of Carlow that persons were next shewn to me, I identified six there, I afterwards identified seven in Maryborough I remained in Mayo about nine days after Good-Friday night I was then taken to Carlow infirmary, I remained in Carlow gaol until I went to Maryborough gaol. I went to Maryborough gaol to identify those prisoners my sister did not tell me any thing she was saying here, I did not hear her saying any thing about her talking about priests, I heard in the house we lodge in, that there was a great deal of talk about priests.

Were you expecting an attack? I did not this night

But did you a few days before? No my mind was altered, I did not think they would call to me

What altered your mind? Those people coming to welcome me to the place

What reason had you to expect an attack before that? Because they were attacking every body that had fire-arms through the country

Do you know Father Kelly? I saw the man after, but to know him, I do not

Did you ever speak to your sister about him, or she to you, before Good-Friday night? I cannot say whether before Sunday, or between that and Good Friday, my sister said she would go to Father Kelly to see if there would be any danger in our living in the country from the Whitefeet.

And she did go to him? Yes

And she came back? You are right enough,—when she came back, she came to my uncle and me to the garden, and we asked her what passed, and she told us a good deal of it.

What did she tell you? That he told her that there would not be any Protestants left in the country, more than another year or two at farthest that he was asking her not to go to church, and that he bid her go to Mass that if she would. there would be no fear of the Whitefeet, that we were devils that if we went to Mass, we would have God at our side, and we would become good christians, that if she did not go to Mass, it was out of his power to protect us

Did she tell you any more? I heard that some of the counsellors here cross-hackled her a good deal about going to Mass

Had your sister ever been at Mass before this? I believe she did go to Mass, when we were living at Carlow, she went to Father Tyrrell's chapel I don't recollect that she went to the chapel at Mayo, I believe she was advised by my uncle to go, and my opinion was asked, and I said that she might go if she liked, I don't recollect that I ever mentioned that to any one before this, the prisoner, Martin Brenan, was the first person that swore me, when I was sworn the second time, I was on my knees, with my face towards the fire still, I saw the prisoner, Owen Brenan often that night, I saw him no where but in the parlour I brought my Mother from Carlow the Sunday before Good Friday, to live at Mayo we intended to live there

Fourth Witness, *William Jacob*, examined by the ATTORNEY GENERAL —I am seventy-four years of age, I remember the night my house was attacked, I cannot see well without spectacles, the people that came in took a sword from me, and they knocked me down several times

Cross-examined by Mr BRADY —I am not acquainted with Father Kelly I don't think I ever sent my niece to him, I don't recollect that she ever told that she had been with him she might have told me, and it might have escaped my memory, I don't recollect that she ever told me that Father Kelly said that I was little better than an old devil, it might have been told to me and I might forget it

The evidence for the prosecution closed here

EVIDENCE FOR THE DEFENCE

The *Rev Eugene Kelly*, examined by Mr BRADY —
You are parish priest of Mayo? I am.

Do you know a young woman of the name of Ellen
Magee? I never knew her but a young woman came to
me on the 19th of April last, she said that she wanted to
go to confession

ATTORNEY GENERAL —Your Lordships will see
whether this line of examination can be pursued I take
it for granted that the object of producing Mr Kelly is to
contradict what has been stated by a witness on the part of
the prosecution, who deposed to a conversation between her
and him If I am right in anticipating that as the object
of producing Mr Kelly, I object to his examination

Mr BRADY —Our object in producing Mr Kelly is
certainly to contradict that witness

ATTORNEY GENERAL —The rule I take to be is this,—
that whenever a witness is cross-examined, as to collateral
matter, for the purpose of impeaching credit, the party
adopting such a course, must abide by the answers which
the witness whom he so cross-examines gives to his questions, and is not at liberty at a subsequent stage of the
trial to call a witness to contradict him

In the case before the Court the question is whether the

prisoners at the bar, or any of them, are guilty of the crime imputed to them by this indictment. In support of the charge, I produce a witness, and that witness has been cross-examined at great length, and to a vast variety of matters, manifestly for the purpose of impeaching her credit. I confess it was with great pain I heard the introduction of the topics to which she was cross-examined: neither in my statement, nor in any part of her direct evidence was any allusion made to them; the prisoner's counsel, however, thought it expedient for his client's case to elicit them on cross-examination; and even if I could have prevented it, it is obvious that I must have felt a repugnance in criminal case to interfere with a course which was deemed expedient for the defence of the prisoners. What is the nature of the evidence given by her? She spoke to particular conversations between her and Mr Kelly, not one of which in itself has the slightest tendency to prove either the guilt or the innocence of the prisoners at the bar. the simplest proof of this is, to suppose every word that she has sworn as to her communication with Mr Kelly, to be utterly untrue, could your Lordships in charging the Jury advert to its untruth as any proof of the prisoners' innocence? On the other hand, how does its truth tend to establish the guilt of the prisoners? supposing every word she has sworn to be true, could I, on the part of the Crown call upon the Jury to derive from it even the remotest inference to the prisoners' prejudice? Indeed my Lords, I would be ashamed to do so, and if I were to make the attempt I would expose myself to be corrected, and must be corrected by the Court.

But while I would thus exclude all further enquiry into

the truth or falsehood of those collateral matters, I will not deny the right of the prisoners to insist on the nature of her testimony in these respects, as matters to be considered by the Jury in examining the credit of the witness, and I know they will be told to give them in this respect all the weight they may be entitled to. Let me however again repeat, that it has given me the deepest concern that the character and conduct of a third person should have been brought forward before the public under circumstances which uttterly precluded the possibility of any satisfactory investigation of the matters which appear to reflect on him.

Mr BRADY.—I think the Attorney-General had laid down the rule too narrowly. All evidence of the kind under consideration is, in a strict sense, collateral to the issue. it goes entirely to the credit of the witness. It is evidence not admissible as substantive matter of defence. it is offered not in denial of the charge, but in contradiction of the witness with a view to the question of his or her credibility. It is not to the purpose therefore to contend that the evidence now offered does not bear immediately upon the guilt or innocence of the prisoners. their guilt is not inconsistent with the truth of what it is proposed to prove. The question is whether it be admissible in contradiction of the witness with a view to her credit. and the rule upon that point seems to me to be this. that if the matter of contradiction be altogether foreign to the subject matter of enquiry, then it is inadmissible. if it relate to the subject matter of the enquiry, then it ought to be received. in other words, if the contradiction tend merely to affect the general credit of the witness, it is inadmissible. if it tend to the credit of the witness in the present enquiry, it cannot be rejected. What is the evidence here? Ellen Magee states that a day or two previous to the attack on Jacob's house she had an interview with the Rev

Mr Kelly, that he made enquiry from her as to the means of defence possessed by the family, the quantity of arms and ammunition in the house, and the place in which they were deposited; that she mentioned the quantity, but *fortunately* concealed the place, and that he told her he had the Whitefeet under his command. She further stated that the persons concerned in the attack acted in such a manner as to make it evident that the information elicited from her, by Mr Kelly, had been communicated to them, and that they failed in discovering the arms, because she had not divulged to him the place of concealment. Now we propose, my Lords, to examine Mr Kelly, in order to prove, that he did not make any such inquiries, or statements, as those attributed to him, and that the narrative of the witness is in those respects an absolute fabrication. And, we humbly submit, that this is a matter of contradiction, not wholly foreign to the subject matter of inquiry, but intimately blended with it, not matter concerning, merely the general credit of the witness, but vitally affecting her credit in this particular case. These circumstances, although they came out in cross-examination, now constitute a portion of her narrative, and if one portion of it be shown to be utterly false, it will be for the Jury to determine whether they can give credit to the remainder

In Jervis's case, 2 Camp. 638, the limits of the rule, with respect to the contradiction of a witness, are defined with precision. There the witness was interrogated upon two points, whether he had not been charged with robbing his master, the prisoner, and whether he had not, in consequence of the charge threatened to be revenged on the prisoner. He answered in the negative, and it was proposed to contradict him on both points. But it was held, that he might not be contradicted as to the former, but, that as to the latter, he was liable to contradiction. Why? Because the former was foreign to the inquiry; the latter concerned his credit in that particular case. But, it is unnecessary to refer to other authorities; your Lordships have ruled this point, during the present Commission; and in another branch of this case—Nash, one of the persons charged with being concerned in this attack, was capitally indicted for stabbing John Magee in the progress of the outrage. On his trial it came out in cross-examination, that the witnesses had charged James Dowling with a participation in the attack on the house. In defence of Nash, we proposed to prove an *alibi* for Dowling. The evidence was objected to by the Attorney-General, but it was ruled to be admissable by your lordships. Now let a distinction be shown between that and the present case! The innocence of Dowling was consistent with the guilt of Nash. The charge against each was different. It was not even sworn that Dowling was present at the commission of the crime, with which Nash was charged. The evidence was therefore collateral to the issue. Why was it received? Because of its tendency to affect the credit of the witnesses in that particular case. Because if they should appear to have implicated one individual wrongfully in the transaction, their testimony with regard to others must have been received with distrust or neglect altogether. In this instance the witness has implicated this respectable clergyman in this abominable outrage, she has represented him as an accessary before the fact, which in this charge of misdemeanour is the same as principal, and we seek to affect her credit as to the prisoners, by proving that she has sworn falsely and corruptly against this minister of God. Will it be said that Dowling stood indicted, but that no bill has been preferred against Mr Kelly? Your lordships will not be induced to draw any such distinction It would amount to this, that the Attorney-General might have deprived Nash of the benefit of the defence made for him, by proceeding to try him before he had preferred his bill of indictment against Dowling But the right to contradict the witness arises from what the witness has sworn, not from the course the Attorney-General may think proper to pursue The Attorney-General might, if he thought proper, send up a bill of indictment against the Rev Mr Kelly

ATTORNEY-GENERAL —I deny that.

Mr BRADY —The Attorney-General may deny it, but I am now in argument, and I insist that he may send up a bill of indictment against that gentleman

BARON SMITH —He might send up a bill of indictment, but no Grand Jury could hesitate the hundredth part of a moment to ignore that bill.

Mr. BRADY —However that may be, I submit that it cannot alter or affect the question of the admissibility of the evidence now offered on the part of the prisoners

BARON SMITH —The rule is a well-established rule, and it is a rule founded upon manifestly rational principles, but the difficulty, if any, is in the application of it

CHIEF JUSTICE —Mr. Brady, upon your argument it appears to me that this follows, that if Mr Kelly is to be examined at all, he is only to be examined for the purpose of contradicting as much of that young woman's evidence as amounts to an accusation of Mr Kelly himself, as being a participator in this transaction. If I should find myself inclined to adopt your argument at all, I would, as at present advised, feel myself bound to confine it within that limit But, as to the question argued by the Attorney-Geneial and you, I think the doctrine has not been quite accurately stated by either, I take it that it is not the rule, that if counsel cross-examine a witness as to merely collateral matters, he is at liberty to do so abiding by the answers I take it that the qualification of abiding by the answers is confined to cases in which a witness had been examined to a matter of a criminatory nature against himself, but that to mere collateral matter he is not in strictness to be examined at all

BARON SMITH —The true interpretation of the rule I conceive to be this that where it is manifest, that the evidence which it is the object of a certain question to extract, is altogether foreign and irrelevant to the issue, and that it therefore can only be asked, with a view to offering evidence in contradiction, that there it is the right of the court to stop the question and this struck me so forcibly that I was very near reserving a question for the twelve Judges upon the subject But some circumstances afterwards prevented my taking such a course Here I did conceive that the main object of a great part of the cross-examination of Ellen Magee, was to lay a foundation for contradicting her answers

ATTORNEY-GENERAL —The view which your Lordships have suggested is really the one which has occurred to me to be right upon a former trial, when the same witness was cross-examined in the same manner, and to the same matters, as on the present trial and the cross-examination was not interfered with either by the Court, or by me But it never occured to me, or I believe to your Lordships that by not objecting to the line of cross-examination then pursued, I was thereby letting in not one, but perhaps fifty collateral issues

The charge now to be tried is the assaulting of the habitation of William Jacob what is the evidence of the witness for the Crown with respect to which they say that it is competent for them to examine Mr Kelly? It is not the evidence, adduced on the part of the Crown in support of the charge, but the prisoners say this, having cross-examined the Crown witness, and obtained from her matter to warrant an indictment against Mr Kelly, we now demand the right of examining Mr Kelly to disprove a charge, which we have thought it expedient for our defence to prefer against him

This is *their* argument, and I must say that I totally dissent from the grounds of it, for in my view of Ellen Magee's evidence it is not possible to say that she has deposed to a single fact warranting any criminal imputation against Mr Kelly.

She has, it is true, been induced to adopt inferences to his prejudice, suggested by the questions put to her on cross-examination but these inferences are not in my opinion borne out by the facts which she states The assurances of protection which she received from Mr. Kelly, and that the family would not require fire arms, is so far from warranting a conclusion that Mr Kelly was connected with the illegal confederacy that prevails, that I should infer his promise to be founded on the natural influence which belonged to his clerical character, and which he engaged to exert in favour of her, and her uncle's family

The Court adjourned at 11 o'clock at night, and their Lordships said that they would take until the following morning to consider the question as to the admissibility of the evidence of the Rev Mr Kelly On the following morning, at the sitting of the Court, Baron Smith delivered the following decision

DECISION AS TO THE ADMISSIBILITY OF THE EVIDENCE OF THE REV. E. KELLY.

Baron Smith.—After the best consideration which, in the course of a few hours, my Lord Chief Justice and I have been able to give this case, our joint opinion is, that the evidence of the Rev. Eugene Kelly, offered to contradict the testimony of Ellen Magee, as to conversations which upon cross-examination, she stated to have occurred between him and her —that this contradictory evidence, I say, cannot be received.

With what might, or might not be desirable, under the particular circumstances of any case, the Court can have nothing to do. A question upon the admissibility of evidence, we must, according to the best of our skill and knowledge, determine according to the established rules of evidence; and the application of those dry rules to the case before us.

It cannot be disputed, that it is the established law that evidence is not admissible to contradict a witness, upon matter that is collateral.

What, then towards enabling us properly to apply this rule, have we preliminarily to do?

To ascertain the meaning which is attached to the word "collateral" in that rule.

Towards ascertaining this, I conceive that we have assistance which is quite sufficient.

We find a collateral fact impliedly defined to be one, 'wholly irrelevant to the matter in issue.'

If it were merely defined to be a fact " wholly irrelevant" there might be an ambiguity, and consequent difficulty, which do not exist

It might be said, how can that be " wholly irrelevant " which affects the credit of a witness, who may, perhaps be the only one, and upon whose credit the question of guilt or innocence will altogether turn?

But the answer to such a question is, that the definition of such a collateral fact as is within the rule is not that it is one " wholly irrelevant " but, that it is one " wholly irrelevant *to the matter in issue* "

Now, how can the conversations to which Ellen Magee has sworn, as having been had between her and Mr Kelly, be relevant to the issue, whether certain prisoners appeared in arms, and assaulted the dwelling-house of William Jacob?

But the question, after being somewhat modified, I admit, may be repeated It may be asked, how can that be wholly irrelevant *to the matter in issue*, which affects the credit of a witness, on whose testimony the question of guilt or innocence may hinge?

The answer is, that by allowing the reasoning which such a question is meant to involve, we must not only conflict with, but overrule distinct decisions

Proof that one witness attempted to dissuade another from attending the trial, must strongly affect the credit of the dissuading witness, and thus, cannot, it may be said, be wholly irrelevant to the matter in issue

Yet it is decided that such a fact is so wholly irrelevant to the issue,—that if the witness deny such an attempt to dissuade,—this denial must be abided by and cannot be contradicted

But it may be said, how can any contradiction of a witness operate, otherwise than by affecting the credit of the person contradicted? This I admit must be one —nay the first of its operations

But what follows? And how does the case stand?

It is common to every contradiction, that it tends to affect the credit of the contradicted witness

But if it does *no more* than this, it cannot be received

But if on the contrary, the contradiction be, as to a fact ' *relevant to the matter in issue,*' then, consistently with Lord Ellenborough's rule, it may be received

Let us put each case

A prisoner is indicted for a burglary —and a witness for the prosecution swears that she never had a child, or is unmarried, or breakfasted yesterday at Athy, or was not at church on Sunday last,—can evidence be called to contradict her by proving that she was married,—and in a year afterwards delivered of a child, or breakfasted yesterday at Maryborough,—or was seen in church on Sunday last?

Yet all these contradictions would be directly relevant and material to her credit, and indirectly therefore (if you please) relevant and material to the issue

But if she said that she saw A B, and C D break into the house and that she had always said so, proof of an *alibi* for C D, or of her having said that one only broke in, or that she did not know the second,—such contradictions, besides being relevant to her credit, could not be alleged to be " wholly irrelevant to the matter in issue "

Suppose there was no evidence for this prosecution, but that of Ellen Magee, and suppose the Jury to believe, that every thing she swore, as to her conversations with Mr Kelly, was utterly and intentionally false —they unquestionably must acquit But why? Not because the fact of those conversations was not wholly foreign and irrelevant to the matter in issue; but because a Jury must expunge from their minds, the testimony of a witness, who, as to any fact, however foreign to the issue, has *intentionally* deviated from the truth.

And why must they acquit? Because there would be a gross and palpable inconsistency, in their at once virtually convicting a witness of perjury, and founding a verdict of guilty on the evidence of such perjured witness.

Suppose Ellen Magee had given one hundred answers on her cross-examination, not one of them as to facts relevant to the issue, but every one, if false, calculated to destroy her credit; shall a hundred witnesses be called and received to contradict her, and one hundred others to rebut their contradiction? And an innumerable litter of subordinate issues be thus propagated, by the one which alone the Jury had been sworn to try?

Then is there indeed *an end* to Lord Ellenborough's rule; but *no end*, that I can imagine, to a criminal investigation.

To say that the fact of the witness's having said, that he would be revenged on a prisoner, and would *fix him in gaol*; to say that this is plainly relevant to the matter in issue, may be to go *far enough*; but that is a reason why we should not go *farther*. Meantime, it is widely distinguishable from this case. It was a fact between the witness and the prisoner. It *approached* a declaration, that the former would avenge himself, at the expense of truth, in a judicial and criminal proceeding, against his victim. It would be going too far to say, that such a fact was *solely* relevant to the witness's credit, and WHOLLY irrelevant to the matter in issue.

Another case, quite similar in principle, is the witness being asked whether he had not declared he would procure witnesses *corruptly* to give evidence in support of the prosecution.

But, if Ellen Magee had one hundred different conversations, with one hundred persons, none of those conversations on the matter in issue, shall the hundred persons be received, to contradict her account of the import of those conversations?

Nay, I not only hold, that the statement by a witness, on cross-examination, of facts irrelevant to the issue, cannot be contradicted, but, sanctioned by the concurrence of my Lord Chief Justice, in an opinion of mine, which, some years ago I suffered to be overruled, I recur to that opinion. It is this: that a party has not a right, on cross-examination, to question witnesses on matters irrelevant to the issue, for the purpose of producing witnesses to contradict their answers.

I think the very language of the cases more than impliedly lays down this.

What is this language? "It is not competent, on cross-examination, to *question* the witness, concerning a distinct collateral fact which is wholly irrelevant to the matter in issue, for the purpose of discrediting him, if he answers in the negative, by calling witnesses to contradict him"—(7 East 108.)

This is not merely to lay down that ANSWERS as to irrelevant matters shall not be *contradicted*, but to take the thing up earlier, and to say, that QUESTIONS as to such irrelevant matters shall not, with such a view, be ASKED. Agreeably to which we find it said —' *though* the witness, even answer the irrelevant question *before it is disallowed* evidence is not allowed to contradict "

Is not this to say, that on cross-examination, such questions may, and ought to be *disallowed ?*"—(2d Campb 628)

And how does Russell express himself ?

" It need hardly be observed, if a question be wholly irrelevant, and, *therefore, improperly asked on cross-examination,* and the witness, *nevertheless,* give an answer to it, the cross-examining party may not call evidence to contradict the answer "

Thus the law takes two positions, for combating irrelevant discussion First, it prohibits a certain class of questions, secondly, if asked and answered, the law makes a second stand, and resists all farther proceeding, by forbidding contradiction

Why then did I suffer this line of cross-examination to proceed ?

Very possibly I was wrong But first, it was but a repetition of one which had come upon us, most irksomely, and altogether by surprise, in a former case, before my Lord Chief Justice some days ago and then no attempt was made to object to, or resist it

Secondly —I should have scrupled to act upon an opinion which I had surrendered but which with the sanction of the Lord Chief Justice I resume

Thirdly —For obvious reasons, I waited for objections to be made

Fourthly — As no contradiction was offered in the former instance, I could not be certain that this line of examination was on the present trial pursued, with a view to offering evidence to contradict the answers But it will be recollected, that while the cross-examination of this young girl was proceeding, I often inquired its tendency; but, trusting that I should by and by discover it, forbore to push inquiries, which might baffle the objects of the cross-examination; and that I distinctly and repeatedly declared, that unless so far as the answers might affect her credit, I did not see how the questions could bear upon the case and issue.

Fifthly,—and especially, supposing no contradiction to be sought, or in contemplation. I conceived that if the Jury thought Ellen Magee's narrative of her intercourse with Mr Kelly to be so improbable as to be incredible, the prisoners were entitled to the benefit of such an impeachment of her credit, by herself.

On the whole, without suffering ourselves to wander into any inquiry or consideration beyond this, *what is the law?* and conceiving the law to be, that such evidence as is now offered is not admissible, my Lord Chief Justice and I, according to the best opinion which we have been able to form, are obliged to decline receiving it.

BARON SMITH'S CHARGE.

Gentlemen of the Jury, many circumstances conspire to render this an anxious trial. The severity of the punishment which may ensue upon conviction, the number of persons involved in the accusation, the connexion of the offence with the disturbances of this county, the symptoms of religious animosity which have so afflictingly transpired, all conspire to give an anxious character to the investigation on which you are about to enter. The rules of Law precluded our admission of the evidence of the Rev. Mr Kelly, to contradict that of Ellen Magee, on matters collateral and irrelevant to the issue which you have to try.

namely, whether the prisoners assailed and entered a certain dwelling-house, ill-treated the inmates, and made a demand of arms. And I scarcely can regret the existence of a rule of law (founded obviously too on sound principles,) which has exempted us from the necessity of dwelling longer upon subjects at once painful and extrinsic. But in declining to receive the testimony of Mr. Kelly, we do not withhold from you the question of the credit of Ellen Magee. If her narrative of what occurred between her and Mr Kelly, appear to you to be so improbable as to be incredible, you will throw her evidence altogether out of your consideration. For if her narrative be false, it must have been so to her knowledge; and if a witness deviate intentionally from the truth, on any point, however collateral it may be, the testimony of such a person must be altogether put aside. A different doctrine would involve a Jury in the palpable and mischievous inconsistency of at once virtually convicting a witness of perjury, and placing dependence on the testimony of such perjured witness. If you discredit and put aside the testimony of Ellen Magee, this, however, will but throw you upon the evidence of her brother John. He has sworn against *all* the persons upon trial, and is corroborated by the evidence of his mother, as to *one*.

The Baron then recapitulated, construed, and observed upon the evidence. Even supposing the Jury to believe that of Ellen Magee, they ought not to confound her opinions with her facts. Some, at least, of the former seemed to be prejudiced and rash; and at all events were not evidence.

The learned Judge concluded thus:—I will not do you the injustice of calling upon you to discard all impressions, which the nature of the charge and its connexion with the state of the country, might produce. Such a call might insinuate that you had given admission to such impressions. You will forget the state of the country or but recollect it for the purpose of guarding yourselves against mistaking the quality of the crime, for any evidence of the prisoner's guilt. Above all, you will remember, that you are called on to administer the *mercy* as well as the justice of the Law. For you are called on heedfully to give the prisoners the benefit of its *merciful* rule, that every reasonable doubt is ground for an acquittal. In directing your attention to this fundamental maxim, I admit that the counsel which I am giving you is trite, but you will recollect that it is trite, *because* it is important.

The prisoners were all found Guilty. The Jury recommended Lawrence Leonard to mercy.

COUNSEL FOR THE CROWN

Mr Attorney General   Mr Clarke
Mr Tickell, K. C.   Mr Arabin
Mr Martley K. C.
     Crown Solicitor — Mr Geale

COUNSEL FOR THE PRISONER

Mr D'Arcy   Mr Murphy
Mr Brady
     Agent — Mr Delany

The King
v
Dunne and others

A bill of indictment was found at the Spring Assizes, 1832, at Maryborough, against the Traversers, for the alleged murder of one Comerford. Mr D'Arcy, as Traversers' counsel, then stated that they were ready for trial, and if not tried, he moved to have them discharged, or admitted to bail, an affidavit was made on the part of the Crown to postpone the trial till Summer Assizes 1832. Baron Smith, upon reading the affidavit and informations, postponed the trial, and refused to admit prisoners to bail.

Mr D'Arcy, at this Special Commission, again applied on behalf of the prisoners, and insisted that if not tried at this Commission, they were entitled to be discharged, contending that the Habeas Corpus Act contained two provisions in favour of the subject.—First, that in case no bill of indictment was found against the prisoner, the next Term Sessions of Oyer and Terminer, or General Gaol Delivery after his commitment, he was entitled to be discharged upon bail, unless it should appear upon oath that the witness for the Crown could not be produced.

Second,—That the traverser, the second time Sessions of Oyer and Terminer, or General Gaol Delivery after his commitment, if not *indicted and tried*, was entitled to be discharged.

And he contended that this case fell within the provision of the statute, for in this case the prisoners were indicted at the first General Gaol Delivery after committal, and were ready for trial, which was postponed on the part of the Crown and they were now ready for trial, and he contended that this Act ought to be *liberally expounded*, and though he admitted the Act used the words General Gaol Delivery, and the Commission under which the Judges then sat did not say General Gaol Delivery, yet it did give them a Commission of General Delivery, and therefore, under the Habeas Corpus, the prisoners must be tried or discharged

The ATTORNEY GENERAL opposed the application, and contended that the Judges sat under a limited authority, and not under a Commission of General Gaol Delivery, that under their present authority they could not discharge a person by proclamation, and that he could adjourn that Commission at his pleasure and try such prisoners only as he thought proper, that the rule made at the Spring Assizes, 1832, was, that the trial should be postponed till the next Assizes and that this was neither a General Gaol Delivery nor an Assizes

The JUDGES took time to consider the question and afterwards gave judgment stating that they sat under a Special Commission, and not under a Commission of General Gaol Delivery and that they were of opinion, that without the consent of the Attorney General, they could neither discharge the prisoners, nor admit them to bail, and as he did not consent, they must refuse the application

SENTENCES

PRONOUNCED BY

THE CHIEF JUSTICE

ON THE LAST DAY OF THE SPECIAL COMMISSION

CLERK OF THE CROWN.—Put John Whelan and Thomas Lawlor to the Bar

CHIEF JUSTICE.—This Commission has sat for thirteen days, and at this moment thirty-eight persons stand at that Bar, to receive sentences proportioned to the crimes of which they have been found guilty We have made every enquiry that we possibly could, and have examined all the evidence given on the different trials, in order to find the means of administering justice effectually, but at the same time in mercy Many of the sentences that are to be pronounced are in their nature discretionary and the duty of pronouncing these devolves upon me there are some not discretionary the most tremendous of all sentences, and the duty of pronouncing them remains for my brother Smith In the pronouncing of those sentences, the public will be apprised not only of each man's punishment but of the class of crimes to which his guilt belongs and the several cases upon which judgment is now to be given will illustrate the history and progress of the insurrection, of which these wretched prisoners are the victims There is in the first instance a list of thirteen persons to receive sentence for the most mitigated of those crimes, namely, the unlawfully assembling and carrying arms, without any particular act of criminality being imputed to them. To those as nearly of the same class, may be added, the two men who have pleaded guilty to a charge of riot and rescue. Fine and imprisonment is the punishment we shall inflict for all the offences of the first class I have mentioned, and we shall not add to it the corporal punishment which the Statute authorizes. We have considered each particular case with a view that each sentence may be adequate, and not more than adequate to the offence; and in the hope that those sentences may be useful as a warning to the wretched persons themselves, and beneficial to the public in the way of example. The first of these cases is that of the two men now standing at the Bar, John Whelan and Thomas Lawlor. They have been convicted of appearing in arms in the streets of Portarlington, at seven o'clock in the evening, and one of them had a pistol in his possession bearing the marks of having been recently discharged. Under the direction and questions left to the Jury, they have found that those two persons "appeared in arms" in the language of the Statute, "to the terror of the King's subjects." It does not appear clearly, that they committed any offence, but the evidence abounds in suspicion that they were implicated in an offence committed on that evening. We do not act upon that suspicion, nor do we allow it to prejudice them, or make any ingredient in their punishment, and for that reason, a very mild sentence will be pronounced upon them. That sentence is that you and each of you, John Whelan and Thomas Lawlor be imprisoned for one month, that you be each fined one pound, and that you give security to keep the peace for seven years, each of yourselves in fifty pounds, and two sureties, each in five pounds.

CLERK OF THE CROWN.—Put Michael Doran and Thomas Murphy to the Bar

CHIEF JUSTICE.—Michael Doran and Thomas Murphy, you have been found guilty of the same offence for which Whelan and Lawlor have just now been sentenced. The circumstances of your case are less favorable, but they are not of an aggravated class, and I trust in God, that the moderation and mercy you will be dealt with now, may have an influence on the rest of your lives. You are each sentenced to six months imprisonment, each of you shall pay a fine of one pound, and each of you is to give security for your good behaviour for seven years, yourselves in fifty pounds each, and two sureties in five pounds each.

CLERK OF THE CROWN.—Put Edward Kilmartin, John Coonan, and John Phelan to the bar

CHIEF JUSTICE.—Edward Kilmartin, John Coonan, and John Phelan you have been found guilty of one of those offences of assembling in arms to the terror of the King's subjects, and your case is a dreadfully aggravated one, it is not the mere riotous movement of the moment, but the evidence in your case traces it up almost to the fountain head, (wherever that is,) of this dreadful conspiracy. You were found at night armed with desperate weapons, fire arms highly loaded, in good order, but what is more, there were found upon your persons notices from that personage that is called Captain Rock, to be served upon two persons, denouncing merciless vengeance upon one of them if he did not give up his property, and upon the other if he did not discharge his servant. If our sentence shall appear heavy, I desire you to remember that you ought to thank God that you were arrested that night. The great probability is, that if your wicked course had been allowed to run another hour, that you would be now in that blacker list to which I am approaching, that list of those who are to be sent from this country for the remainder of their days or perhaps you would have fallen into that class upon whom my brother Smith will just now have to pronounce sentence of death You and each of you shall be imprisoned for twelve months, each of you shall be fined forty shillings, and your imprisonment shall be continued until you give security, yourselves in fifty pounds each and two sureties each in ten pounds to keep the peace, and for your good conduct for seven years

CLERK OF THE CROWN.—Put Patrick Brophy and Jeremiah Kelly to the bar

CHIEF JUSTICE.—Patrick Brophy and Jeremiah Kelly, I have reserved your case to the last of that class to which you belong It is by mere accident that you are not now standing at the bar to receive sentence of death You were found with arms in your hands and arms lying about the place you were found in, many well prepared arms you were found in possession of the parts of unextinguished kindling of fire, which I have little doubt had been applied to a house in that neighbourhood, within half an hour before your arrest that house close to which you were taken was attacked just before you were apprehended and there was not only fire put under the roof of it, but a shot was fired through the door, which might have taken away the lives of some innocent persons If the police who apprehended you just after the dreadful crime was committed, had seized you in the commission of it you would now have to hear sentence of death that sentence you are saved from, but I shall sentence each of you to be imprisoned for eighteen months to pay each of you a fine of £5 and not to be discharged from imprisonment until after you shall have paid that fine, and each of you must give security for the peace, and for your good behaviour for seven years, yourselves in £100 each, and two sureties in £10 each

CLERK OF THE CROWN.—Put Hugh Galvin, and Patrick Hurley to the bar

CHIEF JUSTICE.—Hugh Galvin and Patrick Hurley, you do not belong to the class of cases in which I have been just now pronouncing sentence, but you belong to a class of persons demoralized in the highest degree, and under the influence of the most depraved spirit, and the most unfortunate delusion you belong to that class of persons who seem to have sworn enmity against the laws of their country It is in the general demoralization one of the most deplorable circumstances, that instead of magistrates and dispensers of the law being respected and looked up to, as they are in civilized countries, unhappily in this part of Ireland, every man who assists in the administration of justice is denounced as a public enemy and exposed to violence and outrage Your offence is this, a magistrate of this county had criminals in his care bringing them to prison to have them dealt with according to law, and you made a riot in the streets of this town, and with a set of ruffians you assaulted that magistrate, and did your best to rescue his prisoners I should now pronounce a heavy sentence upon you, but that by your contrition, evinced by your pleading guilty, you have entitled yourselves to a mitigation of punishment I shall therefore sentence you under these circumstances, each of you to be imprisoned for three months, and each of you to pay a fine of ten shillings, and give security for the peace, and your good behaviour for seven years, yourselves in fifty pounds each, and two sureties in five pounds

CLERK OF THE CROWN.—Put William Doody, William Fennell, Michael Barron, and Thomas Humphries to the bar

CHIEF JUSTICE —I am now about to pass sentence upon a class of persons, who have subjected themselves, not to fine and imprisonment, but to be torn from their families and their friends, never again to see the country of their birth, and to pass the remainder of their days in a foreign barbarous land. In every case, but one, in which I am to pass sentence of this nature, the Judges have a discretion left to them to pronounce sentence of transportation for the life of the criminal, or for seven years, or to substitute imprisonment in its place. We have done every thing in our power to enable us to exercise that discretion, with as much humanity as is consistent with justice.

You, William Doody, and William Fennell, have been found guilty upon one indictment; and you, Michael Barron, upon another indictment; and you, Thomas Humphrys, upon another indictment, all distinct cases—but all the same crimes; and, in our judgment, calling for the same punishment; and there belongs to your cases, that which I am sorry to say is a true description of every crime, which has been now brought to justice before us, with the exception of one,—that every one of those crimes was committed in the short interval between the close of the last Assizes, and the opening of the present Commission. What is that crime? The crime of demanding arms—and what use is made of those arms? You will be in Court, and you will hear just now sentence of death pronounced upon some persons belonging to your wicked associations; and to that sentence, that ignominious death, all those are in inevitable progress, who are engaged in the taking of arms. What, in the name of God! do you want with arms? The implements of industry ought to be your only arms; but, when I find in different parts of this county, from one end of it to the other, a simultaneous movement, often on the

x

same identical day, of a great portion of the population rising in search of arms, the prospect of future mischief, independently of existing crimes, is opened before me, and it is one that I am afraid to dwell upon. It is in our power to sentence every one of you to transportation for the remainder of your days. We shall sentence each of you to be transported for seven years, some of you may live to come back, and see those friends, from whom, a word from my lips might have separated you for ever.

William Doody.—Oh, my Lord, I am a poor widow's son. Do any thing with me—but don't send me out of the country. Have mercy on me.

CHIEF JUSTICE.—The only mercy that, consistently' with justice, we could administer to you we have. and that is, to reduce your punishment from transportation for life to transportation for seven years, and mercy beyond that would be cruelty to others.

CLERK OF THE CROWN.—Put forward Arthur M'Donnell, and Andrew M'Evoy.

CHIEF JUSTICE.—Arthur M'Donnell, and Andrew M'Evoy, you have been, providentially for yourselves, convicted only of a crime that subjects you to transportation, that crime is the demanding of arms. But, under what circumstances have you been found guilty? You are not only identified with this reprobate banditti, by the demanding of arms, but your crimes have been accompanied by two most dreadful robberies—robberies of property to a large amount, and. what is worse, there belongs to your crime, that most horrid extreme of a demoralized nature, the lifting of the arm of a man against the person of a woman. We cannot forget the circumstances connected with your defence—a defence not to be imputed to any source, but your own subornation of depraved participators in your vices. The production of a young woman of the name of Anderton, has exhibited a scene of perjury and corruption, of every kind that taints the human character, which calls upon us, in common justice to the offended laws, and to the safety of the country, to remove you both from it, as men unfit to live in it, and, therefore, we sentence you, and each of you, to be transported for the remainder of your lives.

CLERK OF THE CROSS.—Put Thomas Delany, Bartholomew Malone, Jeremiah Weire, Michael Malone, and James Deegan to the bar.

CHIEF JUSTICE.—Thomas Delany, Bartholomew Malone, Jeremiah Weire, Michael Malone, James Deegan, you have been found guilty of an offence which in all its particulars is an exact description of the crime called a "*Whiteboy misdemeanour,*" and illustrates the dreadful mischiefs produced by that association to which you belong. The crime of which you have been found guilty is, the assaulting and breaking into the dwelling-house of a man of the name of Terrott: up to this hour, no one has discovered. I have not been able to conjecture, for what purpose it was, that at least thirty ruffians, in the dead hour of the night, broke into that poor man's house. You broke into it; you demanded arms; your crime was burglary; and you might have been capitally indicted as one of your party was: you treated the inhabitants most brutally, and you then were about to retire. your crime, if it had stopped there, would have been a very bad one, and your sentence which might have been death, would, even under this indictment, have been a severe one, but your crime is now characterized by something more, upon the one hand, it is dreadfully aggravated by what followed, on the other hand, it is but right

to say, that what followed does not appear to have been pre-
meditated by you I mean the brutal and savage attack upon
Mr Miller I will do you the justice to say, that you did
not expect to meet him, and that you met him accidentally
But let your case be remembered by the public, as a proof
of this, that the man who goes one step in a Whiteboy
crime, does not know but that the next step may be to
death

Thomas Delany, your share in this transaction is worse
than that of the others I shall sentence you to be transported for life

Bartholomew Malone, and *James Deegan*, you stand before us, with some claims to a mitigation of punishment to
this extent, that you participated less in the violence upon
Mr Miller than your associates did, but, for the sake of
example, you must be transported for seven years

Michael Malone, I have inquired into your case, and
have heard circumstances favourable to you, there is a circumstance very creditable to you, and that circumstance is,
that you have sent to the Judges a penitent and candid
avowal of your guilt In this well prepared paper, drawn
up, as I am informed, from your own lips, you have
stated the justice of the law, and have thrown yourself
upon its mercy, and you form a contrast favourable to
yourself, when you are compared with those who have, to
the last moment, audaciously and impenitently alleged,
that injustice has been done to them. I shall not turn you
loose upon the country. It is for your advantage that you
should be imprisoned You shall be imprisoned for the
purpose of cutting off any communication between you
and the tainted atmosphere, in which persons of your class,
in this part of the country, now live, and, I trust, that
during the time of your imprisonment, you will avail your-

self of the opportunities that may be afforded to you of re-
forming and subduing your bad passions, and of profiting
by religious instruction, and that at the end of the year,
for which I sentence you to imprisonment you may come
out a better man than you are when going into prison   I
shall require further of you before you shall be discharged
at the end of the year, that you shall give security to be
of the peace and good behaviour for seven years, yourself
in £50, and two sureties, each in £5

Jeremiah Weare, I have had, from the day of your trial
up to this moment, many anxious thoughts about you   I
do not forget—I do not think I shall ever forget the manner in which Mr Henry Smith spoke of you   He stated
you to be young, to be peaceable, and to be humane   and
he swore to that in which I firmly believe he is not mistaken that your natural disposition is averse to cruelty, and
that it is quite opposed to the dreadful crime in which you have
participated, but you are one of those instances, which are
too frequent, of a good natural disposition, depraved not by
bad passions, but by bad associations You are the peculiar
representative now of the fresh, and ingenuous, and thought-
less mind, inoculated and poisoned with this pestilential
infection which has made the country that you live in, if
I may call it so, a *moral pest house*. we feel for you, and
we shall give you an opportunity for my brother Judge
and I, have had many anxious communications upon the
subject of your case   we shall give you an opportunity of
penitence and reformation of which I do not in your case
entertain any doubt that you will avail yourself   But I
have something more to tell you   I have to tell you that
you are much indebted to the representation made of you
by that brave, and gallant, and humane, and single hearted
character Thomas Miller, Thomas Miller that man, who

so nearly lost his life by the brutal and cruel violence of your associates, committed in your presence, has stated you to have been a young person of good conduct, and a good character, and that good character which he has given, shews at once, how well he knew you, how little likely it was that he could be mistaken in swearing to you, and at the same time demonstrates the fairness and kindness of his nature. Your own brother when he was examined, was asked whether he knew Mr Miller, Oh! yes, said he," and we all liked him," that man whom you all liked, that man to whose worth your own family have borne testimony, that man lay bleeding before you, and you did not raise your hand or voice to protect him. What revolution of your nature could have thus metamorphosed your character and can account for this? There is but one way of accounting for it, and that is the dreadful influence and authority of the existing conspiracy.

I had a question put to him since your trial, with reference to that part of his evidence which represented you as stooping over his body and looking in his face, then within four inches of your own, while he lay weltering in his blood—whether this might not be attributed to a return of your natural good feeling, and to your wish to ascertain the extent of his danger. when that question was put to that honest man, he said at once, " I would be glad to think so, " and I believe it was so" You shall be imprisoned for one year. I have ascertained that your health is bad, but I also know that I consult your temporal and spiritual interests, more by leaving you in prison for twelve months, with every care that will be taken of you by the constant attendance of a physician for your body, and the Physician of your Soul, than if I were to allow you to return to that corrupted society from which you are now happily separated

CLERK OF THE CROWN —Put forward Laurence Leonard, Hugh Slattery, Owen Brenan, Martin Brenan, Thomas Dunne, and William Dunne

CHIEF JUSTICE.—You have been all found guilty of an offence of the same class as that for which I have just now sentenced those who immediately before you have been brought to the bar, but your offence differs dreadfully in degree In the former case, the meeting Mr Miller, and the violence to his person was accidental —In your case, the offence was premeditated, and your crime consists in from thirty to forty persons in the dead hour of the night, breaking into the house of an unoffending and unprotected family, determined on their destruction that is an awful distinction between your case and the former

But there are other distinctions—I need not tell you that you might have been capitally indicted, and that the two most guilty of your associates have been capitally convicted, and you must be convinced that you have been mercifully prosecuted, when I remind you, and those who hear me, of one feature in your case the outrage that you committed upon Good-Friday night was the consequence of a most abominable conspiracy, the operations of which commenced on the Sunday evening previous to the attack, by some of you making a treacherous and deceitful visit to the house of old William Jacob, for the purpose of finding out the accessible and weak points for attack for the purpose of seeing how you could lull to sleep the apprehensions of the inhabitants, for the purpose of making them think that they were under under your protection, and afterwards you availed yourselves of those advantages, so acquired, by committing a crime that will be long remembered in this county, for the many extraordinary and shocking circumstances connected with it There are distinctions, however, among you Laurence Leonard, your prosecutors have represented you as a man who acted with humanity towards them, they have represented you as a person who though implicated in the guilt of that treacherous visit, yet interfered, and saved their lives At their intercession, and the intercession and recommendation of the Jury, we have determined that you shall not be transported, but you cannot be allowed to go at large, it is for your own benefit that you should remain in custody, and be separated from the contagious association of your old confederates —You shall be imprisoned for one year, and find security for the peace and your good behaviour for seven years, yourself in fifty pounds, and two sureties, each in ten pounds

Owen Brenan, you also come before the court under mitigating circumstances, you are very young you have this also to say for yourself, that you were acting in obedience to the orders of your unfortunate master. who has forfeited his life by this crime, and you have this to say for yourself also. that until the very moment of your trial, you had expressed contrition for your offence, in my sight you walked up to the place where you now stand having obtained at your own request, permission to withdraw the plea of *not guilty*, and to plead *guilty* to the charge, but you were induced to change your mind, in consequence of communications which we all witnessed. We shall not visit that upon you, but will give you the full benefit of that contrition you originally manifested You were taught to believe, and perhaps justly, that such a proceeding on your part would be injurious to your confederates, and your conduct was prompted by a perverted generous feeling

I am about to pronounce a sentence of longer imprisonment upon you than upon Leonard, not that I think your crime is greater, or so great as his, but for this reason, that in your case, imprisonment may be highly salutary to you, you are young, the prison in which we are going to leave you is commodious, the governor is an attentive and humane person.—You can be kept out of bad company, your mind may be moulded into better habits, and at the end of two years, which I make the measure of your imprisonment, you will, I trust, come out not merely a reformed person, but, perhaps, an improved character, a better man than even before you committed the crime You must also give security, yourself in fifty pounds, and two sureties each in five pounds, for keeping the peace, and your good behaviour for seven years

But there are four persons more in this number, Hugh Slattery, Martin Brenan, Thomas Dunne, and William Dunne—I am not able to state any thing favourable of them of the same nature as I have been happy to discover and to state in favour of Leonard and that young boy, and we see no possible alternative in your case but to sentence you to the very heaviest punishment which conviction on the present indictment has subjected you to Your crime has the horrid aggravation of premeditation and on looking into the notes of the evidence of the three trials, I have looked in vain for any distinction among those who went through that house that night in arms, beating a helpless old man, and attempting the life of an unprotected young woman, and putting to the very verge of death an unoffending young man Our sentence is, that you, and each of you, be transported for the remainder of your lives

Hugh Slattery—I am the father of six children, and, before God and your Lordship, I never knew that he was in the country until the next day   I never had hand, act, or part, in the business   Mercy I crave—before God, I declare, I am innocent.

CLERK OF THE CROWN.—Put forward Francis Adams, and Thomas Langton

CHIEF JUSTICE.—Francis Adams, and Thomas Langton, the gentlemen of the bar who defended you, with great ability, have made an objection in point of law to your conviction, and the Judges, who preside here now, will put that question into a course of inquiry, and, if you shall appear to be entitled to the benefit of it, you shall have it, and in that case, the sentence, which I am to pronounce upon you will not be executed But, I shall now pronounce that sentence as I should have done, if no legal difficulties had been suggested Your crime does not belong to any of those classes, with which I have been hitherto dealing It stands by itself, and manifests an approach still nearer to the source of the wicked and profligate conspiracy that now afflicts the Queen's County Your crime is the administering of unlawful oaths, a crime of the most dreadful character, dangerous to society, prophane towards the Almighty, and calculated to suggest to the minds of persons of your class very perverted notions of the nature of the legal and religious obligations of an oath, it is a melancholy truth, that two species of demoralization seem to be going hand in hand together in this country, one manifesting itself in the fidelity with which unlawful oaths are observed, and the other in the violation and contempt of those oaths that are lawful, and taken in the administration of justice You, with others in arms, by compulsion, administered an oath to a man, calling upon him to give up his property, merely because you ordered it.   That is an offence, in every point of view, atrocious and dangerous, and, we sentence you to the severest punishment the law annexes to it   That you, and each of you, be transported for seven years

The following charge of BARON SMITH, in the case of William Dunne, seems substantially to involve in it a sufficient report of the evidence and case

BARON SMITH, proceeding to charge the Jury, observed, that in this case the evidence against the prisoner was merely circumstantial. Even the proofs which went to identify him were but a collection of circumstances. Evidence of this kind was undoubtedly a legitimate foundation for a verdict of conviction. But as, from its very nature, it involved something resembling doubt, (for the facts and circumstances might be all established, and yet the inference of guilt be a fallacious one,) such evidence ought to be weighed with proportionable scruple and attention. Jane Quin, at whose house the outrage had been committed, did not know who were the perpetrators, and could not identify any of those concerned in it. At near five o'clock on the following morning, Mr Jones, of the constabulary saw three persons, of whom the prisoner was one, but he met them at no very unseasonable hour, on a public road, and which was the prisoner's way home. He saw them, as he approached, turn through a gap into a field, from which, in about a minute, they returned to the road, and continued to advance towards him. He and his party took them into custody, and searched the field and them. Concealed in the field, and very near the gap, he found a piece of calico, and upon them he found a handkerchief, a small quantity of cocoa, and about nine penny worth of tobacco distributed equally amongst the three. This occurrence took place within little more than a mile of Whitefield, where, a very few hours before, the outrage had been committed. The three men appeared in liquor. Two of them, of whom the prisoner was not one, lived near Whitefield. On the prisoner there were also found twelve shillings in the handkerchief and one shilling in another pocket. Compare with this the evidence of Jane Quin and her aunt They identify the calico and the handkerchief The outrage at their house was committed a very few hours before, by three men, of whom two at least seemed intoxicated The calico and handkerchief were then taken, and a small quantity of cocoa was taken at the same time The evidence of Taylor, a publican, brought the prisoner, and the two men whom Mr Jones met with him, together, at his (Taylor's) public house, in the neighbourhood of Whitefield, on the day before the outrage In order to make any acts done by those two men, or the fact of any thing found upon them, evidence against the prisoner, it would be necessary that the Jury should believe, and be satisfied upon the proofs, that they were all three associates and confederates With this caution, the Jury would recollect the finding of the cocoa on the person of one, and of the calico near the gap into which all three had retired, though that this calico had been hidden there by any one of them, there was no direct proof As to the tobacco found upon them, look to the evidence of Mary Lahy She lived in Whitefield, very near to Jane Quin Some few hours before Mr Jones met these three men, she, at the requisition of one or more unknown men, handed out through her window, nine penny worth of tobacco But again, on the prisoner himself, there were found twelve shillings in one pocket, and one shilling in another And what was the evidence of Margaret Collier, who lived within less than a quarter of a mile of Jane Quin ? That a few hours before, some persons came to her window, and asked to borrow twelve shillings, which she gave them. Shortly after, more was demanded, and her little girl handed out one shilling more

Lastly, compare the evidence of Charles and Anne Crawford, with the finding of the prisoner wearing a great coat which wanted a cuff. The Crawfords lived near Jane Quin, at Whitefield. On the night on which Jane Quin was robbed, strangers came to Crawford's house, one of them took off his outer coat and flung it on a door. after some disorderly conduct he put it on again, and left the house. Next morning a cuff was found upon his floor. It got into the possession of the police, was produced upon the trial, and the Jury would determine whether it fitted and belonged to the great coat, also produced to them, and which had been found upon the prisoner.

The prisoner had produced three witnesses to his character, and they had given him a good one. Two, upon a knowledge of two years. The third had known him for but four months. But this third was a serjeant of police, likely to hear any thing ill of a suspected person in his neighbourhood, especially in the present disturbed state of the county. It was also proved that the prisoner had lately married a young wife. Part of the evidence of Jane Quin might render this fact material. She (Jane Quin) swore positively to the calico and handkerchief, on the table. She had sworn to them only to the best of her knowledge before the Magistrate. The Jury would give to the man upon his trial whatever benefit this fact seemed to them to entitle him to demand. To tell the Jury to acquit, if they had any reasonable doubt, he admitted was to address to them a very common place direction. But what had made it common place? Its vital importance, and unquestionable truth.

Considering the peculiar nature of that evidence which is called circumstantial, the great delicacy, if not difficulty of dealing with it, is this, that Juries must not, in acting on it, return a verdict which shall conflict with that most fundamental maxim of Crown Law, that nothing short moral of certainty can justify a conviction   They must steer a course between the rejection of circumstantial evidence altogether and the neglect of that never to be forgotten rule, that a prisoner demonstrates his innocence, by raising a doubt as to his guilt   I mean, demonstrates it to the extent of entitling himself to an acquittal

The Jury returned a verdict of *Guilty*

The three following persons, William and John Dunn, and Patrick Keenan, having been called up for judgment, on the last day of the Commission, were addressed as follows by Baron Smith —

BARON SMITH —William Dunn, John Dunn, and Patrick Keenan, you have all been found guilty of a robbery in the dwelling-house of Jane Quinn, and a part of the evidence seems to impute to two of you, that you aggravated this guilt, by the commission of another crime

The evidence against you was of the circumstantial kind   But to this the attention of the Jury was directed, and they were told by me, that such evidence should be diligently searched

I agree with them, that the case against you was *satisfactory*   I use this word in the melancholy sense, of its being demonstrative of your guilt   I mean your guilt of the offence charged by the indictment —Indeed, a more perfect chain of circumstances, extraordinary and convincing, it has not often been my lot to hear. The time and place where you were met,—the companionship which was shown to have existed between you,—the property found upon you,—the hiding of the calico in the field, and its identification,—the cocoa—the tobacco—the twelve shillings found in one pocket, *separate* from the one shilling in another,—the cuff of a coat, found in Crawford's house, and fitted to the mutilated coat, found upon one of you, these circumstances with others which might be added, formed a mass of evidence, which it would be difficult to resist

Of any aggravations which attended your offence, it was not the business of the Jury to take notice neither did they But now that there has been a convicton, those aggravations, though collateral, may not be immaterial

Of this aggravation, it would appear, that two of you were guilty and, perhaps, there may have been evidence,-- or ground at least for conjecturing that of those two, you, William Dunne, were one

There is evidence that in the house of Crawford, a person wearing the coat, which was afterwards found on you, flung it off, and showed an intention of offering violence to Crawford's wife

Two committed this outrage on Jane Quin But, which of you, John Dunn, and Patrick Keenan, was the second, we cannot tell and, therefore, cannot attach this aggravation upon either

Your offence was not of the Whiteboy kind yet, is it connected with the confederated disturbance, which is disordering this county

Under the shelter of those confederacies, and the intimidation which they cause, such crimes as these of yours grow up, flourish, and prevail Under the supposed protection of an army of combinators which you represented as at your back, you actually pillaged an entire hamlet

Behold the fruits of excitement, and its creature, combination ! Behold the poisonous weeds which are growing up, beneath the shade, perhaps by reason of the contagious influence and atmosphere, of this pestilential tree

Behold the purifiers of our civil polity, the redressers of public grievance ! Who could have expected, that it was amongst robbers, ravishers, and midnight house-breakers, such patriotism would be found! What an unseemly and revolting mixture of the ridiculous with the sad!

But the scene before us now, is one of unmingled awfulness and sadness.

Poor, young, overtaken, and afflicted creatures, adopt a course becoming the solemn situation in which you stand, and penitently recommend yourselves to God, while you hearken to the awful sentence of the law.

Baron Smith then pronounced the sentence. All seemed penitent, and William Dunne especially appeared very much affected

---

Patrick Dunne having been called up for judgment on the last day of Commission, BARON SMITH addressed him in the following terms —

BARON SMITH.—Patrick Dunne, you also have been found guilty of an offence, deeply connected with the system which disturbs this county The charge against you nominally, and indeed substantially is, that you fired at Elizabeth Young, a pistol shot which took effect But this assault ensued upon, and was appurtenant to, an attempt to procure arms, an attempt which proved successful

This was clearly an offence of the Whiteboy character, and one of the most significant and alarming of the insurgent class.

You committed this offence boldly, and in the open day You came accompanied, and prepared to carry your illegal point by force, for you and your companion were both armed You came deliberately, and not uninformed. For you went straight to the room and bed, which contained the objects of your visit

This fact involves some evidence of concert and combination. For you must be presumed to have received from some confederate, the information, which led you to the place where the pistols were concealed

The wounding of the young woman was a consequence of your purpose of obtaining arms, and a proof how determinately this purpose was entertained

I am afraid it may be considered to have appeared, that the shot was not undesigned But, if it had gone off accidentally, in the struggle, while you were in the prosecution of a felonious intent,—I take it that a homicide ensuing would be murder Murder, not in moral turpitude, but in point of law

Connected with this question of the moral extent of your offence, it is but fair to say, that the evidence of Elizabeth Young acquitted you of an intent to murder, and suggested that your object was to wound her arm in order that she might no longer be able to retain the pistol, which she held

A good character was given you

You also produced witnesses to an *alibi* defence, and, though the proof was insufficient, I do not think the verdict has necessarily pronounced that those witnesses were forsworn But your voluntary declaration, reduced to writing, states an *alibi* different from that, to which both of those witnesses swore

It is true that Elizabeth Young had never seen you before you entered her master's house She was somewhat alarmed She had not more than fifteen minutes for observation, and for five of these was engaged in a sort of struggle. Her identification of you, in the infirmary, was attended with some circumstances more or less peculiar At the first short interview she doubted Between that and the second, your clothes were changed She then became

Y

certain of you A pipe was, moreover, put into your mouth In short, with, as I am persuaded, the best intentions in the world, a risk was run, of giving Elizabeth more assistance, than the jealousy of the law approves But to all this, the attention of the Jury was called by me and they were satisfied with her identification of you

You are a young man,— a misguided young man These conspiracies and combinations have been your bane, and for the punishment, poor unfortunate young man, which you have incurred, you will be indebted to those, whoever they may be, in whose encouragement, direct, or indirect, those combinations had their source

For I do feel, and I have more than once admitted myself to feel, that it is a painful duty to punish the instrument, while those who forged and used it, remain untouched and laugh the unavailing law to scorn

But this we cannot avoid Nor does the law operate injustice, though the justice which it accomplishes may be incomplete When the instrument is an animated and free agent, and is only a *tool*, because he allows himself to be made one, he must abide the consequence, and be as responsible as those whose instrument he is

Poor, unhappy, misguided instrument of turbulent agitation, the sentence of the law is that you, Patrick Dunn, &c —

His Lordship here pronounced the sentence in the usual terms, and the prisoner was removed

When their Lordship's had concluded their addresses to the convicts, the Attorney-General rose and thus addressed the Court —

My Lords, I would that the afflicting scenes that we have just witnessed, were to close the labours of this Special

Commission, but the number of crimes which have been perpetrated in this county since your Lordships authority commenced obliges me to move your Lordships to adjourn it to some day intermediate between this, and the ordinary period of holding the Assizes. I assure your Lordships, it is with reluctance that I make this application. I cannot forget the labour, and the anxiety which your Lordships have undergone in the discharge of your individual duties; and though I well know, that all personal considerations should be disregarded on such an occasion. I feel, that as far as is consistent with the interests of the public we ought not, without actual necessity, call upon you to resume them. My reluctance to make this application is increased, when I reflect, that it may possibly add to the labours and inconvenience of the gentlemen who have attended here as Jurors. On a review of the proceedings under this Commission, I will venture to say, that in the history of the jurisprudence of any country it is not possible to find an instance in which justice has been administered with more impartiality, moderation and caution. I wish I could say, that the defence of the convicts had rested on the fair and legitimate aid afforded by able professional assistance; but I regret to say, and I mention this fact as one of the most afflicting circumstances of the times, that almost universally those defences have been sustained by profligate perjury. I am now authorized by the verdicts of successive Juries, thus to characterize the *alibi* defences, in support of which, we have seen whole tribes of witnesses rush forward in this Court of Justice to the commission of perjury without shame or compunction; the signal discomfiture of such wickedness and profligacy appears to me to be one of the most powerful proofs of the value of this Commission. It has demonstrated the utter inefficacy of encountering truth by falsehood, and I trust may lead to the discontinuance of similar practices, by showing the certainty of their failure

My Lords, I would further remark, as a circumstance peculiar to the prosecutions which have taken place under this Commission, that overrun, as this county is, by lawless, extensive, and powerful confederacies, there is scarcely an instance in which a criminal has been brought to justice, in which the crime has been perpetrated against the person or property of any man of power or rank. The objects of aggression have been those who have been unable to protect themselves, the poor, and the defenceless. I could prove this by enumerating the cases one by one. There is not, I believe, in the whole catalogue, a single person prosecuting in the rank of a gentleman. The victims of lawless outrage unable to redress their own wrongs, have seen justice executed on their authors with the most exemplary success, and I trust will have learned, that as the law is ready to afford them protection, so it is their interest, as well as duty, to aid its administration by all the exertions in their power.

My Lords, in saying that the Juries of this county have discharged their duties in a manner reflecting credit upon themselves, and in stating at the same time, that except in one case, they have found verdicts of conviction, I will call the attention of the public to the nature of a Special Commission, because it accounts for that which might otherwise appear singular, and repels a charge which I know there are some not unwilling to make—that the Juries have not acted with caution and discrimination.

Under a Special Commission, a selection is made of such cases as the Attorney General thinks proper to bring forward for trial, under the exercise of this discretion, I have determined, and I believe such has been the practice of my predecessors, never to bring forward a case in which I am not reasonably certain that the evidence, if believed, will warrant a conviction At the Assizes, the practice is totally different. The ordinary Commission obliges the Judges to try all prisoners in the gaol, and all are accordingly tried, whether the evidence be weak or strong, there is therefore of necessity a great number of acquittals. The vast disproportion between the number of acquittals and convictions at the Assizes, compared with those under a Special Commission, is thus simply and satisfactorily explained and accounted for

My Lords, another remarkable circumstance connected with this Special Commission, and one of an unusual character has been the Challenge of the array — Now I think it right to bring before the public the circumstances under which that challenge took place The prisoners, Adams and Langton, were tried on the second day of the Commission, by a Jury taken from this very panel which they afterwards challenged They were acquitted on a defect in the evidence it did not support the form of the indictment preferred against them they were indicted a second time, they postponed their trial until the eleventh day of the Commission this they did upon pretences that proved to be untrue, and on the eleventh day they challenged the array, charging that it was not the act of the Sheriff, and that the Sheriff had so marshalled the names of the jurors, as to prevent the prisoners from having a fair jury to try them The effect of making this objection at that advanced stage of the proceedings, might have been, if it proved well founded to have rendered all the previous convictions abortive and, thus the whole object of this Commission would have been frustrated I need not say, after the investigation which this challenge underwent that never was a more unfounded charge preferred in a Court of Justice, nor a more satisfactory vindication than that of the conduct of the Sheriff.

Let me conclude by expressing my hope, that the effectual administration of justice, the dreadful examples which have been made, and will be made, will tend to restore to the minds of the misguided people, a sense of the danger they incur, and of the impossibility of resisting the law Let me further express my most anxious hope, that this Special Commission may be signalized, not by the number of those convicted, but by the reformation of those who are guilty, and that we shall see, ere long, the authority of the law restored, and the re-establishment of tranquillity and peace

Lightning Source UK Ltd.
Milton Keynes UK
UKHW031102210920
370268UK00010B/1056